How Does God Talk to Us?

How Does God Talk To Us?

The Concept of the "Word of God" in Augustine, Martin Luther, and Karl Barth

by
FRANK HOFMANN

Translated by
GLENN R. SANDBERG

PICKWICK *Publications* • Eugene, Oregon

HOW DOES GOD TALK TO US?
The Concept of the "Word of God" in Augustine, Martin Luther, and Karl Barth

Pickwick Publications
An Imprint of Wipf and Stock Publishers
199 W. 8th Ave., Suite 3
Eugene, OR 97401

www.wipfandstock.com

PAPERBACK ISBN: 978-1-6667-1616-0
HARDCOVER ISBN: 978-1-6667-1617-7
EBOOK ISBN: 978-1-6667-1618-4

Cataloguing-in-Publication data:

Names: Hofmann, Frank, 1962– [author]. | Sandberg, Glenn R. [translator]

Title: How does God talk to us? : the concept of the "Word of God" in Augustine, Martin Luther, and Karl Barth / Frank Hofmann ; translated by Glenn R. Sandberg.

Description: Eugene, OR: Pickwick Publications, 2021 | Includes bibliographical references.

Identifiers: ISBN 978-1-6667-1616-0 (paperback) | ISBN 978-1-6667-1617-7 (hardcover) | ISBN 978-1-6667-1618-4 (ebook)

Subjects: LCSH: Augustine, of Hippo, Saint, 354–430 | Luther, Martin, 1483–1546 | Barth, Karl, 1886–1968 | Word of God (Christian theology)

Classification: BT180.W67 H64 2021 (print) | BT180.W67 (ebook)

10/15/21

Contents

List of Illustrations

1

Introductory Remarks

1.1 The Problem

COMBINED WITH THE TERM "word of God" is the idea that religious experience is bound first of all to language (*word* of God) and secondly is not a planned event but an unconditioned occurrence[1] (word of *God*). The power of this term lies in the fact that, alongside this compact religio-scientific thesis, it gets to the heart of the God image rooted in Judeo-Christian tradition: "God turns towards man concretely and expresses himself to him."[2]

Considerable doubts have been asserted against the application of the term "word of God" as a basic theological category.[3] First of all, the term appears to be historically fraught: from early Protestant orthodoxy to the present the "word of God" has been continually misused in a hijacking equalization with the Christian canon towards a "fundamentalist

1. This statement is based on Ingolf Dalferth's definition: "An occurrence is something that occurs passively, without one's own initiative, and is usually unexpected. Thus, an occurrence is not something that simply confirms and continues a pattern of life and experience; rather, it impacts a life so that it becomes different, so that all that it does or does not do, in its what and in its how, in its character and in its being, is affected by this occurrence and significantly determined by it." (Dalferth, *Radical Theology*, 109–10.) On the concept of unconditionality see also Rosa, *Unverfügbarkeit*, especially 48–68.

2. Lauster, *Zwischen*, 18.

3. On this concept see Körtner, *Theologie*, 13.

remythologizing of the Bible."[4] Closely connected to this, secondly, is the accusation formulated by, among others, Falk Wagner, that a theology built on the word of God leads inevitably to a "positivism of word and revelation," which burdens the "positivity of an historically conditioned word of God theology" with a "hybrid claim to represent the self-givenness of the divine self-word."[5]

Thirdly, the question has been posed if the "word of God" inevitably connotes "unconditional obedience" and thereby an authoritarian relationship with God, as claimed for example by Wolfhart Pannenberg.[6] Fourthly and finally, the image of a speaking God can obviously be understood as a "downright forcible infantilization of the concept of God."[7] As Emanuel Hirsch pointedly expresses it: "That God . . . speaks is an anthropomorphism just as vulgar as God shooting arrows or throwing hammers."[8]

The first three objections are directed against the revelatory-theological aspect of the term—against the word of *God*—while the last takes aim at the *word* of God, thereby against the linguistic phenomena approach. The present study would like to contribute the following: the "word of God" with a concentration on its linguistic significance, thereby preserving it as a central systematic term against these and other reservations—including other insights that "theology and church may forget at their own peril."[9] What those insights are in detail and why they have achieved currency in the twenty-first century is the subject of the concluding sixth chapter.[10]

First of all, the other "fundamental misunderstanding" comes to mind which Gerhard Ebeling designated as a theological "cardinal error" in dealing with the word of God: namely that the word of God is understood as "a separate class of word alongside the interpersonal word" which "therefore is actually not a word in the sense of a normal word event."[11] In fact, the actual sense of the term, the opposition of absolute and finite, can be pinpointed "precisely at the spot of connection of the

4. Lauster, *Zwischen*, 15.

5. Wagner, *Geht die Umformungskrise*, 247–48.

6. Pannenberg, *Problemgeschichte*, 201–2.

7. Lauster, *Zwischen*, 22.

8. Hirsch, *Leitfaden*, 79.

9. Körtner, *Leitbegriffe*, 12.

10. Particularly in section 6.5.3

11. Ebeling, *Wort Gottes*, 340.

unconditional to the conditional"[12]—namely in the consummation of human understanding. According to this idea, the starting point of all theological conversation is a communication situation between humans in which the absolute through linguistic—or at least sign-based—processes enters into a contingent event in appearance as an acting subject.[13] In this "word event"[14] man himself, the world, and God are placed in a relationship: "Thus a human being is defined as that being *with whom* God speaks and from whom God summons and enables an answer. The world is defined as the totality of that *about which* God speaks (to us). God is defined as the one *who* speaks with us."[15]

Since the term "word of God" expresses "the activity of God in the world,"[16] we must deal with a genuine experience-oriented concept. Then God can only be the subject of discussion insofar as he makes himself part of the conversation. "The question of the existence of God, counterpoised to the question of the sense of a discussion of his actions [and language], is secondary."[17] From this flows directly that the word of God is not an "anthropomorphism" nor even less so a "forcible infantilization,"[18] but rather an expression of a rationally responsible and precise limitation to a phenomenon of human *experience* that—in contrast to the *observation* of an aggregate of sensory data—is always understood as being linguistically conveyed.[19] It is then actually the reverse that the allegation of an anthropomorphic (or infantilized) manner of speaking implicitly presupposes an (in principle) empirical and rational non-discursive image of God.

The term "word of God" gained from human communication stands in opposition to a simplified hostility of "revelation versus experience" and links—as will be demonstrated—the idea of unpredictable success of comprehension with the idea of the processing of experience through language.

A contemporary explication of the term naturally must avoid the appearance of any dogmatic or authoritarian claims of final justification.

12. Korsch, *Theologie*, 226.

13. Körtner, *Leitbegriffe*, 15–16. and Webster, *Theologische Theologie*, 252.

14. On this concept see Ebeling, *Wort Gottes*, 326–28.

15. Dalferth, *Radical Theology*, 89.

16. Körtner, *Leitbegriffe*, 16.

17. Körtner, *Leitbegriffe*, 16.

18. See footnotes 7 and 8.

19. Jung, *Erfahrung*, 306.

A consciousness of the linguistic aspect of the word of God is therefore extraordinarily helpful, since the uncontested plurality of religious experiences is mirrored directly in the medium of language: "As God became man and his word becomes comprehensible in human conversation, so does he deliver himself up to a conflict of interpretations which cannot be halted by staking out theological positions."[20]

In this study the "word of God" will be connected consequently to (inner-worldly) "events of speech and language."[21] In doing so it follows a programmatic demand of Dietrich Korsch that expects to obtain from this concept that different dimensions of religious life and theological teaching could be connected non-dogmatically: "When one engages with the consideration of language as a connective quantity of the word of God, then one conceptually already has the view that one must not fit one's self into the traditional alternatives of dogmatics and piety, or theology and religion, or doctrine and life."[22]

Therefore one must orient one's self to three key questions:[23]

1. In the general nature of language, how are special religious interpretations possible—and what are the specific features of Christian interpretations?
2. What empirical findings emerge for the description of self- and world-understanding in "life lived"? Or, formulated differently: What is the relationship between language and way of life?
3. What epistemological status does such a theology of the word of God enjoy?

In the succeeding chapters these ideas will be taken up in an historical-systematic reconstruction of the word-of-God concepts of Augustine, Martin Luther, and Karl Barth. Interestingly, these three thinkers from quite different epochs in the development of Christian theology illuminated and enlarged the linguistic aspects of one another's word of God thought. As will be shown in the concluding chapter, these lend themselves to transposition into the current debate in the philosophy of language.

20. Körtner, *Leitbegriffe*, 20.

21. Korsch, *Theologie*, 228.

22. Korsch, *Theologie*, 228.

23. See Korsch, *Theologie*, 228.

Augustine, the orator and philologist, the gold standard for linguistics in his time, grappled with the building blocks of language like no other Christian theologian and strode a traceable path of evolution in his oeuvre.[24] In thinking beyond his last phase of development as shown in *De trinitate,* an answer emerges to the second of the key questions above (see chapter 3 and section 6.2).

Martin Luther, less interesting theoretically but in practical terms a much more adept word artist, left behind the foundations for a theory of religious interpretation in his own interpretation of idiom communication and his paradosis of communion. Here the linguistic character of religious experiences and the religious element in language become particularly clear: an answer to key question one (chapter 4 and section 6.3).

Finally, Karl Barth created an implicit theory of language[25] with his *Church Dogmatics,* which preceded normative philosophy of language by several years in completing a decisive paradigm change. Barth leaves behind the observation of language as an isolatable structure and proceeds toward a comprehensive view of language as a communication event, which in retrospect can be considered a success (chapter 5 and section 6.4). Without having intended to use this format, Barth made possible a linguistic connectivity to a theology concentrating on the word of God (key question 3).

The three concepts complement each other so well because semiotics (Augustine), semantics (Luther), and pragmatics (Barth) lend themselves to a comprehensive theory of language of the word of God. Chapter 6 attempts to provide such a synopsis with the aid of two tools in particular of modern philosophy of language: metaphor theory and speech act theory. But before all this, chapter 2 will identify the most important semantic threads of the word of God in the Christian canon and place them in linguistic context. The recommended explications in chapter 6 will be measured against the five dimensions of the term gained thereby.

Whenever "language" is discussed in the following study, writing-based, living everyday languages are intended. But it is not said that the word of God can only be demonstrated in this manner. Principally the results apply to all intentional usable sign systems that facilitate communication but leave semantic blurs in their wake. The range extends

24. On this assessment of Augustine's significance as a philosopher of language see Coseriu, *Geschichte*, 122.

25. Korsch, *Religionsbegriff*, 200.

from formal logic[26] and mathematics[27] to art. Supposedly this holds for all possibilities with which we are able to articulate our ideas. Our language ability grows out of a specifically human imaging ability—namely the capacity to differentiate the image from its setting.[28] Without this "capacity for relative negation"[29] neither deciphering of written language nor comprehension of spoken language is conceivable. There is a strong argument that this imaging ability in developed language use has an impact on creative impulses as well as transcending metaphors in the actual manner of speech (partial aspects will be discussed in section 6.3.2). To demonstrate the connections between the religious potential of imaging ability[30] and the potentialities (individually) of language ability, though, goes beyond the scope of this study which orients itself on the *word of God*, on Λόγος τὸν Θεόν and its linguistic and theoretical reasoning aspect.

1.2. Literature Review

As measured by its systematic significance, the theological-historical development of the concept "word of God" has been examined surprisingly seldom. One finds profound articles in the relevant lexica,[31] classic works on biblical exegesis,[32] and studies on the use of the concept by individual thinkers or schools of thought.[33] Furthermore, there is an entire series

26. See for example Kurt Gödel's ontological "proof of God" in formal-logical notation (Bromand, *Gottesbeweise*, 483–87).

27. One thinks of the different interpretations of infinite groups in modern mathematics (see for example Deiser, *Einführung*, 91–194).

28. Krüger, *Das andere Bild*, 151–94.

29. Krüger, *Das andere Bild*, 306.

30. See in detail Krüger, *Das andere Bild*, especially 471–541. Krüger understands the repeatedly established "iconic turn" of cultural studies in recent times not as a replacement for the "linguistic turn," but as a chance for mutual relativization: "For this relativization of language to the image is also a relativization of the image to language (547)."

31. Here should be mentioned especially those in the *Historisches Wörterbuch der Philosophie* (Ringleben, article *Wort*), *Religion in Geschichte und Gegenwart* (Krötke, article *Wort Gottes*), and *Evangelisches Kirchenlexikon* (Dierken, article *Wort*).

32. Such as Dürr, *Wertung*; Grether, *Name und Wort*; Bultmann, *Der Begriff*; Gese, *Johannesprolog*; Wischmeyer, *Wort Gottes*. For further references to the word of God in the Bible see chapter 2.

33. For Augustine, Luther, and Barth see the references in chapters 3, 4, and 6. For the era after Barth see Körtner, *Theologie* and Dietz, *Sprache als Dasein*.

of tendentious fundamentalist publications on the "word of God" whose scholarly value is, at best, minimal.[34] Finally there is the four-volume work by Henning Graf Reventlow on the history of biblical exegesis.[35] But still, a study of this aspect that goes beyond these earlier works and spans multiple epochs—according to the current state of research—is a desideratum.[36] In particular, the era between the canonic texts and the Reformation has hardly been taken into consideration.[37]

Just as fragmentary is the reception of linguistic philosophy in the context of word of God theology. As obvious as the connection may seem, few links have in fact been forged. There are essentially two reasons for this: in the first place, the leading word of God theologians are German systematic theologians—which separates them (not only linguistically) from the English roots of analytical philosophy.[38] On the continent, systematic theology has self-confidently proclaimed itself independent since Idealism, while in England "the extensive permeation of the Christian religion by philosophy of religion" has been accepted well into the twentieth century.[39] In the second place, the first contact between language analysis and theology is indebted not to any bilateral interest, but rather to a one-sided polemic. In 1936 Alfred Ayer's work *Language, Truth and Logic* appeared in which Ayer declared (among other things) religious precepts without the possibility of logical or empirical verification to be absurd.[40] In response to this, English-speaking philosophers of religion developed an entire series of suggestions for salvaging the rationality of religious language in the succeeding decades.[41] These suggestions, how-

34. An exception is Hans Lachenmann's attempt to found a "new theology of the word of God" (*Das Wort*, 8). However, the strength of his book lies less in linguistic, but in psychological reflection on revelation (for this, see specifically 99–103).

35. Reventlow, *Epochen*.

36. See Tobler, *Vielgestaltiges Wort*, 42.

37. An exception is the sketch by Tobler, *Vielgestaltiges Wort*.

38. 1900 is generally considered the "birth year of analytical philosophy," the year in which Bertrand Russell founded logical atomism with the publication of his "A Critical Exposition of the Philosophy of Leibniz" (Carl, *Russell*, 223).

39. Dalferth, *Einführung*, 32.

40. See Ayer, *Language*, 114–20.

41. Survey in Dalferth, *Einführung*, 34–57, and Laube, *Im Bann*, 1–15. Worthy of mention here is George Lindbeck's study on "the grammar of religion" (*Nature*, 81), a study more widely received in the English-speaking world than in Germany. Lindbeck's study played a significant role in the ecumenical dialogue. In this regard see also section 6.5.3.

ever, amounted to at most an epistemic equivalence of articles of faith and they were not able to establish a special claim of validity for religious discourse. In other words, they concerned themselves exclusively with the salvation of the word "God," but not with the word of God.

Some of these texts were made easily accessible by Ingolf Dalferth in his anthology *Sprachlogik des Glaubens* (1974) and Manfred Kaempfert in *Probleme der religiösen Sprache* (1983).[42] As a result, several readable but mostly introductory monographs appeared in Germany on the theme of language analysis and theology.[43] But surely the most in-depth and extensive treatment that tests the analytical approaches of the twentieth century and describes religious language in all its peculiarities and aspirations, comes again from Dalferth: *Religiöse Rede von Gott* (1981).[44] The result of his studies: religious language is "from the linguistic point of view not as qualifiable religiously and religiosity is not a linguistically describable quality of texts."[45] Therefore, Dalferth suggests that instead of speaking of "religious language," we instead speak of "language in religiously structured situations," whose criteria could certainly be "quite different in synchronic and diachronic regard."[46] For the Christian religion, and here the word of God in Dalferth has its systematic locus, "the experience of Jesus as the salutation of God" is characteristic.[47] This solution is unsatisfactory in three ways:

1. Both communications phenomena "address of God" and "religious language" become solely external, but without internal connection to one another. Not every use of the word "God" is necessarily religious.
2. The interpretation of the sensation as "experience of Jesus" and as "salutation of God" already assumes religious language and cannot be applied as its definiens.

42. Nearly a decade before Dalferth, Paul Van Buren presented some germinal insights in his monograph *The Secular Meaning of the Gospel* (1965). In 1972 Uwe Gerber and Erhardt Güttgemanns published *Linguistische Theologie* which connected linguistic findings to exegesis and proclamation.

43. In particular should be mentioned (in sequence of their appearance): Just, *Religiöse Sprache*; Track, *Sprachkritische Untersuchungen*; Grözinger, *Sprache des Menschen*; Halbfas, *Religiöse Sprachlehre*.

44. In addition should be mentioned here the anthology of Gerber/Hoberg, *Sprache und Religion*.

45. Dalferth, *Religiöse Rede*, 355.

46. Dalferth, *Religiöse Rede*, 358–59.

47. Dalferth, *Religiöse Rede*, 397.

3. The most important objection: Dalferth considers language as an isolatable structure from its occurrence and not as a puzzle piece in a human narrative that is to be examined in its entirety.

According to Martin Laube, Dalferth's "failure"[48] shows that the relationship of religiosity and language is faced with the alternative that "religiosity either evaporates into a mist of non-verbal irrationality or acknowledge that religiosity is only mediated by common language and thereby as the special aspect, but it cannot be determined as the other of this language."[49] If Laube's judgment is correct, this is what it would mean for the linguistics of the word of God: one must either refer back to the pre-linguistic phenomenon—and therefore removed from rationality—or the word of God reveals itself finally as a special case of common language usage without any independent claim to validity.

Facing this apparently hopeless background, the undertaking of this study lends itself to being described as an attempt to grasp the *universal validity* of the word of God in the other. The word of God, therefore, is not a special instance of common language but rather human communication proves itself to be a disempowered special case of the word of God.[50]

For further argumentation two linguistic building blocks are especially helpful, both of which have been reviewed in detail in theological circles: metaphor theory and speech act theory. Eberhard Jüngel and Paul Ricœur performed pioneering work on the former in a special issue of *Evangelische Theologie* from 1974,[51] as it was precisely here that faith discourse was pointed toward being defined as "fundamentally and inherently metaphoric."[52] Further evolution of the discussion can be well understood by consulting the anthologies *Erinnern, um Neues zu sagen* by Jean-Pierre van Noppen and *Religion und symbolische Kommunikation*

48. Laube, *Bann*, 12.

49. Laube, *Bann*, 311.

50. The author's intellectual route corresponds to the program of Eberhard Jüngel in *God as the Mystery of the World*: "The goal of the intellectual route adopted in this book is not to demonstrate the thinkability of God on the basis of general anthropological definitions, but rather to think God and also man on the basis of the event of God's self-disclosure which leads to the experience of God, and thus to demonstrate that the Christian truth is universally valid on the basis of its inner power" (Foreword, viii.)

51. Ricœur/Jüngel, *Metapher*.

52. Van Noppen, *Einleitung*, 46.

by Klaus Tanner.[53] Speech act theoretical analyses in theology have to date been fashioned as persuasive and productive for specific exegetical[54] and liturgical[55] issues. However, from a systematic perspective as legitimation of the word of God, the results have been rather disappointing.[56]

53. Specifically on Ricœur see also Korsch, *Paul Ricœur*. From a literary perspective see also Anderegg, *Sprache des Alltags*.

54. See for example Briggs, *Words*, 293–98; Petzold, *Offenbarung*; Wagner, *Sprechakte*.

55. See for example Grabner-Haider, *Glaubenssprache* and Schulte, *Religiöse Rede*, 137–62. A brief research report on this theme can be found in Schulte, *Religiöse Rede*, 45–46.

56. On this point see the essential Dalferth, *Religiöse Sprechakte*.

2

The Word of God in the Bible

2.1. Introduction

The Bible tells consistently of a talking God who speaks to mankind.[1] The explicit thematicization or citation of divine discourse at important portal places ennobles this aspect virtually as a hermeneutical guideline for the entire canon: from the creation account in Genesis 1 through the יְהוָה words in the prophets up to the edict of Cyrus at the end of the Tanach (2 Chr 36:22–23), from the Johannine prologue to the Apocalypse, where the ultimate heavenly judging rider is called ὁ Λόγος τοῦ Θεοῦ (Rev 19:13).

Between the earliest and most recent biblical records of divine discourse lies more than a millennium. Therefore, it is hardly surprising that completely different theological concepts are attached to the term "word of God." Viewed historically, the qualification of divine discourse, and thus determination of its essence, became richer and richer.[2] Nevertheless, a red thread makes itself known—contrary to Wolfhart Pannenberg's criticism of the heterogeneity of the word-concept in the Bible.[3] One can associate all great word of God traditions with particular linguistic functions, which taken together point to profound insight into the essence of language. The task of this chapter is show that this is plausible. It is not

1. See Korsch, *Einführung*, 67 and Haacker, *Wort*, 298.

2. See Noort, "*Wort Gottes*"; Haacker, "*Wort Gottes*"; Klappert, "Λόγος"; Kreuzer, "Λόγος"; Jeremias, *Theologie*, 350–62; Körtner, *Theologie*, 113–19.

3. Pannenberg, *Nachwort*, 132.

about new exegetical insights, nor about an historical line of development, but rather it is about a systematic thesis: the talking God of the Bible is a linguistic God. The creation began with his word, the salvation history of his people with the revelation of his name (אֶהְיֶה אֲשֶׁר אֶהְיֶה).[4] The term "word of God" is an expression of the experience that God:

a. lets himself be comprehended in a spatiotemporal sense solely[5] linguistically—or more generally: conventionally (and not somehow through indicators which in an empirically secure manner point to a cause)[6]

b. is experienced as present solely by processes of communication—and indeed insofar as these processes disclose reality.

The linguistic implications of this thought—which formulates a) from an objective, or b) from a subjective perspective—lend themselves to being read as determinants of the formation of religious language. In the following, five aspects of biblical divine discourse will be differentiated and to each will be assigned a fundamental language function. Of these five aspects, the first three—prophetic, legal, and creative—are recorded primarily in Old Testament writings, while the fourth and fifth—incarnate and critical—primarily in the second part of the canon. All five aspects are intertwined with one another in many ways—and only when taken together do they reveal a witness to how the people of the Bible felt themselves to have been spoken to by God.

2.2 The Prophetic Word

Following Jörg Jeremias and Jan Christian Gertz, the oldest biblical reflections on the word of God are found in the prophetic writings of the eighth century BCE. Micah accuses other נְבִיאִים, that they are making the transmission of God's word dependent on the expected reaction of the addressees. Interestingly, this early text does not separate the word of God from its human articulation, but rather problematizes it directly. The divine לָכֵן is spoken by the mouth of the prophet.

4. Exod 3:14.

5. On the exclusive but not pejorative meaning of this "solely" see Korsch, *Einführung*, 65.

6. On the difference between conventional signs and indicators see Savigny, *Zum Begriff*, 17–21.

We note that 123 of the 225 sources for the construct state combination "word of YHWH/God" in prophetic writings—that is more than 90 percent of the total occurrences in the entire Old Testament[7]—underscore the human transmission using the formula for reception of the word,[8] "the word of YHWH *came to* . . . ." Jörg Jeremias states clearly: "A word of God pure and simple, without the participation of the transmitting prophet, does not exist in the Old Testament."[9] This applies for the formula of God's pronouncement נְאֻם־יְהוָה and the so-called messenger formula כֹּה־אָמַר יְהוָה with its variations, for which Andreas Wagner has shown that behind these an entire system for differentiated theological declarations lets itself be known.[10]

In discussing the prophetic word of God, the discussion cannot be about distilling precise words from texts which were recorded by exclusive witnesses to a supranaturally rendered divine revelation.[11] On the contrary, the discussion should be about the prophetic texts—according to the current prevalent common sense of Old Testament research—and the result of updated interpretation of older traditions by writers' collectives.[12]

Now the question is posed whether or not there is a commonality of texts that one way or another can be identified as "the word of God." For the answer, the observations of Samuel Meier and Friedhelm Hartenstein are helpful. The marking of an order or a decision with the addition "word of . . ." is a prevalent emphasis of the highest authority in ancient Near Eastern history and is connected to the courtly ritual of performance before an audience, which also influenced the YHWH image of the Old Testament.[13] So fundamentally, through its supreme origin, it is about conferring special significance on a proclamation and thereby an outstanding effect. This is not necessary for stories nor for factual texts, but is necessary for proclamations which (should) have actions as consequences—on the order of commands or pronouncements. These

7. On the quantities see Noort, *Wort Gottes*, 291.

8. On this concept see Krispenz, *Wortereignisformel/Wortempfangsformel*, 11.

9. Jeremias, *Theologie*, 353.

10. Wagner, *Prophetie*, especially 330–31.

11. On this see also Maier, *Jeremia*.

12. See Steck, *Prophetenbücher*, 177–204.

13. See Hartenstein, *Angesicht*, 53–62 and Meier, *Speaking*, 316.

precisely are the main categories of prophetic speech, which presents itself as God's word.[14]

The prophetic language of the pronouncement reveals itself prototypically in the form of the verdict on the individual. One example is Amos 7:15b–17 (NRSV):[15]

Commission	"Go (לֵךְ), prophesy to my people Israel!
Call	Now therefore hear the word of the LORD! (וְעַתָּה שְׁמַע דְּבַר־יְהוָה)
Charge	You say, do not prophesy against Israel . . .
Causal Link	Therefore thus says the LORD: (לָכֵן כֹּה־אָמַר יְהוָה)
Announcement	Your wife shall become a prostitute in the city . . ."[16]

This "preliterary form"[17] is varied in many ways in the prophetic texts, especially in the sentencing of an entire people, but "the only thing remaining the same throughout all of these variations is that which constitutes the essence of the judgment-speech directed to Israel—the judgment of God is announced to the people because of specific failures."[18]

The defining characterization of the prophetic word is therefore the pronouncement of a—generally speaking negative[19]—sanction of whose arrival no one should doubt. It is a declarative speech act, which—if it succeeds—changes the world and thereby is a performative language event.[20] If it succeeds, the future demonstrates it. Of course, when the time came for written tradition and updating of prophetic writings, this was in many cases already in the past.

In retrospect, declarative speech acts obtain a totally different function. They explain history and thereby display potential for interpretation towards coping with contingency, with which the expatriates in Babylon may have been able to make sense of events despite their traumatic experiences.[21] The potential for interpretation is therefore that much stronger

14. See Westermann, *Basic Forms*, 90.

15. See Westermann, *Basic Forms*, 131 and Schart, *Prophetie*, 15.

16. Unless otherwise noted, Bible citations in English are from the New Revised Standard Version.

17. Westermann, *Basic Forms*, 172.

18. Westermann, *Basic Forms*, 176.

19. Only after the destruction of Jerusalem in 587 BCE did editors add an occasional word of comfort or salvation in the prophetic books (see Schart, *Prophetie*, 19).

20. On the term "declarative speech act," see Searle, *Classification*, 1–23.

21. See Lange, *Vom prophetischen Wort*, 316–19.

the more credibly the causal connection between pronouncement and real events turns out. And what could be more credible than כֹּה־אָמַר יְהוָה? This is why later redactions, for example of Jeremiah, converted frequently prophetic speeches without a connection to God which turned out to be true, into YHWH speeches.[22] For only as divine speech can the prophetic word disclose reality.

In this way the remnants of magical exaltation of language play a role in biblical texts, as is shown for example in the names portending doom in Hosea 1:4–8, in the renamings commanded by God (Hos 2:35; Jer 20:3), or in numerous etiological word games.[23] But it is precisely the prophetic tradition of the Old Testament which records that the impact of language cannot be compared to any other divination. Paradigmatically, the story of Balaam in Numbers 22–24 (NRSV) gets to the heart of the matter. The heathen seer realizes that at best he can only, with his mantic methods, foresee reality but not influence it. Only God's word creates reality: "Now Balaam saw [וַיַּרְא] that it pleased the LORD to bless Israel, so he did not go, as at other times to look for omens [נְחָשִׁים]," but became the "oracle of one who hears the words of God, and knows the knowledge of the Most High" (Num 24:1.16, NRSV). The story turns out to be a "lesson . . . on true prophesy and the way there."[24]

The most comprehensive reflection on the difference between true and false prophets is offered in Jeremiah 23:9–30, "originating in the immediate setting of the catastrophe of Judea and Jerusalem in 587 BCE."[25] Jeremiah names five criteria by which the word of God may be known:[26]

1. First of all is the unrestrained power with which the "holy words [דִּבְרֵי קָדְשׁוֹ]" (Jer 23:9, NRSV) take over a man and fundamentally and, occasionally, traumatically transform his personality. They work like wine, which makes a man drunk and has him stagger (Jer 23:9, NRSV). In Jeremiah 20:7 Jeremiah speaks of having been persuaded by God against his will (פִּתִּיתַנִי) and in the process plays on the connotation of פתה as "rape" (see Exod 22:15, NRSV).

2. Then there is the inability of false prophets to differentiate between their own thoughts, "visions of their own minds [חֲזוֹן לִבָּם]" and the

22. See Hermisson, *Studien*, 65.

23. See von Rad, *Theologie*, 2, 92–93 with examples.

24. Gaß, *Menschliches Handeln*, 107.

25. Gertz, *Grundinformation*, 351.

26. On this see Jeremias, *Theologie*, 353–55.

words "from the mouth of the LORD [מִפִּי יְהוָה]" (Jer 23:16, NRSV). They project their wishful thinking onto God's will.

3. In this way they invert the intended effect of God's word and confirm the people in their wrongdoing (Jer 23:17, NRSV). Accordingly the word of God should—and this is the third criteria—"turn them from their evil way, and from the evil of their doings" (Jer 23:22, NRSV).

4. The false prophets confuse the basic understanding of the word of God with its proximity to human thinking. They gather up all of God with God's word and overlook the crucial element (Jer 23:23, NRSV): "Am I a God nearby [אֱלֹהֵי מִקָּרֹב], says the LORD, and not a God far off [אֱלֹהֵי מֵרָחֹק]?"

5. Finally Jeremiah once more sharply differentiates the word of God from every non-linguistic vision (חֲלוֹם) and emphasizes the recalcitrance of divine discourse in one of the few passages in the Old Testament which criticizes dreams (Jer 23:28–29, NRSV): "Let the prophet who has a dream tell the dream, but let the one who has my word speak my word faithfully. What has straw in common with wheat? says the LORD. Is not my word like fire, says the LORD, and like a hammer that breaks a rock in pieces?"

What is thematicized in the narrated present at the textual level as a question of the truth of prophecy presents itself—as explained above—at the receptive level of readers as a question of the reasonable interpretation of what happened long ago.[27] From both perspectives, the hallmark of God's word is its performative and effective (while reality-creative) power. In the language of the Old Testament: the divine word is not one which "fails" or "tumbles to earth [לא יפל אדמה]," provided that אדמה can be missing and only so long as the "invalid" (German, *hinfällig*) stands alone and remains.[28] A different description qualifies the word of God as one that does not remain "empty [רֵק]."[29] Both images bring together the famous divine speech at the end of Deutero-Isaiah: "For as the rain and

27. That the narrators of prophetic writings consistently concede more weight to the power of interpretation than historical precision is shown by the example of Hos 1:4–5 (see Gaß, *Menschliches Handeln*, 152–53).

28. Examples: Josh 21:45; Josh 23:14; 1 Kgs 8:56; 2 Kgs 10:10; 1 Sam 3:19. On this see also Dürr, *Wertung*, 67.

29. Deut 32:47; Isa 58:13. See also von Rad, *Theologie*, 2, 95.

the snow come down from heaven, and do not return there until they have watered the earth, making it bring forth and sprout, giving seed to the sower and bread to the eater, so shall my word be that goes out from my mouth; it shall not return to me empty, but it shall accomplish that which I purpose, and succeed in the thing for which I sent it" (Isa 55:10–11, NRSV).

Here it is striking that in this description that word is parted from its human messenger and appears as a hypostasis. It is the same active power which makes life on earth possible. In this one can see, like Gerhard von Rad and Walter Zimmerli, the beginnings of a theology of the word.[30] The pronouncements of justice in Deutero-Isaiah (Isa 43:12–13 and Isa 48:16), in which YHWH defends his unique position against all other gods, presage the understood word almost into a "proof of God":[31] "Since the divinity of God in inconceivable without the direction of historical reality, the prophetic word is the only way to verify the claim of being God."[32]

In the prophetic word of God the reality- and future-forming power of God in the form of its human recognizability from the a posteriori perspective is named: as a linguistic option of interpretation. The function of language, on which this interpretation is based, is performance. Every language event alters reality—one more, the other less. In this sense, the word of God can be thought of as the maximum of this power. Both sections which follow, covering biblical points of view on the word of God, are variations on this theme. The legal word stresses the potential for interpretation, the creative word stresses the constitution of reality.

2.3 The Legal Word

The transition from the emphasis on the prophetic word to the emphasis on the legal word-character in the deuteronomistic redaction of Jeremiah from the post-exilic era becomes especially significant.[33] Here the salvation pronouncements of earlier prophets were held accountable for the catastrophe of 587 BCE because they confirmed the people in their

30. von Rad, *Theologie*, 2, 102–3; Zimmerli, *Ezechiel*, 89.

31. Jeremias, *Theologie*, 356.

32. Jeremias, *Theologie*, 356.

33. See Lange, *Vom prophetischen Wort*, 313–15.

iniquity and their forsaking YHWH.[34] While Haggai and Zecharaia were repeating the Zion-theological message of salvation—and the supposed cause for that judgment of God—after the reconstruction of Jerusalem in 520–515 BCE, the deuteronomistic Jeremiah redaction found "Jeremiah's rejection of all contemporary prophets confirmed" and urged the people to listen to the תּוֹרָה (Jer 26:4) and the revelation on Sinai (Jer 7:9, 22–23) instead.[35] Armin Lange writes: "This rejection of all present-day and future prophecy by the deuteronomistic Jeremiah in favor of the once forgotten word and its exegesis had been carried out comprehensively in the post-exilic era."[36] The historically falsified experiences with salvation prophecy initiated a realignment with traditional prophecy: "Revelation now occurs in the expanded exegesis of the once forgotten word."[37]

This brief historical parenthesis should make it clear that the legal word is no newly appended strand of tradition nor a "second root," as Oskar Grether still believes,[38] but rather it evolved out of the prophetic word in the service of harnessing reality. Even if behind the idea of the prophetic word the idea persists that God continually intervenes in history in a revelatory fashion, from the later point of view of the recipient the overriding insight is that God binds himself reliably and verifiably to his promises and his words possess a timeless validity. Ezekiel 2:8—3:4 paints a vivid picture of this transfer of accent. At God's command the prophet eats an entire scroll almost as if it were several years' supply of God's pronouncements to Israel. The relation between both aspects is to be seen throughout from both directions. In Deuteronomy 28 the legal word is definitively bound to prophetic promises and warnings. "For the deuteronomic theologians, the word of God from Moses and the word of God from the prophets belong closely together."[39]

The legal word certainly has one outstanding characteristic. In contrast to the prophetic word, it cannot be escaped. Think of divine punishments, such as those spoken of in Amos 8:1 and 1 Samuel 28:6.15–18, for example. By contrast, the law is not silent. Thereby it qualifies itself as a reliable basis for every way of living, as Deuteronomy 32:46–47 (NRSV)

34. See for example Jer 5:12–30.

35. Lange, *Vom prophetischen Wort*, 314.

36. Lange, *Vom prophetischen Wort*, 315.

37. Lange, *Vom prophetischen Wort*, 317.

38. Grether, *Name und Wort*, 111.

39. Jeremias, *Theologie*, 359.

tells us: “Take to heart all the words that I am giving in witness against you today; give them as a command to your children, so that they may diligently observe all the words of this law [כָּל־דִּבְרֵי הַתּוֹרָה הַזֹּאת]. This is no trifling matter for you, but rather your very life [חַיֵּיכֶם]; through it you may live long in the land that you are crossing over the Jordan to possess.”

At the same time the law demands complete trust in its exclusivity, like the first commandment of the Decalogue clearly states:[40] “I am the LORD your God [יְהוָה], who brought you out of the land of Egypt, out of the house of slavery; you shall have no other gods before me [עַל־פָּנָיַ]” (Exod 20:2–3, NRSV). Here the included communicative references emerge clearly. The statutory bearer of the word inserts himself in a language act of introduction,[41] which takes up the revelation scene at the burning bush (Exod 3:14–17). The name revelation is a precondition for the following word revelation. Both must be thought of as complementary in order to exclude on the one hand an autonomy of the word as a timeless and authorless idea, and on the other hand a voiceless “mystical immersion in any sort of divine primary source.”[42]

In every self-perception lies a call to the counterpart, to act towards it. One can ignore it (which generally speaking is again an act with communicative consequences) or one can engage with the contact. Then the question presents itself: How does this new relationship alter my understanding of myself and of my world?[43] In this special case of divine self-perception there is no concrete opposite which exists in the same representational sense like other persons, but only as a linguistic phenomenon—the word אָנֹכִי. That is not a liability but rather a great asset for the interpretation of the revealed words. It introduces an “I” that itself is not a part of the circumstances of which constitute the world, but at the same time provides, as an “I,” a reference point toward a relationship with the world to which the recipient himself can relate.[44] “I am your God, you shall have no other gods before me”: the offer of interpretation of God’s unity and singularity which is made here to acknowledged hearers and readers is that of the “oneness and wholeness of life.”[45]

40. On this see also Jeremias, *Gottesbild*, 72.

41. See Korsch, *Einführung*, 63.

42. Grether, *Name und Wort*, 166.

43. See Korsch, *Einführung*, 63–64.

44. Korsch, *Einführung*, 64–67.

45. Korsch, *Einführung*, 67.

If the God-relation is introduced in the first commandment, then the second commandment regulates the connection of God-relation and self-relation. The name of God understood this way may be used for nothing else without losing its all-encompassing power of interpretation. The following commandments can then be read as a shaping of the world-relation for a self-relation which is grounded in a God-relation.[46] In its totality the legal word shows itself once again as a transcendent disclosure of reality over and above the prophetic word. Its prescriptivity allows not only for a collective coping with contingency but also harnesses "the movement of [active] life itself."[47] Completely in line with Deuteronomy 32:47a: "This is no trifling matter for you, but rather your very life."

The divine discourse in the Psalter, as Andrea Doeker describes it in her poetological study, goes even a step further. The dialogic structure of anabatic prayer discourse and katabatic divine discourse, especially in the post-exilic Asaf psalms, serves individual contingency-coping and an almost therapeutic, pastoral function: "Those who pray live in trust of the power of bygone divine words which have not lost their validity, and in trust of the present-day effectiveness of the divine word which is capable of altering negative situations."[48]

In Psalm 119, the longest chapter of the Bible, the functions of divine words are once again hymnic and are skillfully conflated in twenty-two stanzas with each stanza beginning with the same letter. The prophetic word of promise, the power of God's word to direct history, as well as the character of the laws to order reality, which serve to make the life of those who follow and observe them "happy [אַשְׁרֵ]" (Ps 1:1, NRSV).

2.4 The Creative Word

The performative component of the prophetic word in the priestly creation myth (Gen 1:1–2, 4a) gets to the heart of the matter in thoughtfully concise form and thereby expanded by a crucial moment. While in the older, mostly designated "yahwistic" story of creation (Gen 2:4b–25) God appears as a manual creator, who makes, plants, and forms something and then speaks as the humans are dwelling in the Garden of Eden (Gen

46. On this in detail see Korsch, *Einführung*, 81–134.

47. Korsch, *Einführung*, 129.

48. Doeker, *Funktion*, 306.

2:16),[49] in the more recent priestly version he appears only as a speaker. As a rule[50] there follows on the divine command the formula of accomplishment, "and there was . . ." (וַיְהִי). The command itself is in each case kept as short as possible. Corresponding to the performative sense of the Hebrew, the first act of creation in Genesis 1:3 (וַיְהִי־אוֹר) can truly be translated with just one word: "Light!"[51]

In this context the immediacy of the creator's word is unique, even with a view to both of the older and continually discussed Middle Eastern creation myths. The epic *Enuma eliš* from the twelfth century BCE has the Babylonian city-god Marduk extinguish a constellation by command and then puts it back up in the firmament[52]—but here "faith in the magical power of the word" stands firmly in the foreground.[53]

The barely five centuries younger[54] monument to Memphitic theology knows of a deity Ptah whose heart and tongue dwells in all gods, humans, animals, and plants and who called into existence the entire universe.[55] In comparison to the P story two differences are significant, which from a systematic perspective accentuate the special features of the priestly word of creation:

a) Firstly in Genesis 1 it is not commanded, but with language created. In the moment of pronouncement what is said has been fulfilled. Nothing can come between speech and deed, which are united in the term "creation."[56] A *reality-constituting* language event is being narrated, which in the Hebrew text is expressed by its own verb—בָּרָא—instead of עָשָׂה.[57]

b) Secondly in the ancient Egyptian myth the monophysitism is striking, according to which God and man are of the same nature. Ptah does not face his creation but in it he thinks and speaks with *his* heart

49. On the language skepticism of the yahwistic story see Zaborowski, *Aber sprich nur ein Wort*, 64–69.

50. On the inner structure of the story and its irregularities see Kaiser, *Der Gott*, 253–64.

51. Miles, *God*, 26.

52. *Enuma eliš*, table 4.

53. von Rad, *Theologie*, 1, 157.

54. On the dating see Kaiser, *Die Schöpfungsmacht*, 7, and the documents named there.

55. See *Denkmal*, 255–57.

56. See Steck, *Schöpfungsbericht*, 48.

57. See Kaiser, *Der Gott*, 257–58.

and *his* tongue.[58] Otherwise the biblical God: he is not only quantitatively superior to his creation, but categorically detached from it.

Here the theological advantage of the P myth shows itself. Fundamentally there are three possibilities conceivable for thinking clearly of the creation of the universe by a Pantocrator in analogy to everyday processes: a) as biological procreation, b) as a product of manual labor, and c) as a verbal command.[59]

Option a) boils down compellingly to monophysitism, option b) to a vulgar anthropomorphic God-image. Only c) allows for "God and the world to be so fundamentally detached from one another, that . . . the transcendence of God shines through."[60] Here language is the last anthropomorphic remnant, the only bridge between immanence and transcendence. Any further reduction of the anthropomorphic share would lead to voicelessness and thereby into the inconceivability of God, and thus to an agnostic worldview.

Otto Kaiser calls it an "astonishing fact for the contemporary reader" that the Priestly Scriptures start out with the description of God's work of creation without beforehand having established the obviously required fact of the divine in itself.[61] The physico-theological proof of God, which infers from the earthly order the God who puts in order, assumes—as Immanuel Kant has shown[62]—the ontological proof of God. P in no way provides this, but introduces God right away with וַיֹּאמֶר אֱלֹהִים (Gen 1:3) as a speaker and lets it be known that knowledge of God and knowledge of the world cannot be conceived as anything other than linguistically structured. Language constitutes reality—and at the same time enables rapprochement between immanence and transcendence.

2.5 The Incarnate Word

The mediation between God and the world remains abstract if it is not thought of in personal terms. Only the personality makes out of an

58. See Kaiser, *Der Gott*, 249–50 and Kaiser, *Die Schöpfungsmacht*, 7–8.

59. See Kaiser, *Der Gott*, 240.

60. Kaiser, *Die Schöpfungsmacht*, 8.

61. Kaiser, *Die Schöpfungsmacht*, 12–13.

62. Kant, *Critique of Pure Reason*, 555 (A 630/B658): "Accordingly, the physico-theological proof of the existence of a single original being as the highest being is grounded on the cosmological, and the latter on the ontological."

ordering instance of a known quantity a quantity who speaks directly to mankind and is existentially relevant. This thought forms the basis of the wisdom hymns of the Old Testament. In Proverbs 8 wisdom is conceived as the ordering principle of creation and human history and therefore demonstrates human attributes: it was brought forth (Prov 8:24), stands at the side of the creator (Prov 8:27), plays like a child (Prov 8:30), and delights in the human race (Prov 8:31).

This personification of wisdom, as Hartmut Gese has convincingly proven, serves as the "traditio-historical origin" for the logos hymn in the John prologue.[63] Most of all, the parallels to the late wisdom song in Sirach 24 are striking. Here, wisdom is praised as a creative, history-forming, and legal quantity (Sir 23) which comes forth "from the mouth of the Most High" (Sir 24:3) and seeks a resting place (Sir 24:7). The step from חָכְמָה to λόγος is already sketched out. Since John 1 primarily concerns itself with salvation-historical significance, "those components must emerge in the idea of wisdom which has long since connected creation with salvation history, the divine *dabar*."[64]

The incarnation specific to the John prologue[65] is to be understood as a further ascertainment of the personality. While Sirach 24 gives pride of place to the cultural history of Israel, John 1 is all about the "human subjective reference to the revelation."[66] While Sirach tells how God spoke to a people, John proclaims that here God speaks to individual persons—and indeed as a person. In John 1 the religiously pointed language functions are once again tied to a human counterpart: the Jesus Christ who is witnessed to in the gospel is God's word incarnate, naming the experience of having been spoken to by God.[67]

Consequently Jesus' discourse—especially in John and Luke—is seen as the authentic word of God: "He whom God has sent speaks the words [ῥήματα] of God (John 3:34, NRSV). In Luke's two-volume work the equivalence of God's word and Jesus' proclamation runs like a red thread from Luke 5:1 to Acts 19:20.[68] This identification carries with it the fact that the word of God in the New Testament can never be directed

63. Gese, *Johannesprolog*, 179.

64. Gese, *Johannesprolog*, 180.

65. See though the identification of wisdom with the son of man in Ethiopic Enoch 48:3.6.

66. Gese, *Johannesprolog*, 184.

67. See Ebeling, *Dogmatik*, 69–73.

68. See Wischmeyer, *Wort*, 31 (on Luke) and 33 (on Acts).

toward Jesus himself. The voices ἐκ τῶν οὐρανῶν and ἐκ τῆς νεφέλης respectively, which are heard in the baptism scene[69] and transfiguration scene,[70] are directed explicitly at the spectators. Even the Synoptic tradition hands down few sayings of Jesus in which ὁ λόγος occurs[71]—including none in the putative Q material.

The word occurrence formula is found only once in the New Testament in Luke 3:2,[72] where they are connected to John the Baptist. Nevertheless, the Jesus of the Gospels is tied to the prophetic tradition—in the manner of surpassing that same tradition. The antitheses of the Sermon on the Mount following the pattern "You have heard that it was said to those of ancient times . . . But I say to you . . ." (Matt 5:21–22, NRSV), just like the phrase "Truly I say to you,"[73] which is "without analogy in Jewish literature," verifies the "divine self-authentication of his word."[74] If the tradition of the legal word is taken up here, then the stories of healing, in which only Jesus' discourses are effective, stand in the tradition of the creative effect of the word.[75]

The John prologue reflects this surpassing[76] with a new interpretation: Jesus does not only fulfill the prophetic writings, he is also not only the one authoritative prophet—in him as the "revelator is the origin of all things existent."[77] He is the pre-existent word that created everything: Moses, the prophets, the Baptist, they all had their truth through him. They *proclaimed* the word of God; Jesus *is* the word of God.

By this thought the λόγος first achieves autonomy from דְּבַר־יְהוָה as Rudolf Bultmann has proven: "In the Old Testament word and history soon fall to pieces. The history is that which the people have experienced . . . and the prophetic or legal word intervenes in the here and now. . . . The history of Christ is not one already past but fulfills itself in the

69. Matt 3:17; Mark 1:11; Luke 3:22.

70. Matt 17:5; Mark 9:7; Luke 9:35.

71. Along with the interpretation of the parable of the sower (Matt 13:18–23) there are only Mark 7:13, Luke 8:21, and Luke 11:28.

72. ῥῆμα θεοῦ ἐγένετο . . .

73. Seventy-four occurrences in the gospels.

74. Klappert, "Λόγος," 1939 and 1940.

75. Above all in Matt 8:8b (NRSV): "But only speak the word, and my servant will be healed."

76. The Jesuanic surpassing of the prophets is also the point of departure for the word of God concept in the Letter to the Hebrews (see above all Heb 1:1–4).

77. Theißen, *Religion*, 258.

proclaiming word."[78] But as a result the effect on those who hear becomes a crucial component of the word of God whose history only now begins with its recognition by the recipient.[79] "Everyone then who hears these words of mine and acts on them," they are called by Jesus a "wise man," but those who hear and do not act, on the other hand, are "foolish" (Matt 7:24 and 26, NRSV). "When Jesus makes judgment dependent on the hearing and acting (or not acting) on his own words, it differentiates his word from the highest claims of the ancient prophets. These prophets consider themselves nothing less than the bearers of the word of God. But none of them say that 'his words' will not pass away or that the judgment of those hearing depends on those words."[80]

God's discourse does not alter external circumstances but aims in its personality at the center of human self-understanding—almost between ψυχή and πνεῦμα, as Hebrews says—and God's word demands a judgment and is active, "sharper than a two-edged sword," "able to judge the thoughts (ἐνθυμήσεων) and intentions (ἐννοιῶν) of the heart" (Heb 4:12, NRSV).

This new aspect of interpretation is decisive for Paul. The earliest historical mention of the word of God in a writing of the New Testament—as λόγος ἀκοῆς τοῦ θεοῦ in 1 Thessalonians 2:13—emphasizes its effect ἐν ὑμῖν, namely the conversion of the addressees to the faithful.[81] How this conversion was accomplished by the word and its consequences is most vividly described by Paul in 1 Corinthians 1:18–25. This pericope is fathomed separately in section 2.6 below in which the personal function of the word of God, which leads to self-knowledge, is taken one step further to a critical function. The discourse requires a reaction from the person addressed, and on which in turn further communication wholly depends.

2.6. The Critical Word

A sentencing whose judgment is made dependent on the behavior of the hearers is also known in the Old Testament—even though such stories are counted as exceptions.[82] The most prominent example is mentioned

78. Bultmann, *Begriff*, 292.

79. Bultmann, *Begriff*, 293.

80. Schniewind, *Matthäus*, 105.

81. See also Rom 10:13–17.

82. Westermann, *Basic Forms*, 186–87 names the examples of Isa 7:1–7 and Isa

in Jonah 3, where the annihilating divine judgment within the forty-day period leads to a surprising conversion of the inhabitants of Niniveh and this finally leads to the salvation of the city. Here it concerns the behavior of a group, not an individual decision.

This critical[83] function of the word of God, to initiate among addressees a behavior of recognition or rejection with existential and eschatological consequences, is especially conspicuous in the New Testament in connection with theology of the cross. This is documented firstly in the gospel of Mark in which the proclamation of Jesus' sufferings in Mark 8:31–32 concludes the previous imagery in parables (καὶ παρρησίᾳ τὸν λόγον ἐλάλει)—and in the rebuke of Peter the greatest polarity conceivable is promptly called into action: "Get behind me, Satan!" commands Jesus (Mark 8:33, NRSV). And after the news of the resurrection (Mark 16:6–7) the paradoxical Mark ending—καὶ οὐδενὶ οὐδὲν εἶπαν (Mark 16:8)—provokes readers to their own conclusion: Do you believe or do you not believe?

On the other hand—and this is the *locus classicus* of the theology of the cross[84]—the Pauline text 1 Corinthians 1:18–25 stands for a radical reinterpretation of the discourse of God:[85] "Within the ancient world the 'message about the cross' constitutes something completely new and singular."[86] Here a "provocative and yet extraordinarily creative act of early Christianity"[87] is shown which decisively shapes the interpretation, proclamation, and textualization of the new faith.[88]

These verses, supposedly from early 55 CE,[89] are directed at the historical provenance setting of the church community founded by Paul in Corinth in 50 CE.[90] In a socially heterogeneous community[91] consisting

28:14 "expansions" of the prophetic word of judgment. In the broadest sense one could also count the story of the bronze serpent among them (Num 21:4–9).

83. In our context the literal sense of "κρίνειν" as differentiate, separate.

84. On the historical independence on 1 Corinthians from Mark see Luz, *Theologia*, especially 120–21.

85. See Vollenweider, *Weisheit*, 43.

86. Schnelle, *Die ersten 100*, 460.

87. Schnelle, *Die ersten 100*, 460.

88. On the Pauline theology of the cross as a "prototype of the manifold variations of paradox theology" in the New Testament see Vouga, *Kreuzestheologie*, 325.

89. See Schnelle, *Einleitung*, 74.

90. See Acts 18:11–18.

91. See Schnelle, *Paulus*, 198–200.

of Jewish Christians, proselytes, and former adherents of Hellenistic-Middle Eastern cults, differences of opinion on various issues of fact had been inflamed,[92] which Paul tries to clarify with this letter.[93] In doing so he especially grapples with a speculative wisdom theology of Judaistic-Hellenistic provenance which hopes to create exclusive access to certainty of salvation beyond the new doctrine—without the crucified at the center.[94] The rejoinder of the apostle is consolidated in the few sentences of 1 Corinthians 1:18–25 which elevate themselves from their context by inclusive use of first person plural.

The promise of divine presence—here as δύναμις θεοῦ—is the central content of the *propositio* (verse 18) and is included at the conclusion of the *argumentatio* (verse 24).[95] Salvation is bound to the acceptance of an almost unheard of interpretation: the new play on words is λόγος τοῦ σταυροῦ (verse 18)—replaces the old play on words σοφίᾳ λόγου since this has not stood the test. The world did not know God through the wisdom which comes forth from God (verse 21)—so accordingly, Paul modified a motif from Judaic wisdom theology.[96] It disappeared for a certain period and then reemerged in a configuration both foreign and obnoxious to all conventional forms of discourse. In verse 20 obsolete discourses are characterized on the one hand as diachronically understood wisdom based on scriptures and tradition (γραμματεύς), and on the other hand as synchronous, dialogic, and word-based wisdom (συζητητὴς). This is similar to verses 22–23 where Paul counterpoises divine logic of salvation to both "basic idolatries."[97] Prophetically-oriented thought requires from the divine a sign as an exception to the rule; order-oriented thought conversely enquires after wisdom as GPS coordinates in the cosmic harmony.[98]

The rules of the new play on words are formulated in verses 23–25. Christ is the crucified. He is to be proclaimed exclusively as the crucified.

92. For this reading of 1 Corinthians (contrary to the long-held thesis in reception history of Paul's "enemies") see Schrottroff, *Brief*, 25.

93. Of the numerous partial hypotheses on 1 Corinthians our pericope remains intact: 1:1 to 2:5 is viewed unanimously as a single entity in literary criticism (see Schnelle, *Einleitung*, 80).

94. See Sellin, *Streit*, 67–68.

95. On the rhetorical characterization see Schrage, *Brief*, 167.

96. See Sir 24:3–7, Eth. En. 42, and the post-Pauline John 1:10–12. For further sources on the motif of absent wisdom in Judaic literature see Williams, *Wisdom*, 48.

97. Fee, *Epistle*, 75.

98. See Baidou, *Paulus*, 55 and Vollenweider, *Weisheit*, 48.

He who accepts this faithfully, for him Christ is God's power and God's wisdom. Indeed, those who believe in the foolishness of our proclamation are already saved (infinitive aorist in verse 21!). Thus their existence is fundamentally altered—and right at the moment in which they accept the good news. Here the word takes on a soteriological function.[99]

The *parallelismus membrorum* in verse 25 conveys the comparative that this foolishness and this weakness does not simply express the "paradoxical otherness of God,"[100] but rather faith in the message about the cross opens up a new, "broad . . . dimension of experience."[101] In the foolish message about the cross more wisdom is shown than in every human understanding of the world—and the weakness of God in the crucified Christ turns out to be the strength that even conquers death. Since Paul always keeps in mind the resurrection of all in the resurrection of Christ,[102] verse 25 closes the arc to verse 18. The salvation of those who believe in the message about the cross resides in the transcendence, originating in God, of their mortality.

With a view to other key Pauline passages the play on words with the cross as the "central narrative abbreviature"[103] can be expanded still further. From 1 Corinthians 1:8 arises the equation with Romans 1:16 of "message about the cross," "power of God," and "gospel." One reads with 1 Corinthians 2:1–2 and Romans 16:25: the "crucified Christ" is the "mystery of God" and the "gospel." From 2 Corinthians 5:14–17 finally follows the existence-altering impact of this demonstrable power of God in the crucified: "So if anyone is in Christ, there is a new creation: everything old has passed away; see, everything has become new!" (2 Cor 5:17, NRSV).

Whoever can say that about themselves, for them the interpretation option has become a definition of existence which brooks no alternative. This becomes significant in the pericope when one follows the reading of the oldest manuscript P46 for 1 Corinthians. According to this 1 Corinthians 1:24—in contrast to later codices—is a standalone sentence.[104] The crucified Christ is not proclaimed to those called as God's power and wisdom, he *is* God's power and wisdom. It is about more than the

99. See Wischmeyer, *Wort Gottes*, 39.

100. Vollenweider, *Weisheit*, 50.

101. Vollenweider, *Weisheit*, 50.

102. 1 Cor 15:13.20–22. See also Käsemann, *Perspektiven*, 75 and 99.

103. Schnelle, *Die ersten 100*, 460.

104. See *NT Graece*, 520.

communication of an interpretation, it is about a synchronous event of hearing, recognizing, and being saved. The cross as "basis and standard for metaphor formation appropriate to God"[105] was believed by the first Christians to be a "turning point of the world."[106] This God "can not be talked about as if everything remains as it was."[107]

The subsequent verses 1 Corinthians 1:26–31 provide to some extent the empirical proof for the entire line of thought. Precisely the community in Corinth shows for sure, with their few sages, aristocrats, and power brokers, according to Paul, that God had chosen the fools.

The message about the cross proves to be an experience of a linguistically communicated option of interpretation which in the moment of its acceptance necessarily alters the entire horizon of experiences—and guarantees individual salvation. In the Pauline proclamation the crucified Christ stands for an interpretation situation which, with reference to the canonic texts,[108] demands a border crossing of present-day plays on words and thereby an innovative semantics. The connection to familiar plays on words consists precisely in the fact that the meanings of defined terms—wisdom, strength, power—are inverted to their exact opposites.

The eight verses of 1 Corinthians are worthy of a closer examination because it is here that the Judeo-Christian concept of the word of God soars to a higher level of reflexion. Here the promise of salvation is defined as a new reality into which one enters by the acceptance of an expanded new semantics of the word of God. That word is the key to soteriology.

2.7. Summary

The talking God of the Bible is a linguistic God. The term "word of God" owes its origin to the experience that God can only be recorded in language and only be experienced as active in communicative contexts. This presence of the absent one is demonstrated in speech acts of various kinds. This is, then, the basic thesis of this chapter which highlights and outlines five aspects of divine discourse, interrelated and bound

105. Jüngel, *Metaphorische Wahrheit*, 117.

106. Gogarten, *Jesus*.

107. Jüngel, *Metaphorische Wahrheit*, 118.

108. The reference is made explicit (γέγραπται γάρ) in verse 19, where Paul cites Isa 29:14cd LXX, and it is oblique in verse 20, where the three-fold anaphora evokes Isa 19:11, Isa 33:18 (the only three-fold ποῦ question in the LXX), and Bar 3:16.

together by intellectual evolution. These five aspects then become five language functions:

Aspect	Language Function	Purpose
Prophetic word	Performance	Coping with contingency
Legal word	Prescription	Interpretation of reality
Creative word	Access to transcendence	Constitution of reality
Personified word	Personality	Self-knowledge
Critical word	Semantic creativity	Soteriology

Figure 1. The word of God in the Bible

The prophetic word emphasizes the performance of linguistic acts and serves the collective coping with contingency in its retrospective textualization and canonization. The legal word evolves out of the prophetic in which the reliability of divine discourse is defined as a prescription and so can be used as an individual interpretation of reality. The creative word draws on the performative power of the prophetic and elevates this to a constitution of reality, whereby a connection emerges between immanence and transcendence by means of language. The personified word shifts the focus to the personality of the language event and stresses the possibility of self-knowledge, which can be the result of two communicators in opposition to one another. Finally, the critical word connects the reality interpreting components of the first three aspects with the individual directionality of the fourth. It claims for itself the creation of a new, eschatological reality to which the recipients have immediate access by acceptance of the innovative interpretations being offered. One can read this as a linguistic-philosophical definition of "gospel."

Overall these concepts demonstrate by which language functions the special nature of collective or individual experience can be connected to an absolutely conceived universal. The five language functions are constituents of divine discourse and therefore also of religious experience dependent upon symbolic communication. On this basis three Christian theologians in particular reflected further, deeper, and creatively on the connection between the word of God and human language and discourse: Augustine by means of the ancient philosophy of language (chapter 3), Martin Luther by means of his profound insight into the potential for interpretation of language (chapter 4), and Karl Barth with his resolutely theocentric and christologically based theory of language (chapter 5).

3

The Word of God in Augustine

3.1. Introduction

WHETHER AS *VERBUM DEI* or *verbum divinum*, the word of God appears in Augustine in three essential contexts with, at first glance, different meanings.[1] First comes the creative word of God, that is dealt with in particular in Augustine's interpretations of Genesis (see section 3.2). The second interpretation complex is the *verbum*, which originating in John 1 is thought of as an inner-trinitarian relation and to which is especially dedicated *De trinitate* (see section 3.3). Finally we will deal with the specifically postlapsarian ways of speaking of God, which to a greater or lesser degree make extensive use of human sign systems. In doing so, Augustine differentiates between (1) external speech of God ordered by visible or audible means, (2) imaginative speech "in sleep or ecstasy," and (3) internal speech which is performed in waking,[2] which can be called "revelation" (*illuminatio*) in the narrower sense.[3] These empirical forms of appearance are, however, only seldom objects of Augustine's studies. He is much more interested in the imaginary interface between *verbum*

1. See Pintarič, *Sprache*, 31, where, however, the creative word is missing, and Wieland, *Offenbarung*, 99–100, which for its own purposes differentiates only between "creative" and "revelatory." Our classification is oriented on *De genesi ad litteram libri duodecim* 8,27 and *Sermo* 12,4.

2. *De genesi ad litteram* 8,27.

3. Wieland, *Offenbarung*, 101.

dei and human language: the "inner word" whose concept is developed in *De triniate* (see section 3.5).

In this respect the fall from grace is of systematic significance for this differentiation, as it has a crucial epistemological consequence for Augustine. Original sin understood as *superbia*[4] indicates a "renunciation of the inner source of truth and therefore . . . a binding of thought to materiality."[5] In prelapsarian fashion, Augustine uses an image inspired by Genesis 2:5[6]—"God watered the soul by an interior spring, speaking to its intellect [*in intellectu eius*], so that it did not receive words from the outside." After sin God speaks only "from the clouds," by which the writings of the prophets and apostles are intended:[7] "They are correctly called clouds, because these words which sound and pass away after they strike the air become like clouds when there is added the obscurity of allegories like a fog that has been drawn over them. When they are pressed by study, the rain of truth, so to speak, is poured out on those who understand well."[8]

In this cloud image can be heard that critical attitude towards human words—whether written or spoken—which remains a constant from his early work *De dialectica* through *De magistro* and *De doctrina christiana* all the way to his late work *De trinitate*, a trademark of Augustine's sign theory and language theory. This engagement shows itself like a red thread by his far-flung reflection. Like no other Christian theologian before him, the trained rhetor and philologist systematically unfolded his sign concept and made pagan language theory fruitful for religious contexts.[9] The linguist Eugenio Coseriu acknowledges him as "the third great philosopher of language of antiquity" (after Plato and Aristotle).[10] Section 3.4 on the human word is dedicated to the main features of Augustine's sign theory.

In doing so, it will be shown that Augustine's conception of language stands in a strange tension with his appreciation of the word of God. Its resolution divides Augustine research into two camps. For the larger

4. *De genesi contra Manichaeos*, 2,5.
5. Wieland, *Offenbarung*, 185–86.
6. On this see also Walter, *Ertrag*, 139–41.
7. *Manichaeos*, 2,4.
8. *Manichaeos*, 2,4.
9. See Pollmann, *Doctrina christiana*, 191.
10. Coseriu, *Geschichte*, 122.

group, the *verbum dei* is just a graphic manner of speaking that Augustine takes over from the prologue to John without being able to make it theoretically fertile.[11] For example, Kurt Flasch judges: "He either remains stuck on single issues of grammar and deals with them unoriginally, keeping with the Stoic tradition, or he practices metaphysics of the divine and inner-intellectual 'word,' whereby the word, this pure thought, more traditionally—by accident bears the title 'word,' without Augustine making clear the analogy with the word of language or with language at all."[12]

On the other hand, for some few scholars the intersection of human and divine discourse in the "inner word" described in *De trinitate* remains a consistent *language* event,[13] which the bishop of Hippo interpreted in an innovative fashion. An example of this is the appreciation of Hans-Georg Gadamer: "When Augustine and the scholastics treat the problem of the *verbum* in order to gain the conceptual means to deal with the mystery of the Trinity, they are concerned exclusively with this inner word. . . . Thus it is a quite specific side of the nature of language that emerges here."[14]

Section 3.5 goes into these different appreciations of a foundational thought of Augustine's in which the symbolic mediation of the *verbum divinum* stands at the center. Section 3.6 attempts to apply these acquired insights to Augustine's textual production itself, namely the narrative structure of *Confessiones*.

3.2 The Creative Word of God

In his five attempts,[15] spread out over more than two decades, to interpret the biblical account of creation, Augustine increasingly allows more

11. Representative are Brachtendorf, *Struktur*, 307–14; Duchrow, *Sprachverständnis*, 144–48; Flasch, *Augustin*, 121–26; Kahnert, *Entmachtung*, 154–56; Kuypers, *Zeichen- und Wortbegriff*, 66; Lorenz, *Wissenschaftslehre*, 238; Schindler, *Wort*, 89–91; Strauss, *Schriftgebrauch*, 78–79; Wieland, *Offenbarung*, 227.

12. Flasch, *Augustin*, 121.

13. For example Herzog, *Non in sua voce*, 228; Johnson, *Verbum*, 50–53; Kreuzer, *Pulchritudo*, 252–53; Pintarič, *Sprache*, 126–28; Pollmann, *Doctrina christiana*, 247. Outside of research on Augustine in the narrower sense should be counted the greatly respected account of Hans-Georg Gadamer in *Wahrheit und Methode*, 422–31. For examples from older literature see Krause, *Studien*, 225.

14. Gadamer, *Truth and Method*, 380 [trans. Bowden and Cumming].

15. *De genesi contra Manichaeos* (between 388 and 391 CE), *De genesi ad litteram liber unus inperfectus* (393/394), *Confessiones* XI-XIII (ca. 400), *De genesi ad litteram*

space and importance to the *talking* God. His great commentary on Genesis, which already in the title acknowledges the obligation of literal exegesis, poses the question right away in the first book: "Why moreover is it stated 'In the beginning God created heaven and earth' and not 'In the beginning God said, Let there be heaven and earth,' and heaven and earth were made? For in the case of light, the words are: 'God said: Let there be light. And light was made.'"[16]

Here the origin of language in the biblical story is localized exactly. What new quality comes through this *Deus dixit* in the creation? What is the difference between before and after? What effect does language have?

Augustine proposes the answer that the word brings *forma*. Heaven and earth as spiritual and corporeal matter[17] in their incompleteness and formlessness strive to return to nothingness—*informitate quadam tendit ad nihilum*.[18] By the creative word the unformed attains its form in such a way that it is oriented to the creator, it is turned toward him. "And so, when scripture declares 'God said, Let there be . . .' we may understand this as an immaterial utterance of God in his eternal word [*verbi eius coaeterni*], as the word recalls his imperfect creature to himself, so that it may not be formless but may be formed according to the various works of creation which he produces in due order."[19]

Creation is completed by the word because the creatures were initially formed by the divine *revocatio*. This call causes an alignment of the creature "in its own way" to a "form which is eternally united with the Father [*pro suo genere imitando formam sempiterne atque incummutabiliter inhaerentem patri*]."[20] It is the "ideal exemplary being of worldly things"[21] that is conceived as oneness in *verbum dei*.[22]

God's creative talking is the interface between eternity and temporality. His word, the form of the things he has made, is removed from

libri duodecim (ca. 410–415), *De civitate dei* XI (412–26). On dating see Drecoll, *Chronologie*, 253–61.

16. *De genesi ad litteram libri duodecim* I 3,8 [trans. Taylor].

17. On this understanding of *caelum et terra* see *Confessiones* XII 13,16.

18. *De genesi ad litteram libri duodecim* I 4,9.

19. *De genesi ad litteram libri duodecim* I 4,9 [trans. Taylor].

20. *De genesi ad litteram libri duodecim* I 4,9 [trans. Taylor].

21. Schmaus, *Trinitätslehre*, 358.

22. Here is yet another echo of the origin of the concept *forma* as a translation of the Platonic "idea" (see *De diversis quaestionibus* 46.2: *Ideas igitur latine possumus vel formas vel species dicere, ut verbum e verbo transferre videamur*).

ephemerality, but the act of utterance to the form of the corresponding temporal quality: "whatever you say shall be made, is made; nor do you make otherwise than by speaking; yet all things are not made both together and everlasting which you make by speaking."[23]

The point in time "'when' something must come into being" is also deposited in any other eternal word.[24] Augustine emphasizes this thought in his Genesis commentary and in his *Confessiones* by a comparison of the words of creation with the voice from the clouds which, according to Luke 9:35 (NRSV), speaks at Jesus' baptism: "This is my Son, my chosen." At the Jordan River a voice was actually audible, "the syllables sounded and passed by."[25] Otherwise in the word of creation: "For what was spoken was not finished, and another spoken until all were spoken; but all things at once and forever."[26] For the totality of the creative *verba*, in *De civitate dei* Augustine introduced the concept of *scientia dei*—a complete knowledge "so perfect as to receive no addition from his finished works."[27]

In the language event of creation Augustine obviously recognizes three components: 1) a timeless and unchanging *word*, 2) use of the word constituting time in *speaking*, and 3) the formed creature as an *expression* or *sign* of the word in space and time. Here we are interested especially in the aspect connected to component 3): the world experienced through the senses is, so to speak, a symbolic and linguistic expression of the act of creation. In fact, Augustine stands as the inventor of the metaphor from "The Book of Nature."[28] In one of his sermons can be found this passage: "Others, in order to find God, will read a book. Well, as a matter of fact, there is a certain great big book, the book of created nature. Look carefully at it top and bottom, observe it, read it. God did not make letters of ink for you to recognize him in; he set before your eyes all these things he has made. Why look for a louder voice? Heaven and earth cries out to you, 'God made me.'"[29]

23. *Confessiones* XI 7,9 [trans. Pilkington].

24. *De genesi ad litteram libri duodecim* I 2,6 [trans. Taylor]. See *Confessiones* XI 12,10.

25. *Confessiones* XI 6,8 [trans. Pilkington]. See also *De genesi ad litteram libri duodecim* I 2,2.

26. *Confessiones* XI 7,9 [trans. Pilkington].

27. *De civitate dei* XI,21 (Documenta Catholica Omnia; no translator listed).

28. Fuhrer, *Schöpfung*, 235.

29. *The Works of St. Augustine. Sermons. III*, trans. Edmund Hill, 225–26.

In a letter written shortly before beginning his great commentary on Genesis, Augustine coins the phrase "divine rhetoric [*divina eloquentia*]" which expresses itself in "amazing deeds [*facta mirabilia*]."[30] Every creature becomes a sign of its creator.[31] In these pan-semiotics[32] in which "every creature, every human life, every action and expression of mankind [is] ultimately divine discourse," the "world text of creation" appears as the most comprehensive book of all, richer even than the Bible.[33] These signs are legible for all, which is why Augustine can say about the universal referential character of all creatures in allusion to Romans 1:20: "Heaven and earth, and all that is therein, behold, on every side they say that I should love you; nor do they cease to speak unto all, so that they are without excuse."[34]

Augustine defines a sign in this manner: "A sign is a thing [*res*] which, over and above the impression it makes on the senses, causes something else to come into the mind as a consequence of itself [*faciens in cogitationem venire*]."[35] Where that something else leads to, Augustine discusses with the example of a person who hears an unknown sign.[36] As soon as this person realizes that what he heard is a sign, he will want to know "with eagerness what manner of sign it is."[37] What drives him on? It cannot be love for an as yet unidentified *res*, "for certainly nothing can be loved unless it is known."[38] Augustine believes it is knowledge of the "beautiful and practical form" or rather the shape (*forma/species*) with which "human fellowship mutually communicates its own perceptions," which inquirers seek so zealously.[39] In other words, it is the knowledge of the significance of the sign, of its meaningfulness, in the communication

30. *Epistula* 102, 33 [my translation]. Augustine's inversion of *eloquentia* from a superficial rhetorical art to a type of divine inspiration is clearly indicated already in *De doctrina christiana* 4.

31. On the fundamental sign character of sensory reality which makes reference to spiritual reality see *De vera religione* 42.

32. On this term see Eco, *Models*, 11.

33. Fuhrer, *Schöpfung*, 241.

34. *Confessiones* X 6,8 [trans. Pilkington].

35. *De doctrina christiana* II,1 (Documenta Catholica Omnia; no translator listed).

36. *De trinitate* X, 2–3 [trans. Haddon].

37. *De trinitate* X, 2 [trans. Haddon].

38. *De trinitate* X, 2 [trans. Haddon].

39. *De trinitate* X, 2 [trans. Haddon]. Here Augustine uses the terms *forma* and *species* synonymously.

community. That is the human perspective on every *forma* which, from a divine perspective is completed in the understood creation in the image of language. It assigns the *res* its purpose.

To this extent one can understand the linguistic interpretation of the creation process initiated by the biblical *Deus dixit* in Augustine, that the *res* is determined by its specific *formae* and therefore becomes, in space and time, a perceptible sign for the *verbum dei* which embraces all *formae.* In modern terms: the creation corresponds to a process of designation in which out of the totality of interpretive possibilities (*verbum*) a speaker (*res*) is assigned to a particular signifier (*forma*), which thus becomes a signified of the *verbum dei.* Or, once again with Augustine: "The word finds a voice [*verbum fecit sibi vocem*]."[40]

3.3 The Word of God as Inner-Trinitarian Relationship

In his early writings (up to 397 CE) Augustine never used the term *verbum* as a proper name for the λόγος—Christ. Indeed, he seems to almost purposely omit the term in all appropriate contexts, as Douglas Johnson has shown in his study "*Verbum* in the early Augustine."[41] Johnson supposes the reason to be that Augustine was initially unable to integrate the λόγος-theory into his concept of language: "It is . . . possible, that from the very beginning Augustine the rhetor intended to present the divine *verbum* as God's active self-expression but was unable to do so because of this insufficient doctrine of language."[42] The way forward, λόγος—just as correctly translated with *ratio* in Latin—was discarded by Augustine because only the linguistic interpretation of *verbum* stresses the relationship between Father and Son on the one hand, and between God and his creatures on the other.[43] In doing so, Augustine follows the common practice, with few exceptions, in the Latin-speaking church of saying *verbum* or *sermo* in John 1:1 instead of *ratio* or *lex.*[44]

40. *Sermo* 288,2.

41. Johnson, *Verbum*, especially 36.

42. Johnson, *Verbum*, 33.

43. *De diversis quaestionibus*, 63. This contradicts the thesis of Otto Scheel which wants to identify the *verbum* of Augustine consistently with the neo-Platonic νοῦς (*Anschauung*, 180–81; for a critique of Scheel see also Johnson, *Verbum*, 34 and Schmaus, *Trinitätslehre*, 355–61).

44. Schindler, *Wort*, 115–16.

Nevertheless Augustine was only haltingly able to feel his way to a linguistically consistent understanding of λόγος. After 393 he writes: "Let us ask whether the words were spoken to the only-begotten Son [*filio unigenito dictum est*], or whether the words were themselves the only-begotten Son [*filius unigenitus est*]."[45] He leaves the answer open. A further approach is found in *De fide et symbol*: "The reason of his [the Son] being named the word of the Father, is that the Father is made known [*innotescit*] by him."[46] Here is displayed a revelatory function of the word, which Augustine connects with the creative word of God in the *Confessiones* and in his great Genesis commentary: "The word answered the question as to who it is: 'the beginning, that is why I also speak to you [*principium, quia et loquor vobis*].'"[47] An idiosyncratic rendering of John 8:25b,[48] but it does make it possible for Augustine to identify in the *verbum* terms from Genesis 1 and John 1 a common language function: "This beginning, remaining unchangeably in himself, would certainly not cease to speak by interior inspirations and summons to the creature of which he is the beginning, in order that it might turn to its first cause. Otherwise such a creature could not be formed and perfect."[49]

Here the thought emerges once again that the divine word generates the definition and interpretation of all creatures by harkening back into timelessness. "The word as the Son" includes this *forma* to the extent that it brings "the immutable truth [*sapientia incommutabili*]" to mankind without which "their lives are foolish and wretched, and that is their lifelessness [*informitas*]."[50]

Augustine unfolds a new, independent solution to the λόγος interpretation in *De trinitate*. The first important step in this direction is the relational interpretation of the Trinity. Coming out of Aristotle's differentiation of substance and accident, Augustine argues that the unchanging God could not be able to assign any accidentals if God is also not a substance.[51] Therefore Augustine suggests using the term essence

45. *De genesi ad litteram liber unus inperfectus* 5,19 [trans. Isabella Image, rogerpearse.com].

46. *De fide et symbolo* III,3 [trans. S. D. F. Salmon, logicmuseum.com].

47. *De genesi ad litteram libri duodecim* I 5,10. See also *Confessiones* XI 8,10.

48. NT Graece: Τὴν ἀρχὴν ὅ τι ͗ καὶ λαλῶ ὑμῖν. Even the earliest Latin codices expand a *quia* before the *et*/*καὶ*.

49. *De genesi ad litteram libri duodecim* I 5,10.

50. *De genesi ad litteram libri duodecim* I 5,10 [trans. Taylor].

51. *De trinitate* V,3–6.

[*essentia*] instead of *substantia*[52] (without however adhering consequently to this terminology).[53] But how do the three consubstantial persons of the Trinity stand in relation to one another now, if indeed the relation is an accident in the Aristotelian sense? In this case, according to Augustine, the relation can be an accident because it is unalterable.[54] It is, however, not a substance because in other respects it would have to do with three substances. Out of this emerge two perspectives from which the persons are to be addressed: From the perspective *ad se* the same is to be expressed about all three, from the perspective *ad aliquid relative* the specific connections appear among each other.[55] The Father and the Son are connected to each other by the procreation, and then again as donors bestowing the Spirit as a gift [*datum* and *donum*].[56]

Now Augustine is free to reinterpret the relationship between Father and Son, between *Deus* and *verbum*. He understands procreation as speaking: When we express something of our knowledge, then "the word is born [*nascatur verbum*]."[57] Knowledge remains undisturbed by linguistic abandonment—and in discourse knowledge is duplicated. God the Father and God the Son are to be understood analogously: "Therefore the Father procreated, while in the same manner he expressed himself [*tamquam se ipsum dicens*], his word which resembles him in everything."[58] In another passage Augustine even says: God spoke the Son.[59]

Augustine attempts to explain this divine discourse on human language as far as possible. Of course it requires for this neither voice nor concrete language, but it is comparable to the impertinent thought process which forms the concept: "You have in your heart [*in corde habes*] the word that you speak, and as it is with you, and is none other than the spiritual conception [*conceptio spiritualis*] itself (for just as your soul is spirit [*anima tua spiritus est*], so also the word which you have conceived

52. *De trinitate* VII,10.

53. See Brachtendorf, *De trinitate*, 365.

54. *De trinitate* V,6.

55. *De trinitate* VII,10.

56. *De trinitate* V,15–17.

57. *De trinitate* XV,19.

58. *De trinitate* XV,23.

59. *Quomodo auditus est a Filio, cum ipsum Filium sit locutus Deus?* (*In Evangelium Iohannis tractatus* 14,7).

is spirit; for it has not yet received sound to be divided by syllables . . . ; so God gave out His Word, that is, begot the Son."[60]

This concept of *verbum cordis* or *verbum intimum*[61] is explained more thoroughly in section 3.5 when it involves the question of where the word of God touches human language processes. In this place it should be emphasized: the circumstance remains as the greatest difference between divine and creative discourse, that human thought and language are bound to a temporal sequence, while God speaks eternally, before all time. In this way his *verbum* comprises the whole truth, which humans by contrast must parse their knowledge in data blocks for linguistic transmission.

In a sermon on John 3:29–36 Augustine closes the arc conclusively between *verbum dei* and *verbum humanum*: "the Son is the word of God, and the Son spoke to us not his own word, but the word of the Father, he willed to speak himself to us when he was speaking the word of the Father. This it is that John said, as was fit and necessary; and we have expounded according to our ability."[62] The sequence of the language events here is significant. The Father speaks the word, the Son; the Son speaks to mankind, which John records and centuries later is passed on by the Bishop of Hippo in his words. Augustine was undoubtedly truly interested in interpreting the word of God linguistically as an inner-trinitarian relationship. In Augustine's word theory the incarnation, the historical Christ, plays practically no role at all.[63] It is merely the "compression of the reference structure"[64] onto the creator in whom all creatures reside (see Section 3.2). "The transcendental ontological constitution of God remains . . . undisturbed by the incarnation."[65]

What is metaphysics of language here, what is linguistically comprehensible? In the modern age the motif of procreation through speaking has been taken up by Paul Ricœur. In the act of expression is constituted the difference between the "I" as addressed subject and the "I" as subject of the expressed sentence. The talking "I" and the "I" of conversation are two different perspectives on the same persons. The latter refers

60. *In Evangelium Iohannis tractatus* 14,7 [trans. Gibb].

61. On the various expressions which Augustine used for the "inner word" see the survey in Schindler, *Wort*, 250–51.

62. *In Evangelium Iohannis tractatus* 14,7 [trans. Gibb].

63. See Mayer, *Zeichen* 2, 212–33.

64. Walter, *Ertrag*, 145.

65. Wieland, *Offenbarung*, 226.

symbolically to the former[66]—just as the Son refers to the Father but indeed is not identical to the Father. In this respect the inner-trinitarian procreation is still linguistically communicable. Still the question poses itself: If one understands (in the modern sense) language as an interpersonal form of sign behavior,[67] then after these considerations it remains open how the *verbum dei* is to be regarded as a sign. In that regard we will look at Augustine's theory of signs.

3.4. The Human Word as Sign

3.4.1 *De dialectica*: the Semantic Triangle

Augustine formulated four significant approaches to the theory of human language-formation in which the entanglement with the word of God plays an ever more important role.[68] The first approach is found in *De dialectica* from 386, whose long-disputed authenticity is considered settled[69] since Jan Pinborg's article from 1962.[70] The *verbum dei* still plays no role here, but nevertheless a glance at Augustine's compact and precise definitions is worthwhile for the language event:

> A word is the sign of some thing which can be understood by the hearer when pronounced by the speaker. A thing is whatever is felt (sensed) or understood or "latent" (is hidden, inapprehensible). A sign is something which presents itself to the senses and something other than itself to the mind. To speak is to give a sign in articulate voice. I call that articulate which is capable of being comprised in letters. [. . .] That of the word which is not sensed by the ears but by the mind and is held enclosed in the mind itself is called *dicibile* (the expressible, the sayable; Stoic lekto/n). When the word is uttered not for its own sake,

66. See Ricœur, *Selbst*, 65–68.

67. See Eco, *Zeichen*, 109.

68. Individually these are *De dialectica, De magistro, De doctrina christiana*, and *De trinitate*. See the survey in Hennigfeld, *Geschichte*, 125–67. Among the language-theoretic writings overall should be counted *Contra academicos, De diversis quaestionibus, In Ioannis evangelium tractatus*, and some of the *Sermones* (on this see also Kahnert, *Entmachtung*, 6–18; on the relevant sermons see the list of Clemens Weidemann in Augustine, *Sermones Selecti*, 106).

69. Ruef, *Augustin*, 13–14.

70. Pinborg, *Sprachdenken*, 149–50.

> but to signify something about something, it is called *dictio* (an expression, a saying).[71]

Here is possibly the first description of the triadic relationship, without ontological (as in Plato) or epistemological (as in Aristotle and in the Stoa) prerequisites, simply on the basis of the process of designation, which today we call the "semantic triangle."[72]

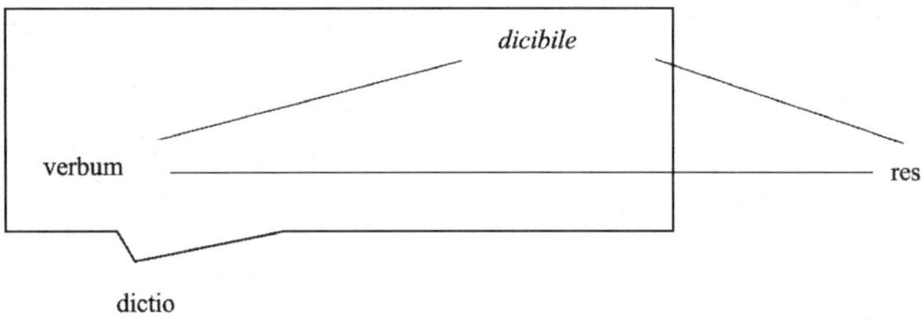

Figure 2. The Signification Process according to *De dialectica*

In any case, the following should be kept in mind regarding Augustine's deep penetration of the sign character: a sign does not only refer to a thing but it must signal something to the mind. This means it must be capable of being understood *as a sign* for a thing, thus bearing a meaning (*dicibile*). The linguistic use of a word and meaning as a unit is limited by its own term (*dictio*) against a metalinguistic application of signs (more or less in the sentence "'Word' has four letters"). The thing for which the sign stands can be something perceived by the senses (a different sign), something purely intellectual, or even something fictitious.

Beyond semiotic analysis Augustine assigns a "power [*vis verbi*]" to the word in a language event, which can originate from the sign itself, from *dicibile*, or from both together, and thus from the *dictio*. As an example for the first he cites the names Artaxerxes and Euryalus to whom a person who knows nothing about them might connote "supreme crudeness" or "gentleness" respectively. In contrast similar sounding names (*Cotta*/*Motta*) could call forth opposite feelings on the basis of different

71. *De dialectica* 5 [trans. Jackson].

72. See Simone, *Sémiologie*. On the language philosophy of Plato, Aristotle, and the Stoa see Hennigfeld, *Geschichte*, 23–124, as well as Coseriu, *Geschichte*, 31–120. On the "alleviation" of language theory from "gnoseological tasks" in Augustine see Schulthess, *Bedeutung*, 93.

associations. When the sound and the meaning together stimulate the listeners, the *vis verbi* has its basis in the *dictio*.[73]

Augustine's approach to *spoken* language is noteworthy. We are talking about a listener, a speaker, and sounds. Only in order to elevate human sounds from animal sounds, Augustine refers back to written language as a criterion for "articulated sounds." To him, written words function as signs for written language.[74]

There is some controversy about the extent to which Augustine went beyond Stoic language theory with this model.[75] This can hardly be ultimately decided on account of the insufficient sources for the Stoa.[76] His concentration on the abstract sign character of the *verbum* with concurrent consideration of the real-world language event is unique.

3.4.2 *De magistro*: the Admonitive Language Function

Written nearly three years after *De dialectica*, the dialogue *De magistro* begins with the programmatic question: "What . . . do we wish to do when we speak?"[77] The fictitious dialogue between Augustine and his son Adeodatus soon comes to concentrate on the epistemological function of language: How do words help us to acquire knowledge?

What follows directly is an astute analysis of the referential character of signs in which both father and son come to agree that, in every case, other signs can be taught through signs. Words can sometimes be explained through directional signs or other words.[78] Therefore signs can stand in different relationships to one another. A sign can refer to a subset of that designated from another sign (all *verba* are *signa*, but not vice versa); a sign can refer to the same thing as another sign but illuminate another aspect (like *nomen* and *verbum*);[79] a sign can in its

73. *De dialectica* 7.

74. *De dialectica* 5. *Omne verbum sonat. Cum enim esi in scripto, non verbum sed verbi signum est.*

75. The controversy especially concerns the question of whether or not Augustine's *dicibile* corresponds to the Stoic λεκτόν. On this see Ruef, *Augustin*, 108–11, Hennigfeld, *Geschichte*, 129 and 132, Pollmann, *Doctrina christiana*, 165–67, and Kahnert, *Entmachtung*, 80–81.

76. See Hennigfeld, *Geschichte*, 104.

77. *De magistro* I,1 (trans. Tourscher].

78. *De magistro* II-VII.

79. At first glance it may seem surprising that only all Nomina are also *verba*, but

object reference and in its significance be the same as another sign—like *nomen* and "ὄνομα."[80]

So the dialogue partners are still in the realm of logic independent of experience, and thus analytical truths. Up to now no insight has been gained which would yield evidence about the knowledge of things themselves. The maximum of that which is teachable about signs seems to have been for quite some time word definitions. In this process it pushes us to those things which Augustine makes clear with the following query: "Tell me whether man is man [*utrum homo homo sit*]."[81] The sentence seems to be tautological, but is not when one thinks of it in this way: ". . . whether 'man' is a man." In this case, the question is connected to a word sign with three letters and is to be answered in the negative. But according to a *placita loquendi regula* we are inclined to comprehend language from the perspective of things (*ex parte rei*) and not from signs.[82] The agreement with the statement that men are living beings is easier for us than agreement with the sentence "'Man' is a word."[83] It is virtually a necessary precondition of successful communication that we obey the other "law of nature":[84] "When the signs are heard, our attention is drawn to the things themselves."[85] Out of this flows the crucial insight of *De magistro*: "The things which are signified are esteemed more highly than the signs. Whatever is on account of something else must be of lesser worth than that for which it is."[86] Just as the knowledge of things [*cognitio rerum*]

not inversely that all *verba* are also Nomina. Augustine argues nevertheless that every *verbum* "x" modelled on "'x' is a beautiful word" and could become a *nomen* (*De magistro* V,12–16). Of course, here Augustine retreats behind his differentiation outlined in *De magistro* VIII,24 between "use" and "mention" (respectively object-language and meta-language). Today one might perhaps choose for that intended by him the example of Saul Kripke for "necessary truths *a posteriori*:" "The morning star is the evening star." Both names are fixed designators with the same extension in all possible worlds, though it took centuries of astrological experience for the discovery of their identities (see Kripke, *Identity*, 135–64.)

80. *De magistro* VII,20.

81. *De magistro* VIII,22.

82. *De magistro* VIII,24.

83. *De magistro* VIII,24.

84. *De magistro* VIII,24: *regula, quae naturaliter plurimum valet.*

85. *De magistro* VIII,24.

86. *De magistro* IX,25.

is of greater significance than the signs—but not the *knowledge* of signs [*cognitio signorum*].[87]

Can one come at all to an insight into things without traversing the detour over signs? Adeodatus doubts this—with good reason.[88] For example, anyone who wishes to explain the phrase "walk around" by saying someone simply "walks around," will always remain ambiguous. Its counterpart could be considered essential, for example: the demonstrated amount of steps.[89] Just prior to this, father and son had agreed that there is no possibility during "walking around" to refer to this same activity. If one were to accelerate one's steps, its opposite "hurry up" would possibly be considered the sought-for definition.[90]

The father answers with an example that admittedly cannot entirely rebut this argument. If someone who has no idea about bird hunting with rods and glue were to observe a bird catcher just long enough, this spectator would have to have learned without any further signs what the whole business is about. The objection of Adeodatus that these observations could also be interpreted in various ways is fended off by the father. The spectator must be intelligent enough to grasp the totality from what he has observed. It is with this capability that man recognizes things in nature which the creator has put before his eyes: sun, moon, stars, continents, oceans "and whatever lives in them without number."[91] From here it is only a small step forward to his central thesis which bursts open the dialogue with an *oratio perpetua*: "I shall try to prove this to you first of all, that by signs, which are called words, we learn nothing. For it is more true, as I have said, that we learn the force of the word [*vim verbi*], that is the meaning which is concealed in its sound [*sono*] by knowledge of the reality, which is signified, than that we perceive the reality by such signification [*significationem*]."[92]

87. Augustine leaves this relationship open (see *De magistro* IX, 27).

88. This is strikingly similar to the thought of Willard V. O. Quine on indeterminacy of translation, that is to say, an expression in a foreign language is not translatable into a known language because there is an indeterminacy as to what the expression refers to in the foreign language. Not even pointing to an object creates unambiguity because, for example, only a partial structure or a temporary quality of the object can be intended (see Quine, *Word*, 59–147).

89. *De magistro* X,29.

90. *De magistro* III,6.

91. *De magistro* X,32.

92. *De magistro* X,34.

The reference function of signs is then only of use to us when we know to which things the sign is connected. Consequently Augustine accentuates the quantities in the semantic triangle differently than in *De dialectica* and introduces a new terminology. The meaning of the word, the *dicibile*, is resolved in the thing itself—and in such a way that the disempowered sign is divided into sound and signification function (see Figure 3): *in . . . signo . . . duo sint, sonus et signification.*[93]

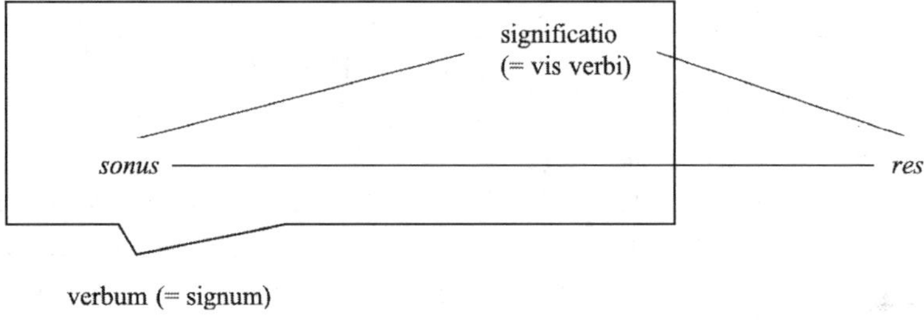

Figure 3: The Signification Process according to *De magistro*

Sound is only vibration in air which one first recognizes in its sign character when one already knows about the signified thing.[94] It is precisely this limitation which takes from the word its meaning in the sense of *dicibile*. The *significatio* in *De magistro* is finally the outstretched pointer finger, which in fact can only become significant when it is clear as to what it is pointing.[95] *Significatio,* used here synonymously with the power of the word, *vis verbi*,[96] has become rather weak in comparison to its use in *De dialectica*. It encompasses only the reference as such, no longer the impact of the word in the language event. Burkhard Mojsisch translates *significatio* appropriately as "signification function,"[97] while other interpreters understand the term against the text and equate it with "word meaning."[98] It is possible that they do so because a proper understanding of Augustine's idiosyncratic analysis of signs raises questions which the

93. *De magistro* X,34.

94. *De magistro* X,34. We comprehend "the signification function by looking at the thing [*re aspecta*], which is signified."

95. Hennigfeld, *Geschichte*, 146.

96. *De magistro* X,34.

97. On this see the notes section of his German translation of *De magistro*, 127 and 132–33, and in the postscript, 152. In similar fashion Duchrow, *Sprachverständnis*, 63.

98. For example Borsche, *Macht*, 141.

dialogue does not answer. For example, it remains unclear in this model why we grasp even words which do not relate to any *res* in their meaning and can communicate meaningfully with them (like "unicorn" or "squaring the circle"). According to *De magistro*, these words must be considered strictly speaking to not be signs at all, but meaningless sounds.[99]

If the *verba* teach nothing, how is it then possible that one can be informed by oral or written witnesses to past events? Does the Bible teach us nothing? As an example Augustine uses the story of the three young men in the furnace (Daniel 3) to demonstrate that "everything that has been signified by those words was already in our cognizance."[100] In order to understand the story, one has to know something about what "three young men," "fire," "furnace," and "unharmed" mean. After the story the men named Ananias, Azarias, and Misahel remain unknown to us. That the events concerning the three men took place as Daniel 3 records them, "I believe admittedly more than that I know [*credere me potius quam scire confiteor*]."[101] One does not negotiate with the narrator over the believability of that which was linguistically communicated but with the "teacher" who dwells within: "Referring now to all things that we understand, we consult, not the one speaking, whose words sound without, but truth within, presiding over the mind [*intus ipsi menti praesidentem consulimus veritatem*], reminded [*admoniti*] perhaps by words to take note (to mark evidence). But he teaches who is consulted, Christ, who is said to "dwell in the interior man": that is, the changeless power of God and the everlasting wisdom [*incommutabilis dei virtus atque sempiterna sapienta*]."[102]

The knowledge of truth is not dependent on a sign. Words can teach us nothing but only admonish us that we should seek what we ought to see with our eyes wide open.[103] In the end, language has an admonitive function.[104] Everything that we experience, "we perceive either by a corporeal organ of sense [*sensu corporis*], or by a power of the mind

99. In *De magistro* the question is debated to which *res* a word like *nihil* is connected. Augustine's answer: Not the non-existent thing is signified here, but "a particular way of thinking [*affectionem animi*] when the mind does not see a thing and nevertheless encounters its non-existence or believes to have encountered it" (II,3).

100. *De magistro* XI,37.

101. *De magistro* XI,37.

102. *De magistro* XI,37 [trans. Tourscher].

103. *De magistro* X,35.

104. See Mayer, *Zeichen* 1, 241, and Mojsisch, postscript, 146.

[*mente*]."[105] We require *verba* neither for the perceptible [*sensibilia*] nor intellectual [*intellegibilia*] knowledge. The *res* of our senses either stand directly at our disposal, or—as with *intellegibilia* fundamentally—we bring to mind their "images [*imagines*] which are impressed on our memory [*memoriae*] and have been stored there."[106]

Therefore it is an illusion if one believes they are able to learn anything from human instructors through symbolic transmission. In reality it is the students themselves who, inspired by the discourse of the instructor, discover the truth in their own persons which dwells within.[107] According to Matthew 23:10 (NRSV),[108] only the teacher within is permitted to call himself "teacher," and that is Christ and—here in its Johannine λόγος meaning[109]—dwells in us as "eternal wisdom."

In the concluding *recapitulatio* of his *oratio perpetua,* Augustine makes a decisive turn which unmasks the entire discrediting of language as only apparent. It is every inner teacher "from whom we are admonished [*admonemur*] from without by means of signs through persons by inner turning [*intro conversio*] to him in order to learn."[110] In other words: In the *admonitio* of human language the divine admonition emerges, that *vocatio*, which calls out to every creature its *forma*, its purpose.[111] Even if the signs teach us nothing directly, "for the fallen creature signs are . . . the only possible way to truth, even if it is mediated and in itself inadequate to the task. The a*dmonitio veritatis*—the appeal to truth—happens necessarily . . . by sensory signs."[112] The *admonitio* is the trace of *verbum dei* in human language, to a certain extent a divine finger pointing to the *res*—and therefore a sign. How tightly bound human and divine statements are, Augustine only works out decades later in *De trinitate* with the concept of the "inner word" (see Section 3.5).

Seen from this surprising point of view, Augustine's critique of signs appears in a different light. Without signs our path to God would be blocked. Only that which is conducive to signs is God's work. Man's

105. *De magistro* XII,39 [trans. Tourscher].

106. *De magistro* XII,39.

107. *De magistro* XIV,45.

108. "Nor are you called to be instructors, for you have one instructor, the Messiah."

109. See Ott, *Schrift*, 17.

110. *De magistro* XIV,46.

111. For evidence of the frequent synonymic use of *admonitio* and *vocatio* in Augustine see Wieland, *Offenbarung*, 173–74.

112. Borsche, *Macht*, 148.

portion is that which makes signs incomplete, ambiguous, and improper. Of course, Augustine can only arrive at this linguistic result because in his analysis, words are isolated from their context. If he had emphasized in *De dialectica* that ambiguities can be severed from their respective contexts,[113] the author of *De magistro* would appear to take language for a mere list of words. This becomes especially significant in his argument that we learn nothing by narration of past events or things which are alien to us. Still it is crucial, as Jochem Hennigfeld correctly criticizes, "that we experience something in the narrative context which would not be known to us without words."[114]

3.4.3 *De doctrina christiana*: Semiotic Biblical Understanding

Augustine's discrediting of the human portion of language suggests the question of how he, as a Christian philologist, understands holy scriptures. Is even it only a collection of signs which are ambiguous and misleading? Can we really learn nothing from reading it, but at most be warned to remain vigilant? Is it then redundant for those who have already found another way to access the things signified there?

With his biblical hermeneutics *De doctrina christiana*, Augustine devoted an entire work to these questions, a work which came into being in two separate phases of thirty years each. The prologue and Books 1 through 3,25 were written in 396/397, soon after his consecration as a bishop and about seven years after *De magistro*. The second part came into being thirty years later at the height of his anti-Pelagian efforts.[115]

For our theme, the first part is the most interesting—although even here Augustine employs a broad palette of accentuations, leading some scholars to suppose that it was first written in the second phase.[116] In point of fact, in the first book Augustine draws the following radical consequence from *De magistro* that the Bible can be superfluous to right faith: "And thus a man who is resting upon faith, hope and love, and who keeps a firm hold upon these, does not need the scriptures except for the

113. *De dialectica* 9–10.

114. Hennigfeld, *Geschichte*, 145.

115. See Lettieri, *De doctrina*, 378.

116. For example Duchrow, *Prolog*, and Hennigfeld, *Geschichte*, 150. Today the debate is considered settled in the sense of the aforementioned separation, and thus an early origin to the prologue (see Lettieri, *De doctrina*, 378, and Pollmann, *Doctrina christiana*, 67).

purpose of instructing others. Accordingly, many live without copies of the scriptures, even in solitude, on the strength of these three graces."[117]

The appeal to the Bible can "only be the illustration of an insight which as an intelligible insight does not need to be acquired through the scriptures."[118] By contrast the prologue seems to argue for a position diametrically opposed to this statement. There Augustine ridicules those who believe that thanks to "the divine gift of inspiration [*divinus munere*]"[119] they can flout the conventions of exegesis and are able to comprehend all of Scripture without any instruction. He reminds them that "it was from human teachers they themselves learnt to read"[120] and that the word of God almost without exception has through the ages sought a human voice: "And without doubt it was possible to have done everything through the instrumentality of angels, but the condition of our race would have been much more degraded if God had not chosen to make use of men as the ministers of his word to their fellow-men."[121]

This seeming contradiction can be resolved to the effect that the Bible like all signs is a means to an end. The Bible is not an exclusive path to proper knowledge, but it is the only one which leads by way of linguistic testimony and contains the "speech of God [*deus loquendi*]."[122] The holy scriptures bear witness to the "will of God [*voluntatem dei*].[123] The authors wrote under divine inspiration—but what they wrote are signs of a human, imperfect language. The Bible is inerrant insofar as it reflects divine purpose. Its dark and ambiguous passages are on the one hand the result "of a particular sin of human disunity [*peccato quodam dissensionis humanae*],"[124] which thwarts a unified language, and on the other hand God's strategy: "I do not doubt that the entirety is foreseen by God in order to constrain human arrogance by tribulation and preserve the mind from boredom, since what is easily traced usually depreciates."[125]

117. *De doctrina christiana* I, 39 (Documenta Catholica Omnia; no translator listed).

118. Strauss, *Schriftgebrauch*, 150.

119. *De doctrina christiana* Prologue, 4.

120. *De doctrina christiana* Prologue, 4.

121. *De doctrina christiana* Prologue, 6.

122. *Sermo* M 27/D 10,56: *Teneamus scripturam tamquam deum loquentem; non ibi quaeramus hominem errantem.*

123. *De doctrina christiana*, II,V.

124. *De doctrina christiana*, II,IV.

125. *De doctrina christiana*, II,VI.

The innovation of Augustine's understanding of the canon is then that the Bible text enjoys no special status hermeneutically. For him, the same rules of exegesis apply as those for pagan texts.[126] Karla Pollmann assumes that "no one prior to Augustine grasped the biblical text so strictly as a collection of linguistic signs."[127] He prefers not to comprehend the biblical text as a mimetic construction which imitates reality or portrays it literally, but as a semiotic composition which tacks from sensory reality and points to the word of God itself.[128] Who, after reading of the miracles of Jesus comes to a halt in astonishment, as Augustine says in one of his sermons on the gospel of John, is compared to an observer of a manuscript who admires the beauty of the handwriting and praises the wrist of the writer, but does not even start to read it:

> Let us interrogate the miracles themselves, what they tell us about Christ: for they have a tongue of their own, if they can be understood. For since Christ is himself the word of God, even the act of the word [*factum verbi*] is a word to us. Therefore as to this miracle, since we have heard how great [*magnum*] it is, let us also search how profound [*profundum*] it is; let us not only be delighted with its surface [*superficie*], but let us also seek to know its depth [*altitudinem*]. This miracle, which we admire on the outside [*foris*], has something within [*intus*].[129]

After this follows an allegorical interpretation[130] of the feeding miracle according to John 6 in which the five loaves (heavy with their marrow separated from the chaff) are interpreted as the Pentateuch. The boy who brings the loaves to Jesus is the people of Israel (because he has the bread but does not eat it), the two fish are the priests and kings of Israel, Jesus is the one who explains the five books of Moses in the breaking of bread, and finally the leftover crumbs, which dwell in the twelve loaves awaiting the twelve apostles, are the mysteries which are still difficult to understand.[131]

126. *De doctrina christiana*, 223 (annotation by Pollmann).

127. Pollmann, *Nachwort*, 284. See also Pollmann, *Doctrina christiana*, 176 and throughout. Jackson came to the same conclusion in his *Theory*, 49.

128. See Walter, *Ertrag*, 146 and Pollmann, *Nachwort*, 284.

129. *In evangelium Ioannis* 24,2 [trans. Gibb].

130. On Augustine's concept of allegory or figurative interpretation see Holl, *Welt*, 89–91, and Strauss, *Schriftgebrauch*, 131–48.

131. *In evangelium Ioannis* 24,5–7.

The purpose of Books II and III of *De doctrina christiana* is to establish guidelines for a close reading of the texts.[132] The signs which impede an understanding of the Bible are divided into four groups by Augustine and suggest different hermeneutical strategies:[133]

Incomprehensible Signs [*signa non intelligibilis*]	Proper [*s. propria*]	Improper [*s. translata*]
Unknown [*s. ignota*]	Language Skills (II,11–15)[134]	Expertise (II,16–42)
Ambiguous [*s. ambigua*]	Textual Criticism (III,2–4)	Rules of Tyconius (III,5–37)

Figure 4: Strategies for Interpretation in *De doctrina christiana*

As a criterion for differentiation between proper use of signs in the *locutio propria* and improper use in the *locutio figurata* Augustine states: "Whatever there is in the word of God that cannot, when taken literally, be referred either to purity of life or soundness of doctrine, you may set down as figurative."[135] With words used in the proper sense, deeper language skills can be helpful in discerning unfamiliar words and a text-critical version of different versions can help smooth over unwanted ambiguities. With figuratively used sign (strings)—like metaphors drawn from the animal and plant worlds—unknown expressions could be deciphered by historical or cultural expertise.

The most difficult cases are the ambiguities of words used in a figurative sense whose meanings "require extraordinarily great care and energy."[136] Augustine discussed some cases primarily from the Old Testament and then devotes himself to the *Liber Regularum* of Tyconius, written in 383 CE and the earliest extant hermeneutics of the Latin West.[137]

132. On this see Strauss, *Schriftgebrauch*, 74–148, and Mayer, *Zeichen* 2, 302–34.

133. *De doctrina christiana* II,10.

134. *De doctrina christiana.*

135. *De doctrina christiana* III,10 [Documenta Catholica Omnia; no translator listed].

136. *De doctrina christiana* III,5.

137. On this see Pollmann, *Doctrina christiana*, 32–65.

Augustine is able to follow six of the seven rules of the North African, "who, although a Donatist himself, has written most triumphantly against the Donatists."[138] In fact, he expressly recommends rules four through six,[139] which however offer little more than a classical doctrine of tropes with biblical examples.[140] Silke-Petra Bergjan states that "Augustine, while paraphrasing the Rules of Tyconius" must not make reference to "lessons in grammar or rhetoric" but can certainly refer to a doctrine of tropes "which is tightly intertwined with the biblical text with exclusively biblical examples."[141] So here as well, in the most obscure passages of the canon, no special hermeneutics of theology is needed. The encoding of divine discourse in the holy scriptures follows pagan rules. God is the master of all rhetoric. A Bible-specific rule, if need be, provides guidance for all cases of doubt which are not to be decrypted with his recommendations for interpretation. The Bible interprets itself. One must "proceed to open up and investigate the obscure passages, and in doing so draw examples from the plainer expressions to throw light upon the more obscure, and use the evidence of passages about which there is no doubt to remove all hesitation in regard to the doubtful passages."[142]

Augustine repeats the points of his biblical hermeneutics in the fourth book of *De doctrina christiana* for Christian proclamation. The same demands apply to the Christian preacher and teacher as apply to the secular orator. It has to do with duties of the orator as spelled out by Cicero:[143] "to teach [*docere*], delight [*delectare*], and persuade [*flectere*]" and the corresponding manners of speaking "restrained [*genus tenue*], temperate [*genus medium*], and noble [*genus grande*]."[144] These principles of *eloquentia* are not "heathen inventions" but "a natural system and doctrine which emerges from the natural activity of the intellect and language," as Gaetano Lettieri summarizes, for whom the "extraordinary innovation" of the fourth book consists in comprehending "God as the supreme orator."[145]

138. *De doctrina christiana* III,30.

139. *De doctrina christiana* III,37.

140. See Bergjan, *Liebe*, 74.

141. Bergjan, *Liebe*, 75.

142. *De doctrina christiana* II,9.

143. Cicero, *Orator*, 21.

144. *De doctrina christiana* IV,12.

145. Lettieri, *De doctrina christiana*, 388. See *Sermo* 17,1: *Lector ascendit, sed ipse non silet. Tractator loquitur. Si vera loquitur, Christus loquitur.*

In the context dealt with here it is also interesting to observe the shift in accent of Augustine's sign theory. While in *De magistro* the pedagogical aspect stands in the foreground, the language functions *docere aut commemorare*,[146] *De doctrina christiana* emphasizes the communicative meaning of signs.[147] Augustine differentiates the *signa* which are natural [*naturalia*] and stand in a causal connection to the signified (smoke—fire) from the given [*data*] and defines the latter as follows: "Conventional signs, on the other hand, are those which living beings [*viventia*] mutually exchange for the purpose of showing, as well as they can, the feelings of their minds [*motus animi*], or their perceptions [*sensa*], or their thoughts [*intellecta*]. Nor is there any reason for giving a sign except the desire of drawing forth and conveying into another's mind what the giver of the sign has in his own mind."[148]

Among all these given signs the linguistic have pride of place, because all other signs could be replaced by them (but not vice versa).[149] To Augustine words are virtually signs *par excellence*.[150] In contrast to *De magistro* here the admonitive function of language is turned from the epistemological perspective into the ethical perspective.[151] And if no word for God is adequate because God remains ineffable [*ineffabile*], he has "allowed the recognition of the human voice [*humanae vocis obsequium*]" in order that we may admonish ourselves to praise God and know God: "In fact he does not recognize himself in the sound of these two syllables [*de-us*] but nevertheless this sound triggers those trained in Latin, when he has touched their ears, to reflection on a certain, completely and especially outstanding and eternal nature."[152]

On the whole *De doctrina christiana* reconciles the language-skeptic approach of *De magistro* with the discourse of God in a "dialectic of language,"[153] which forms a "bridge to transcendence"[154] for fallen man-

146. *De magistro* I,1.

147. See Pollmann, *Doctrina*, 183.

148. *De doctrina christiana* II,3.

149. *De doctrina christiana* II,3.

150. See Markus, *St. Augustine*, 64.

151. See Pollmann, *Doctrina*, 184.

152. *De doctrina christiana* I, VI.

153. Walter, *Ertrag*, 146.

154. See Markus, *Communication*, 180. Otherwise Brachtendorf, *Struktur*, 301: "Language in itself possesses no relevance to salvation."

kind who is dependent on incomplete signs in just these provisional semiotic structures. Augustine formed this idea in *De trinitate.*

3.5. God's Word and Man's Word: the *verbum intimum*

The relationship between *verbum dei* and human language in the concept of "inner word" is deeply interwoven in the filigree argumentation of *De trintate.* Even in its reconstruction no consensus can be detected in the literature.[155] Correspondingly the assessments break down under two headings: the *verbum intimum* as a continuation of Augustine's philosophy of language[156] or as a building block only to be understood metaphorically in his "metaphysics of the mind."[157] Despite its brevity, the following sketch attempts to precisely localize the systematic locale of the word.

It is of primary importance to differentiate in understanding *verbum dei* in *De trinitate.* Augustine does not focus here, as he did in *De doctrina christiana,* on the word of God proclaimed by the prophets and apostles. This is only the case "because a divine doctrine [*doctrina divina*] is handed down, not a human": "we are now seeking to see, in whatsoever way we can, by means of this likeness, that word of God of which it is said, 'the word was God;' of which it is said, 'all things were made by him;' of which it is said, 'the word became flesh;' of which it is said 'the word of God on high is the fountain of wisdom.'"[158]

'Within the framework of his speculation on the Trinity, Augustine is concerned solely with the *verbum* in its creative and inner-trinitarian function. As such it is a composite part of a unique ontological construct whose structure is enfolded by Augustine in Books V to VII. Father, Son, and Holy Spirit are

a. of one substance [*una essentia*]

b. inseparably the same [*inseparabili*], therefore

c. a divine unity [*unitas divina*]

155. See among the newer accounts only Brachtendorf, *Struktur*, Pintarič, *Sprache*, and Kreuzer, *Einleitung*. A survey is offered by Kany, *Typen*, 13–28.

156. See Kreuzer, *Sprachlichkeit*, 197–98, and Pintarič, *Sprache*, 132.

157. Somewhat following Flasch, *Augustin*, 348–49.

158. *De trinitate* XV 11,20 [trans. Haddan].

d. are only to be differentiated by their specific relationships to one another.[159]

In order to be able to speak about these entities without drawing false conclusions, Augustine introduces language rules. To begin with, he distinguishes two manners of speaking: Predications in *ad se* statements are connected to the substance and thus to the Father, Son, and Holy Spirit in the same degree; *ad aliquid relative* statements accentuate the relationship aspect and can be exclusively connected to the Father, Son, and Holy Spirit.[160] Furthermore, a "pluralization prohibition"[161] applies to *ad se* definitions, meaning that they may be stated for the three relationships of the Trinity only in the singular and nothing may be added:[162] "So the Father is omnipotent, the Son omnipotent, and the Holy Spirit omnipotent; yet not three omnipotents, but one omnipotent."[163]

The Trinity defies our language logic. So the question becomes even more urgent—From where did we get the concept? Obviously it does not belong to any *natura insita*,[164] which makes the laws of logic, arithmetic, and geometry evident to the human mind.[165] The concept, however, does not accrue to us from sensory perception since we still "walk by faith, and not by sight [*per speciem*]," as Augustine quotes from 2 Corinthians 5:7.[166] Every attempt to promote divine qualities like *veritas*, *bonum*, or *iustitia* into the Trinity fails, since these attributions are only *ad se* predications and allow for no access to a tripartite structure.[167]

But if we ought to love this trinitarian God, we must have a pathway to this Trinity. For one can only love what one knows—otherwise our faith is merely "imagination [*ficta*]."[168] "But the question is, from what

159. *De trinitate* I 4,7.

160. *De trinitate* V 8,9.

161. Brachtendorf, *Geist*, 158.

162. *De trinitate* V 8.9. Because "personal nature" for Augustine is an *ad se* statement, the term is not really well-suited to the relationships of the Trinity. However, he concedes this manner of speaking with a view to the dilemma of human discourse (*De trinitiate* V 9.10).

163. *De trinitate* V 8,9.

164. *De trinitate* VIII 5,7.

165. On this see *Confessiones* X 12,19.

166. *De trinitate* VIII 4,6.

167. The entirety of Book VIII of *De trinitate* is dedicated to proving this.

168. *De trinitate* VIII 5,8.

likeness or comparison of known things can we believe."[169] Augustine searches for this image of likeness in the structure of the human mind itself. For only in connection to his mind, to the *mens humana*, is man called *imago dei*.[170]

In this way Augustine goes out from the *Ternar* lover–love–beloved with which "that being sought has not yet been found," but it serves as a basis from which one can "ascend further and search after the highest."[171] With the first step Augustine wishes to "tread down the flesh"[172] and ascend to the human mind [*mens*]. Since intellectually we want to approach a unity, we posit lover = beloved. The mind loves itself. What can that mean? Augustine answers: To love one's self means "to wish to help one's self to the enjoyment of self."[173] The *frui*, the enjoyment of a thing for its own sake, stands in opposition to the *uti*, the instrumental use of a thing for a purpose which lies outside of its self.[174] The mind which loves itself is consequently the mind which is present to itself—from which follows that the mind knows itself.[175] This means that out of the original *Ternar* a new one has been gained: the mind, its self-love, and its self-knowledge—*mens, amor sui, notitia sui*.[176]

For this triality Augustine establishes in Book IX that they actually possess the same "structural features"[177] as the divine Trinity: *mens, notitia,* and *amor*. They are:

a. substantial, since *ad se* statements are possible about all three,[178]

b. ontologically equivalent,[179] because the mind "comprehends itself in the complete sense"[180] in its self-knowledge and self-love,

169. *De trinitate* VIII 5,8.

170. *De trinitate* XV 7,11.

171. *De trinitate* VIII 10,14.

172. *De trinitate* VIII 10,14.

173. *De trinitate* IX 2,2.

174. On this see *De trinitate* X 10,13 and *De doctrina christiana* I, 4.

175. *De trinitate* IX 3,3: "For how can it love what it does not know?"

176. *De trinitate* IX 12,18.

177. Brachtendorf, *Geist*, 161.

178. See *De trinitate* IX 5,8.

179. See *De trinitate* IX 3,3.

180. Brachtendorf, *Geist*, 160.

c. a unity, "marvellously inseparable from each other,"[181]

d. and still different relationally: the *mens* brings forth together with *amor* the *notitia*.

In this act the triality *mens, notitia,* and *amor* proves its common bond. As the self-loving mind turns to itself, it recognizes itself and the true form of things. The result is defined by Augustine as "word": "a word then . . . is knowledge together with love."[182] With the equivalence of *notitia* and *verbum*, Augustine achieves a further convergence on the divine Trinity: "And so there is a kind of image of the Trinity [*imago trinitatis*] in the mind [*mens*] itself, and the knowledge of it [*notitia eius*], which is its offspring [*proles eius*] and its word [*verbum eius*] concerning itself, and love as a third, and these three are one, and one substance."[183]

With this "word," the conversation turns to the highest sense that *verbum* can have. Augustine discerns three meanings of "word" without differentiating them explicitly: the word as a symbolic combination of sounds or letters—*verbum3*; the word that stands for every arbitrary knowledge (*verbum2*); and finally that subset of *verba2*, which expresses knowledge pleasing to the mind (*verbum1)* under which falls the justifiably disapproved (because its disapproval is pleasing).[184]

The difference between *verbum2* and *verbum1*, since both express knowledge and are to that extent congruent with reality,[185] does not become completely clear. Normative and formal aspects are mixed together in Augustine's examples. He classifies *verbum2* in the proper sense as, on the one hand, the Christ salutation which according to Matthew 7:21 names the κύριος but does not follow his will, and on the other hand, the use of solecisms, thus violations against the syntactic structure.[186] *Verbum1* is most likely to be construed as a truly intended *verbum2*—a knowledge that, intentionally, the mind willingly and to that extent lovingly, expresses. This matches that which the inner word (*verbum1*) precedes in every case: "We do nothing, therefore, through the members

181. *De trinitate* IX 5,8. See in the same vein: "Since the mind loves itself as a whole, and knows itself as a whole, and knows its own love wholly, and loves its own knowledge wholly, when these three things are perfect in respect to themselves."

182. *De trinitate* IX 10,15.

183. *De trinitate* IX 12,18.

184. *De trinitate* IX 10,15.

185. On this see also Brachtendorf, *Struktur*, 268–77.

186. *De trinitate* IX 10,15.

of the body in our words and actions [= *verbum3*; author], by which the behavior of men is either approved or blamed, which we do not anticipate by a word uttered within ourselves [*verbo apud nos intus edito*]. For no one willingly does anything, which he has not first said in his heart [*in corde suo prius dixerit*].[187]

In this efficacious function the human word as *verbum1* touches the creative word of God which gives the creatures their *forma*. The knowledge of this form and its definition "we have so to speak as a word among us."[188]

The differentiation between *verbum2* and *verbum1* no longer plays a role in the further argument of *De trinitate*. In the new iteration of the thought in Book XV, Augustine continues to speak only of *verbum* in the sense of *verbum1* during which *verbum3* is then called *vox*.[189] In the scholarly literature "inner word" or *verbum intimum* has gained acceptance, although this usage has been limited to anything derived from the source texts.[190]

However, before Augustine comes back to the *verbum intimum*, he develops a further *Ternar* out of the triality *mens, notitia,* and *amor* which converges even more closely on the divine Trinity. The capability for analogy of the self-loving and knowing mind suffers from the fact that this act is an event in time, while the elements of the Trinity stand alongside one another in a timeless, unchanging relationship. Upon closer examination the *mens/notitia/amor* structure shows that even the mind must also be constituted by a triality already present. The event, which brings forward *notitia*, presupposes that the *amor* necessary for that can already connect itself to the self-knowledge of the *mens*.[191]

Augustine illustrates this by means of the demand of the Delphic Oracle γνῶθι σεαυτόν. If the *mens* ought to know itself, it must already have a certain knowledge of itself, otherwise it would not know what it was searching after. "For it knows itself as seeking and as not knowing itself, in that it seeks to know itself."[192] In order to make plain the difference between the "knowing" prior to the searching and the "recognition"

187. *De trinitate* IX 7,12.

188. *De trinitate* IX 7,12.

189. See *De trinitate* XV 11,20.

190. Augustine used *verbum cordis, verbum in cordis verbum in animo, verbum intimum,* and *verbum intus manens* synonymously. See Schindler's list of Augustine's designations for the inner word in *Wort*, 250–51.

191. *De trinitate* X 3,5.

192. *De trinitate* X 3,5.

after the searching, Augustine differentiates the self-comprehension of the mind into an (implicit) *se nosse* plane from the explicit *se cogitare* plane.[193] The triality *mens, notitia,* and *amor* is thereby assigned to the latter. For the plane of implicit self-knowledge, Augustine proposes the *Ternar* of *memoria/intellegentia/voluntas.*[194]

This *memoria* is more closely specified as a *memoria interior*, which in contrast to a *memoria exterior* (memory) does not bring to mind something experienced but directs the attention of the mind in the present to the current self-relation.[195] Out of the self-relation put down in the *memoria interior* follows the prior self-recognition [*intelligentia*] of the mind of all thought [*cogitare*] and the "deliberate confirmation, the self-wanting"[196] of this knowledge [*voluntas*].[197] For this newly gained triality as well the above-named four features of the Trinity a though d are valid, as Augustine rather briefly outlined them. We are dealing with a substance which makes possible *ad se* statements to all three parts; otherwise memory, insight, and will would always be "expressed as 'in relation to.'"[198] In comparison to the triality *mens/notitia/amor*, which is realized only in temporal implementation, here the structural feature of sempiternity has still been gained—and with it the maximum convergence on the divine Trinity.[199] The implicit self-reference of the mind is unalterable on account of the constantly available content of memory of an assured relationship.[200]

The distance from the divine Trinity is of course maintained. For one thing, the triality does not describe the entire person but only the *mens*, while God is the Trinity.[201] For another thing, the human capabilities of memory, insight, and will are not interchangeable functions. The memory cannot want, the will gains no insight, and insight cannot remember. Totally otherwise with God: "But in that Trinity, who would dare to say that the Father understands neither himself, nor the Son, nor the Holy Spirit, except by the Son, or loves them except by the Holy Spirit; and that he remembers only by himself either himself, or the Son, or the

193. *De trinitate* X 3,7. On this see also Brachtendorf, *Struktur*, 163–77.

194. *De trinitate* X 11,17.

195. *De trinitate* XIV 7,10 and 11,14.

196. Hennigfeld, *Geschichte*, 159.

197. *De trinitate* X 10, 13–16.

198. *De trinitate* X 11,18.

199. See *De trinitate* XIV 10,13.

200. See Brachtendorf, *Geist*, 165.

201. *De trinitate* XV 7,11.

Holy Spirit; and in the same way that the Son remembers neither himself nor the Father . . . ?[202]

Here the limit of human understanding has been reached—more of the divine Trinity than in that human triality cannot be known *per speculum in aenigmate*.[203] In order to make this demarcation clearer, Augustine returns to the inner word at the conclusion of *De trinitate*. Despite this—and this is easy to overlook in Augustine's filigree argument[204]—the *verbum intimum* resides on the *se cogitare* plane of *mens/notitia/amor*, not on the *se nosse* plane of implicit connection to the mind.[205] The inner word, "that we speak in the heart,"[206] is as directly-thinking-of-something an actualization of memory and therefore subject to time.

The word, "that illuminates within,"[207] nevertheless, has a prominent systematic significance because it is the clearest mirror in which "the word of God, even if from a distance, is seen as if in an enigma."[208] Augustine describes five structural features in which the inner word coincides with the *verbum dei*:

1. As the word of God became flesh, "in order to be perceived by the senses of mankind," so the inner word (*verbum1*) expresses itself by the *vox* in an exterior word (*verbum3*).
2. By this statement of the word in the *vox*, *verbum1* has not vanished—as little as the *verbum dei* in the incarnation.
3. Like the word of God, the inner word is necessarily true, "because it is conceived from knowledge . . . even if this knowledge is expressed inwardly, as it is."
4. The inner word proceeds from every good human deed—and therein is comparable "through which everything became as it is."
5. Conversely a deed need not follow *every* inner word, just as the word of God could have existed before all creation without the same.[209]

202. *De trinitate* XV 7,12.

203. *De trinitate* XV 8,14 in connection with 1 Cor 13:12.

204. Thus for example Hennigfeld, *Geschichte*, 160.

205. *De trinitate* XV 15,24.

206. *De trinitate* XV 10,19.

207. *De trinitate* XV 11,20. On the connection of word and light motifs in Augustine's complete works see Warnach, *Erleuchtung*, especially 432–33.

208. *De trinitate* XV 11,20.

209. All arguments and citations are from *De trinitate* XV 11,20.

Ethical and epistemological aspects obviously intersect with one another in these characterizations of the inner word. By its connection to the "innermost knowledge [*intima scientia*],"[210] the inner word is always good and true. As examples of assured, undeniable insights, Augustine names "I know that I live," "I want to be happy," and "I do not want to make a mistake."[211] It is rather significant in this passage, first of all, that the "inner word" is connected to statements, not sentence elements. Secondly it is shown that the representational relationship between *notitia* as concrete content of *memoria* and its actualization in the thought process of the *verbum intimum* is fixed. The *verbum intimum* is a reflection of the *notitia*.[212]

Where do these assured insights come from? "The exhibition of the mind" sees them in every "eternal truth," from which all things temporal were created:

> We have the true knowledge of things [*rerum veracem notitiam*], thence conceived, as it were as a word [*tamquam verbum apud nos*] within us, and by speaking we beget it from within; nor by being born does it depart from us [*nec a nobis nascende discedit*]. And when we speak to others, we apply to the word, remaining within us [*verbo intus manenti*], the ministry of the voice [*ministerium vocis*] or of some bodily sign, that by some kind of sensible remembrance [*commemorationem sensibilem*] some similar thing may be wrought also in the mind of him that hears [*animo audientis*]—similar, I say, to that which does not depart from the mind of him that speaks. . . . And this word is conceived by love, either of the creature or of the creator, that is, either of changeable nature or of unchangeable truth.[213]

This verbalization of knowledge content is, in this image, a work in progress at the end of which stands the bodily or phonetic sign (*verbum3*). Before that, this word remaining inside (*verbum1*) is to be classified systematically (though not necessarily temporally), which for its part, however, is only an expression of that true knowledge that we "*so to speak as a word*" carry with us—and which is stamped by the word of

210. *De trinitate* XV 12,21.

211. *De trinitate* XV 12,21. On the relationship between Augustine's critique of Skeptics in *De trinitate* and in the early writing *Contra Academicos*, see Brachtendorf, *Struktur*, 273–76.

212. Brachtendorf, *Struktur*, 278.

213. *De trinitate* IX 7,12. See *Sermo* 187,2: *sed cum ante omnem linguarum diversitatem res ipsa quae dicenda est, adhuc in cubili cordis quodam modo nuda est intelligenti, quae ut inde procedat loquentis voce vestitur.*

the creator received in love. In this way, the inner word shows itself as a result of the divine "analogy"[214] which Augustine describes rather more vividly in his *Confessiones*: Truth speaks "in the chamber of my thought [*in domicilio cogitationis*] . . . without the organs of voice and tongue, without the sound of syllables,"[215] but still understandable to those who open their "inner ear [*auris interior*]" to God's eternal word.[216]

The word of God cannot be translated in human language as *verba3*, because it is only *one*. *Unicum dei verbum*[217] does not lend itself to being partitioned and dismantled into several words. The word is God "in all the same": "He would not have uttered himself wholly and perfectly, if there were in his word anything more or less than in himself."[218] Certainly this word is the ground from which springs the diversity of knowledge content which pours out in time and space. This diversity in turn entails that we as human beings can have with finite memory [*memoria exterior*] only selective knowledge—the first great difference between the human *verba* and the divine *verbum*. The limitation of temporality takes care of the second difference. We can direct our attention to one topic, while to God all things are simultaneous. Out of this follows for Augustine that "the word of God exists without the thinking of God [*sine cogitatione dei*].[219] He then balances his comparison of the human word and God's word:

> And that word, then, of ours which has neither sound nor thought of sound, but is of that thing in seeing which we speak inwardly, and which therefore belongs to no tongue; and hence is in some sort like, in this enigma, to that word of God which is also God; since this too is born of our knowledge, in such manner as that also is born of the knowledge of the Father: such a word, I say, of ours, which we find to be in some way like that word, let us not be slow to consider how unlike also it is, as it may be in our power to utter it.[220]

214. Warnach, *Erleuchtung*, especially 439–43. One finds further text passages there which show the thought of "analogy" of God in man as a constant in Augustine's thinking.

215. *Confessiones* XI 3,5.

216. *Confessiones* XI 6,8. On "speaking truth" see also *De libero arbitrio* II 8,21.

217. *De trinitate* XV 17,31.

218. *De trinitate* XV 14,23.

219. *De trinitate* XV 16,25.

220. *De trinitate* XV 14,24.

So now the question arises to what degree an "inner word" understood in this way can still be understood in any way as language. First the further question should be clarified as to what can be characterized in *verbum dei* as linguistic. On this point there are in essence three different positions which have been advocated:

1. The inner word is not at all conceived from language but is a workaround in which Augustine connects various lines of tradition and which "rather than traditionally quite by chance bears the name 'word.'"[221]
2. The inner word is to be conceived as linguistic insofar as it singles out an element of the signification process and thinks the Stoic λεκτόν further[222] or rather is to be compared with the *dicibile* of *De dialectica*.[223]
3. The inner word is genuinely of a linguistic nature because it gets to the heart of the dependence on language of human knowledge and communication.[224]

In the following it will be attempted to make thesis 3 a stronger argument and to refute thesis 1. It is helpful to first of all rid one's self of the notion that the "inner word" can be situated within the semantic triangle (contrary to thesis 2). There is absolutely no way of making an identification of *verbum intimum* with the *dicibile*, which is why Augustine makes no reference to *De dialectica* in *De trinitate* but instead mentions earlier writings quite often.[225] Actually, against the equation speaks the obvious objection that the inner word is always connected to knowledge, while the *dicibile* can be adjudged as a word definition as well as imaginary products about which we can communicate.

The difference is certainly of a fundamental nature. While the term *dicibile* was gained from an analysis of the signification process, the *verbum intimum* has its systematic place in the language situation itself. It

221. Flasch, *Augustin*, 121. Similarly Duchrow, *Sprachverständnis*, 144–48.

222. For example Pintarič, *Sprache*, 128.

223. For example Markus, *Communication*, 179 (footnote). In his earlier article "St. Augustine on signs," Robert Markus moves closer if anything to Group 3: *De trinitate* makes a first step toward overcoming a conventional language theory but shies away from making the second step.

224. For example Gadamer, *Wahrheit*, 422–31, and Kreuzer, *Sprachlichkeit*, especially 191–93.

225. Such as the reference to *Contra Academicos* in *De trinitate* XV 12.21.

connects speaking with hearing and answers the question of "what we understand, if and when we understand."[226] Here Augustine turns against the idea that to understand a word means to ascertain its hidden meaning in a fictitious dictionary. Against such a reductionist understanding of language, such as that for which Ludwig Wittgenstein scolds Augustine,[227] it is argued in *De trinitate*: "For as a word indicates something, and indicates also itself, but does not indicate itself to be a word, unless it indicates that it does indicate something."[228] Since we use signs, we express that we want to make ourselves understood. That which we want to say with other words is not—as always understood—the sum total of word definitions. If that were so, we could communicate among ourselves without any loss of understanding. What we want to say is rather the "word remaining inside" that cannot be translated into signs but accompanies the entire language process, the choice of sensory perceptible significations which guides (but does not precisely define) so that "in the mind of the hearer something similar arises,"[229] like that which the speaker "spoke with the heart."[230] The similarity is even greater the more willingness there is on both sides to understand one another. So Augustine's dictum means that the inner word, which in love completes the self-connection to the mind, yields access to its content: *Verbum est igitur . . . cum amore notitia*."[231] At the same time it is significant here that language arises from the self-reflection of the mind which is not at all imaginable as anything but linguistic: "when it is turned to itself by thought, there arises a trinity, in which now at length we can discern also a word; since it is formed from thought itself, while the will unites both."[232]

In this context the *verbum intimum* is not a word nor an element of the signification process, but a function which is indicated by the exterior word. It does not precede the exterior word but "appears wordless" in it.[233] The inner word, which is spoken with the *os cordis* while the *os corporis* articulates sounds,[234] is success in a conversation—that which

226. Kreuzer, *Sprachlichkeit*, 183.

227. Wittgenstein, *Philosophische Untersuchungen*, 16 (§2).

228. *De trinitate* VIII 8,12.

229. *De trinitate* IX 7,12.

230. *De trinitate* XV 10,19.

231. *De trinitate* IX 10,15.

232. *De trinitate* XIV 10,13.

233. Kreuzer, *Sprachlichkeit*, 195.

234. *De trinitate* XV 10,18.

we cannot designate with signs.[235] With this concept Augustine "put in concrete terms" the linguistic nature of all content and movements of the mind, its "intentionality and relationality."[236] Our thought, even that which is not current—"that which one knows, even when one is not thinking about it"—cannot be conceived as anything else but "a constantly successive word [*verbum perpetuum*]."[237] Hans-Georg Gadamer links up to this definition when he writes: "So the inner word, by expressing thought, represents the finiteness of our discursive understanding. Because our understanding does not embrace what it knows in one single comprehensive glance, it must always produce out of itself what it thinks, and present it to itself as if in an inner dialogue with itself. In this sense all thought is a speaking to oneself."[238]

When the essentials out of which language is made is seen in its contentuality and capability for order, then the "inner word" is of a genuinely linguistic nature. It gets to the heart of the matter that the linguistic expression of an issue does not demand a space in the mind alongside this, but "that is where knowledge consummates itself."[239] In the word the issue comes up, we have the issue linguistically at hand. The world is "only the world inasmuch as it comes up for discussion."[240]

Of course, if the sign concept is seen as fundamental to language, the inner word remains exterior. It becomes the logical impossibility "a language before language"—and thereby at most comprehensible in the figurative sense. But this—in view of Augustine's pan-semiotics[241] problematic—interpretation is not fair to the point of his thought. As Karl-Otto Apel formulated it, here lies "the seed of a philosophy of language which thinks not in terms of the static 'classification' of cosmos and sign

235. Kreuzer, *Et ecce est ante nos*, 41.

236. Kreuzer, Introduction to *De trinitate*, XLVII.

237. *De trinitate* XV 15,25.

238. Gadamer, *Truth and Method*, 382. His statements concern Augustine and Thomas Aquinas. Not all of Gadamer's conclusions touch on Augustine (see Brachtendorf, *Struktur*, 312–14, which in its critique of Gadamer goes too far. That Augustine places language before thought follows from God's not being able to think in *De trinitate* XV 16,25).

239. Gadamer, *Wahrheit*, 430.

240. Gadamer, *Wahrheit*, 447.

241. On this see section 3.2.

system, but instead from the point of view of identity of speech act and world-constitution in sense-occurrence."[242]

This thought, as it functions anachronistically in connection to the source, leads back once more to Augustine's original purpose—to come as close as possible with the "inner word" to the word of God: "We must pass by this, in order to arrive at that word of man, by the likeness of which, be it of what sort it may, the Word of God may somehow be seen as in an enigma."[243] As decisive parallels of *verbum dei* and *verbum intimum*, Augustine highlighted this potency. Just as the creator's word constituted the world, so does the inner word precede every human deed.[244] The word is the "creative principle."[245] The crucial difference is that the divine word "had not been malleable beforehand and afterwards had not been shaped"—it is not thought before it is spoken and it needs no sensory sign for its communication.[246] In it "sensory and intelligible appearance" are "congruent."[247]

In the eschaton we will approach this language. Certainly, before and after "we shall not be equal to him in nature" but all the disadvantages of using signs—misunderstandings, deceptions—will be lifted from us, just like the limitation to our memory. "We shall see all our knowledge at once, and at one glance." Our word, then, in the unity of *verbum1* and *verbum3*, "will not indeed be false, because we shall neither lie nor be deceived."[248] The *verbum dei* is the basis of our hope in a language without the disadvantages of a sign system and limited by the capacity of the *mens*. Simultaneously the *verbum dei* mirrors for us, even if shattered, a presentiment of the divine Trinity in our inner word in which we may store our "knowledge achieved in love" and we will be able to communicate among ourselves.[249]

The word of God on one side, the *verbum intimum* on the other side—these are the pillars of a "bridge to transcendence" which is constructed from language. It spans the trenches between our "private

242. Apel, *Idee*, 79.

243. *De trinitate* XV 11,20.

244. *De trinitate* XV 11,20.

245. Kreuzer, *Sprachlichkeit*, 187.

246. *De trinitate* XV 15,25.

247. Kreuzer, *Sprachlichkeit*, 411–12 (Kreuzer annotation).

248. *De trinitate* XV 16,26.

249. *De trinitate* only deals briefly with the communicative function of language in X 1,2.

worlds," between a "closed world of brutal objects" and a "world seen and treated as creatures of their maker" and the trenches that rupture "our limited consciousness."[250] We are dependent on language in the use of our mind, but we experience directly its limitations—and we yearn for a fulfillment of the promises which the *verbum dei* augurs. Rowan Williams describes it strikingly in his study on *De doctrina christiana*: "The word incarnate and crucified represents the absence and deferral that is basic to *signum* as such, and represents also, crucially, the fact, that absence and deferral are the means whereby God engages our desire so that it is freed from its own will towards finishing, towards presence and possession."[251]

3.6. In Conversation with God: *Confessiones*

In his *Confessiones* Augustine has demonstrated how language can serve as just such a bridging function. According to Reinhart Herzog, this text can be read as the "gradual constituting of a conversation" with God.[252] Augustine directs himself to God right in the first section: "*Invocat te, domine, fides mea.*"[253] Still, the first attempt seeking contact fails. Motivated by his reading of Cicero's *Hortensius*, he takes up the holy scriptures, but cannot discern the word of God in them: "As I turned to the scriptures, my senses did not grasp the manner of speaking [*modo loquor*] . . . . My view did not focus on its depths."[254] Nevertheless this failed early attempt at establishing dialogue is described with a linguistic image. Augustine mocks [*inridere*] the scriptures, God mocks Augustine.[255]

Instead of speaking directly to him, God speaks firstly in the dream vision of Mother Monnica—and indeed with the wording from Luke 7:14: "*Iuvenis, tibi dico, surge.*"[256] Augustine himself must first be prepared for the knowledge of the truth in the Bible by means of a further linguistically communicated intermediate step: "You procured for me, by the instrumentality of one inflated with most monstrous pride, certain books

250. Markus, *Communication*, 180.

251. Williams, *Language*, 148.

252. Herzog, *Non in tua voce*, 215.

253. *Confessiones* I 1,1.

254. *Confessiones* III 5,9.

255. *Confessiones* III 9,17. On this see also Herzog, *Non in tua voce*, 223.

256. *Confessiones* VI 1,1. See also the account of the vision in III 10,19–20.

of the Platonists, translated from Greek into Latin."[257] In these Augustine discovered, "supported by many and diverse proofs,"[258] the same message as that in the John prologue. Now he has matured from "milk" to "solid food" and, as things develop, recognizes which passages of John 1 go beyond the Platonists.[259]

It first arrives at an initial direct exchange when Augustine comes to terms with his inner cognitive faculty [*intravi in intima mea*] and "above my mind" saw "an unalterable light." He calls out "Is there then no truth whatsoever?" and he receives an answer from God: "Yes indeed! I am, that I am." A sentence that Augustine understands as inner word: "I heard this, as things are heard in the heart."[260] Even here the Bible text—Exodus 3:14—forms the linguistic interface of God's discourse.[261]

In the famous Book VIII of the *Confessiones* the intensity level of the dialogue with God is raised even higher. Augustine attains the *verbum dei* in the *vox humana*. It is only two words which a child's voice from a neighbor's garden carry to his ear: *tolle, lege*![262] Augustine takes the book which is leaning on another book, a collection of Paul's epistles, and reads a sentence from Romans 13:14 which he immediately feels was directed to himself: "Make no provision for the flesh, to gratify its desires."[263] If he had not had the holy scriptures to begin with, and then only understood by the intermediate step of the Platonic writings their general message, he can now recognize the word in the Bible immediately directed at himself. As if the thought still needed a confirmation, the same exact thing happens to Augustine's friend Alypius. In the subsequent scene he also finds the one sentence which for him points the way.[264]

The next twist in the *Confessiones* from the point of view of divine conversation constellations occurs in Book IX, when Augustine introduces his recipient as a listener to his dialogue with God. In the process he reflects first of all on possible modifications to his conversational relationship by the presence of a third party—but then remains in his

257. *Confessiones* VII 9,13.

258. *Confessiones* VII 9,13.

259. Augustine himself uses the image from 1 Cor 3:2 in *Confessiones* VII 10,16.

260. *Confessiones* VII 10,16.

261. See Herzog, *Non in tua voce*, 233.

262. *Confessiones* VIII 12,29.

263. *Confessiones* VIII 12,29.

264. *Confessiones* VIII 12,30.

direct discourse with God.[265] From Book X forward the listener is then "officially" integrated and emancipates himself as a "second addressee of the work."[266] "I wish to do the truth—in my heart before you, and in my writing before many witnesses."[267] The confession itself is soundless and serves nonetheless as the basis for further speaking and writing: "My confession, therefore, O my God, in your sight, is made unto you silently, and yet not silently. For in noise it is silent, in affection it cries aloud. For neither do I give utterance to anything that is right unto men which you have not heard from me before, nor do you hear anything of the kind from me which yourself said not first unto me."[268]

Here one again recognizes the *verbum intimum*: as the condition of truth and understanding in human communication. After Augustine has assured himself of these conditions for understanding in connection to God and to his readers, he can conclude the *Confessiones* with a "Bible meditation"[269] on Genesis. The step-by-step constituted dialogue with God has become, with the help of the holy scriptures, a trialogue. Augustine wishes to achieve nothing less than "permitting entry of your word inside them [his listeners]."[270] From this perspective Books 11 to 13 of the *Confessiones* complement one another, though these books seem out of place to Peter Brown from the hermeneutic perspective of an autobiography of Augustine, not only harmonically with the entire corpus, but following from them almost in compelling fashion.[271] The Bible combines the eternity of God and the postlapsarian mortality and limitation of mankind[272] to form the *firmanentum auctoritatis*. The Bible can do that because, as an unprofitable system of signs, it remains ambiguous and draws authority directly from its multivalence by context-dependent and recipient-dependent actualizations:

> Thus, when one shall say, Moses meant as I do, and another, nay, but as I do, I suppose that I am speaking more religiously when

265. *Confessiones* IX 4,8. On this see Herzog, *Non in sua voce*, 235.

266. Herzog, *Non in sua voce*, 237.

267. *Confessiones* X 1,1.

268. *Confessiones* X 2,2.

269. Herzog, *Non in sua voce*, 241.

270. *Confessiones* XII 16,23.

271. On the didactic motives of Augustine to crown the *Confessiones* with an exegesis of Genesis see Mayer, *Caelum caeli*, 590.

272. See Frederiksen, *Confessiones*, 306.

> I say, why not rather as both, if both be true? And if there be a third truth, or a fourth, and if any one seek any truth altogether different in those words, why may not Moses be believed to have seen all these, through whom one God has tempered the Holy Scriptures to the senses of many, about to see therein things true but different?[273]

The Bible is the model example of that "bridge to transcendence" whose pillars emerge from the word of God and the inner word of mankind (see section 3.5). If the disadvantages of sign-based language use stand in the foreground of Augustine's earlier linguistic works, the *Confessiones* are virtually a "song of praise to the power of the word,"[274] because they show what language can trigger: "People meet in the word; it expresses friendship and lets it ignite; it bridges and confirms in one the infinite distance between God and man; finally it reveals the inner quandary with the person addressed precisely because it offers itself as a medium by which man is reconciled to himself as he is to God."[275]

The word of God is constantly the first impulse of linguistic impact from which human language forms evolve and then function themselves. In the elaborately constructed "conversion scene" in Book VIII,[276] this impulse transmission can be well followed by completely different *language acts and artefacts*:

1. The beginning and the end of the effective radius consisting of six conversions forms a *collection of Paul's epistles*, thus a part of the holy scriptures.[277]
2. This codex, lying on a table in the home of Augustine and Alypius, is an occasion for the visitor Ponticianus to *tell* them both a story:
3. Two courtiers go for a walk in Triers and by chance discover in a monk's cell a *codex with the conversion story* of Antonius, a colleague who converted to the monastic life.

273. *Confessiones* XII 31,42.

274. Van Hooff, *Dialektik*, 343.

275. Van Hooff, *Dialektik*, 343.

276. That this description is to be understood as an interpretive narration and not as an historical report is suggested by the comparison to *De beata vita*. In this document, written immediately after the conversion from betrothed rhetor to celibate Christian, the reversal is triggered by lung disease [*pectoris dolor*]. In the *Confessiones*, written about fifteen years later, the disease plays only a minor role (IX 2,4).

277. *Confessiones* VIII 6,14.

4. The first courtier is so impressed by the *reading* that he immediately wishes to become a "friend of God" and in an *exuberant speech convinces* the second courtier to follow him in the monastic life.
5. Subsequently both betrothed courtiers *convince* their brides-to-be that instead of marrying to consecrate their virginity to God.[278]
6. This *story* of Ponticianus reminds Augustine of his earlier *Hortensius reading* and of his repeatedly postponed decision to forsake earthly happiness.[279]
7. In a *monologue* filled with "sentences like whip cracks" he frets over and shames himself for his long procrastination,[280]
8. *screams* his despair to Alypius,[281]
9. *calls out* desperately to God: "How long? Why not right away?"[282]
10. hears then the child's voice "*tolle, lege*"
11. through that remembers a detail of the *Antonius story*, namely that he was once encouraged by a single sentence *from the Gospel* in his decision,
12. goes to the *Paul book*, takes it, opens it—and *reads* that passage which frees him from his hesitation and provokes his decision to dedicate his entire life to God.[283]
13. His friend Alypius does the same thing, *reads* the passage appropriate to him—and follows Augustine in his decision.[284]

This shows the power of the word of the Bible, which can (but does not have to) unfold directly (11, 12, 13) and can be transmitted by faithful witnesses (4, 5). Nothing in this cycle of effect happens out of its compelling inner logic, the events are consciously arranged as coincidences—the visit of Ponticianus ("I really do not know what he wants from us"),[285] the discovery of the walkers, the child's voice, the Bible opened to certain

278. *Confessiones* VIII 6,15.
279. *Confessiones* VIII 7,17.
280. *Confessiones* VIII 7,18.
281. *Confessiones* VIII 8,19.
282. *Confessiones* VIII 12,28.
283. *Confessiones* VIII 12,29.
284. *Confessiones* VIII 12,30.
285. *Confessiones* VIII 6,14.

passages. It is not the systematic reading of the canon that brings about Augustin's turning point in life, it is God's grace, which finally pulls his vacillating will over to the right side.[286] The impact of God's word lies solely in God's hand. He can bridge over the provisional arrangements of human sign formation and create "successful conversational and comprehension implementation."[287] The decisive element of successful communication situations does not play out on the plane of signs, but on the plane of the inner word.

A further example of this is the final conversation of Augustine with his mother Monnica in Ostia as it is recorded in Book IX of the *Confessiones*. The author does not remember the exact wording anymore, but he has a clear recollection of the content: "Thus we conversed, if not in this exact manner and with these words."[288] For Johann Kreuzer this is being expressed paradigmatically: "What was imparted in conversation does not depend on the words with which the conversation is conducted. It expresses itself in the words. It is the *volubilis motio* of the 'inner word' which expresses itself wordlessly."[289] The inner word does not lend itself to being expressed as such, but it does lend itself to being retrieved from *memoria*: "The truth itself, which you are, was present," Augustine remembers.[290] The communication between him and his mother also functions in that place, where no words were to be heard: "And we rose ever higher, in silent reflection, in conversation, in admiration of your works."[291] The dialogue seems to take place at two different levels—on the inner and on the not unambiguously inferable outer plane: "And while we were thus speaking, and straining after, we slightly touched this wisdom with the whole effort of our heart [*ictu cordis*]. . . . We returned to the noise of our own mouth [*strepitum oris nostril*], where the word uttered has both beginning and end. And what is like your word, our Lord, who remains in himself without becoming old, and makes all things new [*innovanti omnia*]?"[292]

286. *Confessiones* IX 1,1.

287. Kreuzer, *Sprachlichkeit*, 197.

288. *Confessiones* IX 10,26.

289. Kreuzer, *Sprachlichkeit*, 197. See also Kreuzer, *Pulchritudo*, 263–65.

290. *Confessiones* IX 10,23.

291. *Confessiones* IX 10,24.

292. *Confessiones* IX 10,24.

The word of God reaches into our exterior discourse by the inner word so that, in spite of the fundamental deficiency of human language, understanding becomes possible. Finally, all successful speaking is a conversation with God: "You call us, therefore, to understand the word [*intelligendum verbum*], God with you, God, which is spoken eternally, and by it are all things spoken eternally [*eo sempiterne dicuntur omnia*]."[293]

The *Confessiones* prove this by its narrative framework which is held together at key points of canonically motivated speech acts or documents. But even in its stylistic composition the thirteen books are an impressive proof of the power of language and its potential to enable understanding, as Adolf von Harnack characterized the *Confessiones* of Augustine about 1,500 years after they were written: "The religious language which we speak, entrusted to us from songs, prayers, and devotional books, bears the stamp of his [Augustine's] mind. We still speak, without knowing it, with his words, and in expressing the most profound feelings, imparting words to the dialectic of the heart, this he was the first to teach."[294]

3.7. Summary

Augustine's initial reluctance in regard to a linguistic comprehension of the *verbum dei*, as it is expressed by the sparing use of the term in his early writings, increasingly gives way to the insight that there is no more appropriate image for the binding of immanence and transcendence than language. The linguist thinks beyond the John prologue when he grasps the creative power of God's word as invocation [*invocatio*] in the creature. This power, through the *Deus dixit* of the Old Testament, gives things their form and, through the *verbum* of the New Testament, gives mankind its purpose (sections 3.2 and 3.3).

Conversely, from the perspective of creatures, a view is opened by means of language to the mirror in which the word of God appears as in an enigma. For with the outwardly pointing word, sensorily perceptible in letters or sounds, is bound that inner word which as "knowledge associated with love" not only sketches out the divine Trinity in its relational framework, but furthermore ideal-typically comprises the functions of language: the inner connection to what is intended, truth, and truthfulness of those speaking as well as their goal to wish to be understood.

293. *Confessiones* XI 7,9.

294. Harnack, *Augustin's Confessionen*, 8.

From the interpretation of the inner word as—surely distorted, but without alternative—a mirror for the word of God, it also follows that all pathways to God to this extent are of a linguistic nature, since they must come forth from the inner word. Language is the bridge to transcendence whose pillars are the inner word and the *verbum dei*. The holy scriptures represent this in exemplary fashion, as they were inspired by God and their *eloquentia* conceals an encoding (decipherable for us) with pagan methods (sections 3.4 and 3.5). We have reached back to this canon in excellent manner where God's word is expressed in intrinsic biographical contexts—the narrative structure of Augustine's *Confessiones* is a fine example of this (section 3.6).

Nevertheless the cascade of Augustine from *verbum dei*, over the inner word to the outer word, in which the meaning dissipates, remains in this respect unsatisfying, since this model provides us with no criteria with which the loss of meaning can be measured. Everything that is to be said would be formulated in the deficient mode of exterior words. Here is shown the egg shell of Augustine's neoplatonic conditioning[295] as well as the legacy of his earlier critique on the signification process which also influences his language-friendly attitude in *De trinitate*. To Augustine, the certainty of the word of God remains in the end an extralinguistic postulate. Martin Luther was the first to show that one can also think differently about this, as long as one takes a radically serious approach to the linguistic character of the *verbum dei*, from the roots upward.

295. On this see Kamlah, *Christentum*, 207.

4

The Word of God in Martin Luther

4.1. Introduction

The word of God is the center of Martin Luther's theological thought. For him there is no *locus*, no individual theological theme is delineated, rather he identifies "that which . . . makes theology theology, and from that what represents the essential and constitutive in all theological statements, the foundational dimension of all theological discourse."[1] Compared to Augustine, for whom the linguistic character of the *verbum dei* matures only in his later works, one may speak directly of a paradigm change.

As much as Luther shares with Augustine the foundation of the "theological opposition of God and man,"[2] just as much separates them with regard to the approach to the divine revelation. While Augustine gives primacy to the act of the *res* and accepts the linguistic *signa* only as the second-best solution,[3] for Luther the ascertainable linguistic character by means of hearing or reading is ineluctable. It is the only pathway to transcendence, to that which can only be believed: "Faith is the reason why we cannot demonstrate our goods in any other way than by the

1. Ringleben, *Gott*, 2.

2. Korsch, *Luther*, 49. On the influence of Augustine on Luther, see Pesch, *Hinführung*, 82–84, and Andreas, *Luther*, especially 11–12 (theses review) and 14–16 (literature survey).

3. See for example Augustine, *De trinitate* XIV 16,22: "Nothing can be said, unless the images of the corporeal sounds anticipate the sound of the voice in the thought of the spirit."

word, because faith has to do with things that do not appear, things that cannot be taught, shown, and pointed out except by the word."[4] In his exegesis of the Tora Psalm 119 Luther answers the question he himself posed, why is the word so intimately called upon, only the word—not the things themselves, but the signs of things:[5] "But since in the words by faith there are hidden things that do not appear, having the words by faith, they have everything, though hidden."[6]

Both quotations come from Luther's first lectures on the Psalms from 1513 to 1515, the *Dictata super Psalterium*. This is worthy of special mention here because the *Dictata*, alongside his sermon on the John prologue from 1514,[7] are the only noteworthy writings of Luther in which the *verbum intimum* of Augustine plays a role.[8] Nevertheless the seed of Luther's mature language concept is planted in the *Dictata*,[9] which leads to a "radical abandonment of Augustine's understanding of signs"[10] with his distinction of inner and external word[11] which culminates in the sentence: "Whoever has the word, has the entire divinity."[12]

The unique interweaving of God and God's word is pursued in more detail in the first of the following sections (4.2) which taken together with Luther's language concept, is illuminated by posing different questions. In section 4.3 the question of the genesis of the word is the main focus, and in 4.4 the question of its validity and effectiveness. Section 4.5 thematicizes the appropriate use of the word of God, especially as holy scripture and

4. *Dictata super Psalterium*, WA 4, 272,22–24 [trans. Bouman].

5. *Dictata super Psalterium*, WA 4, 376, 14 [trans. Bouman].

6. *Dictata super Psalterium*, WA 4, 376,15–16 [trans. Bouman].

7. WA 1, 20–29.

8. See Beutel, *Anfang*, 149 and zur Mühlen, *Nos extra nos*, 80–90.

9. Gerhard Ebeling shows in his *Anfänge* (especially 33–39) the degree to which Luther, already in the *Dictata* is aiming beyond the plane of language towards an understanding of existence.

10. Bayer, *Promissio*, 188. Oswald Bayer localizes the departure of Luther from Augustine and Luther's new understanding of the word in the 38th thesis (*Promissio*, 175–80). For a critique of Bayer, see Junghans, *Wort*, 172.

11. See *Weihnachtspostille*, WA 10.1.1, 188,18–22: "There have been many pointed arguments over the inner word of the heart in man which remains within and after which man is created in God's image. But it has remained so deep and dark, and will remain so, and those arguing do not themselves know what it is all about; so we will leave it alone."

12. *Weihnachtspostille*, WA 10.1.1, 188,8. That the spoken word is intended here is abundantly clear from the preceding sentences.

sacrament. In the process it will be shown that with the condescendence of God in language a *nova lingua*[13] of faith comes into being.

The word of God in Luther is not quite a desideratum of theological research. In the previous four decades at least three important monographs on this theme have appeared[14] and a great many individual studies.[15] Nevertheless the following chapter sections claim to be more than a summary of previous research, indeed the primary epistemological interest of this work is, in total, the reciprocal correlation of language and the word of God. It is just this interdependence which has long been hardly appreciated. Among the monographs Joachim Ringleben's[16] was the first to think along these lines, and the work before you has profited most from studies on singular linguistic aspects in Luther's theology. Two examples should be named: Thomas Wabel's dialogue between Luther's hermeneutics and Ludwig Wittgenstein's later philosophy[17] and Stefan Streiff's analysis of *nova lingua* on the basis of the disputation *Verbum caro factum est.*[18]

4.2. God and God's Word

The fundamental function of the word of God in Luther's theology[19] and its forced derivation from the image of God are shown especially clearly in Luther's *De servo arbitrio* from 1525, a work directed at Erasmus of Rotterdam which Gerhard Ebeling has remarked "could justifiably be called *De Deo.*"[20] The differences between Erasmus and Luther over the question of human freedom unfold against the backdrop of the problem of what we can generally know and understand about God. In his *Diatribe* Erasmus takes up an almost pragmatic position. God hides some things completely from the human yearning for knowledge, some things

13. *De divinitate*, WA 39.2, 94,21 (Thesis 22).

14. Beutel, *Anfang*; Führer, *Wort*; Ringleben, *Gott*. For earlier publications see the research survey in Führer, *Wort*, 16–32.

15. See Ringleben, *Gott*, 621–26, and Wabel, *Sprache*, 386–414.

16. Ringleben, *Gott*, 30–91.

17. Wabel, *Sprache*.

18. Streiff, *Novis linguis loci*.

19. See Jüngel, *Gott*, 90: "The term word of God and with it the term *deus praedicatus* define . . . what one could call the theological axiomatics or Luther's fundamental theology."

20. Ebeling, *Luther*, 299.

he reveals partially, and other things he reveals completely. Alongside lies a gray area of things whose truth can be argued but are intended *ut etiamsi vera essent et sciri possent* and not for *promiscuis auribis*[21] because they "could not be expressed to the ignorant masses without causing great shock."[22] The comprehension of these things, if at all possible, is not mandatory for proper faith—indeed, it could be counterproductive: "There are certain diseases of the body which are less difficult to bear than their cure."[23] The faith and the comprehensibility of its contents are clearly separated by Erasmus: "so great is my dislike of assertions that I prefer the views of the sceptics wherever the inviolable authority of scripture and the decision of the church permit—a church to which at all times I willingly submit my own views, whether I attain what she prescribes or not."[24]

So, *using human criteria*, Erasmus draws a line between knowable and unknowable divine things. There is on the one hand the question of usefulness, and on the other hand the question of individual capability. Luther summarizes this position polemically in the adage "what is above us, is nothing to us."[25] "Your words sound as if it were completely indifferent to you what is believed by whom and where."[26] For Luther, certainty of faith is unthinkable without anterior understanding: "A Christian would certainly be cursed if he is uncertain and does not understand what is required of him! For how will he believe, if he does not understand?"[27]

This understanding is made possible by divine revelation, which one can imagine in various ways—but for which God has selected *one* medium, namely his word: "So it has pleased God, that not without a word, but through the word of the Spirit, imparts that he has us as his co-workers [*cooperatores*]. We bring outwardly through sounds that which he himself alone breathes into wherever he will. Of course, he could have done this without a word. But he does not want that."[28]

21. Erasmus, *Diatribe*, I.a.9.

22. Erasmus, *Diatribe*, I.a.9.

23. Erasmus, *Diatribe*, I.a.9.

24. Erasmus, *Diatribe*, I.a.4 [trans. Winter].

25. *De servo arbitrio*, WA 18, 605,16. On the history of this proverb as well as its reception by Erasmus and Luther see Jüngel, *Quae supra nos*.

26. *De servo*, WA 18, 605, 15–16.

27. *De servo*, WA 18, 605, 6–8.

28. *De servo*, WA 18, 695, 28–31.

God allows us to know him as a *deus loquens*,[29] a *verbatus deus*,[30] indeed as a *deus verbosa*.[31] And only through the linguistic signs given by him can we grasp him with the senses, as Luther stated in a sermon from 1529: "Reason knows well how to speak of God and shows that there is a God, but it cannot quite hit the mark because it does not know who he is. . . . On account of this uncertainty, God's word must come to our aid and God must reveal himself and define himself in an outer word and sign so that one may hear him, see him, grasp him, hold him, and know him. Otherwise we go astray."[32]

However, it does not follow from this that we can equate God with God's word. That would mean reducing God to human dimensions. We only do justice to God when we think of him as greater than that which we can understand of him: "Nor is he kept bound to his word, but has kept himself free over all things."[33] In contrast to Erasmus, Luther leaves to God the differentiation between discernible and undiscernible—this limit is not drawn according to human criteria. Consequently Luther accuses his opposite number: "The *Diatribe* deceives in its ignorance when it does not differentiate at all between the preached God and the hidden God [*Deum praedicatum et absconditum*], that is, between the word of God and God himself. God does a great deal which he does not indicate to us by his word. . . . We must now pay attention to the word and set aside any inscrutable will [*voluntas imperscrutabilis*]."[34]

The God who does not reveal himself to us does not concern us. That *Deus in maiestate et natura sua*[35] does not wish that we should have anything to do with him. As the point of his argument with Erasmus, Luther can only protest, using the adage with which he polemically summarized Erasmus' approach previously: what is above us, is nothing to us.[36] While Erasmus interprets the sentence philosophically, from mankind that seeks knowledge, Luther views it from a theological perspective. It is

29. *Genesisvorlesung*, WA 44, 574,36. On Peter Meinhold's questioning of the authenticity of Luther's lecture on Genesis (Meinhold, *Genesisvorlesung*, especially 427–28) see Schwanke, *Creatio*, 37–40.

30. *Psalmenauslegungen* 1529/32, WA 31.1, 511,29.

31. *Disputationen* 1533/38, WA 39.2, 199,5.

32. *Reihenpredigten* 5. Mose, WA 28, 611,36–612,15.

33. *De servo*, WA 18, 685,23–24 [trans. Winter].

34. *De servo*, WA 18, 685,25–31.

35. *De servo*, WA 18, 685,14.

36. *De servo*, WA 18, 685,6–7.

God himself who determines what remains *supra nos*, and what remains *nihil ad nos*.[37]

Of course, this may not be understood this way since we are dealing with two different essences of one God. The hidden and revealed God stands in an "absolute personal identity."[38] Whoever hears God's word recognizes his essence: *Qui audit verbum meum, intuetur cor meum*.[39] The differentiation between *verbum dei* and *deus ipse* is rather to be interpreted that "'God himself' is the indispensable conceptual limit without which the God become man cannot be thought of as the self-determination of God but must be misunderstood as divine skill."[40] A God who reveals himself in history out of free will before us—and for us—must be able to be thought of as a God that not (yet) is for us.

The sense of the "often misunderstood"[41] delimitation in Luther's concept of God is not "the indefinability of God, but to assert the definitiveness . . . [of his] revelation"[42]—and thereby maintain the insight that his hiddenness is essential to God: "God is the one who is hidden. This is only appropriate."[43] To this extent as well, his self-revelation can be read as a function of his hiddenness: "So that is revelation: the hidden God hides his divine hiddenness."[44] But now this second hiding occurs in a manner directed towards mankind, and indeed God shows himself "under the opposite object, the opposite sensory perception, and the opposite experience [*sub contrario obiecto, sensu, experientia*][45]—namely in the crucified Christ. The presence of God in man is the *summum mysterium*,[46] for it presents "a manner of hiddenness, which from the reasoning mind which reckons God as the ultimate reason of the world, is felt to be an absurdity."[47] This hiddenness of God reaches its high point *within the world* in the death of Jesus, which "represents the outermost

37. See Jüngel, *Quae supra nos*, 205.
38. Rückert, *Anschauung*, 100–101.
39. *Predigt* 1523, WA 11, 225,27–28.
40. Jüngel, *Quae supra nos*, 223.
41. Korsch, *Luther*, 79.
42. Jüngel, *Quae supra nos*, 229.
43. *Genesisvorlesung*, WA 44, 110,23–24.
44. Jüngel, *Quae supra nos*, 239.
45. *De servo*, 633,8–9.
46. *De servo*, 606,26.
47. Korsch, *Luther*, 78.

venue of God's presence."[48] "Therefore in the crucified Christ is the true theology and knowledge of God."[49]

Eberhard Jüngel has proposed the terms "precise" and "absolute hiddenness" for both of these aspects of the hiddenness of God.[50] Precise is the *sub contrario* revealed and, for us, understandable hiddenness to the extent that, aside from the sermon on the life and death of Jesus Christ, there is no other pathway to faith in God. The absolute hiddenness of God emerges compellingly from this faith, which also understands its own challenge and negation as engendered by God.[51]

Because the faith, which "concerns itself with things unseen,"[52] is the form of consciousness which God, despite his hiddenness, allows himself to be present as the one absent, the central position of the word of God in Luther is illuminated: "And because only the word of God enables this sort of human configuration, because only the essence of God makes it possible, the absent one to be present as the absent one and the hidden one to be revealed as the hidden one, for that reason Luther calls the *deus revelatus* a *deus praedicatus*, therefore the event of the revelation of God is an event of the word, and God himself becomes the word of God."[53]

The *sub contrario* principle applies likewise to the exclusive revelation of God in the word. It excludes the obvious pathway to transcendence as a naturally guided recognition of God by way of reason[54] exactly like a certainty of God as being feeling.[55] The word stands *extra nos*,[56] "tears us away from ourselves,"[57] and gives us as a result certainty completely independent of human factors. The word, which as a sign almost hides

48. Korsch, *Luther*, 78.

49. *Heidelberger Disputation*, WA 1, 362,18–19.

50. Jüngel, *Quae supra nos*, 239.

51. On this see Korsch, *Luther*, 79–87.

52. *De servo*, WA 18, 633,7.

53. Jüngel, *Quae supra nos*, 250.

54. *Prophet Jona*, WA 19, 206,33–34: "That reason can neither partake nor submit to the deity is borne by reason alone. Reason knows that God exists. But who or which it is that is properly called God, that it does not know."

55. *Predigt* 1532, WA 36, 497,19–21: "It is quite true that if it were all about feelings, I would be lost. But the word shall hold true over mine and the whole world's feelings and remain true, no matter how slight it may seem."

56. *Galatervorlesung* 1521, WA 40.1, 589,8.

57. Iwand, *Theologie*, 207.

the presence of God, makes him at the same time manifest. And vice versa: "What God makes manifest . . . is what hides him concurrently."[58]

The word of God that touches us from without, the event of which we are unable to do anything about, corresponds to our existence *coram Deo*. In this, according to Dietrich Korsch, consists Luther's "central religious idea," that "the salvation of mankind" is understood as the "establishment of immediacy of mankind's connection to God through God himself."[59] That radically contradicts a natural self-understanding of mankind,[60] which Luther recognizes in Erasmus' *Diatribe*: "The *Diatribe* dreams of a safe and sound mankind [*hominem . . . integrum et sanum*], as he is in his things for human reflection."[61] If that were really the case, the word of God would fit in coherently with our coherence of reason and would not be able to bring about anything. By contrast Luther stresses: "But truly the word God, when it comes, comes contrary to our senses and our desires.[62] Only when it is "taken seriously as God's word, when it . . . comes as our 'antagonist,' that is to say, as the word which brings about in us, what we are."[63]

From this thought forward, that God's word imparts nothing informative or uplifting, but wants to cause something earthshaking in us, follows Luther's differentiation into the two reifications of the *verbum dei*: "I call the law as well as the gospel the 'word of God.' In the law, works are demanded, in the gospel, faith."[64] As the law, the word of God destroys "self-righteousness and self-assertion before God," as the gospel, "it speaks righteously to the sinner."[65] In both cases it is about an unmediated direct address of God to mankind. It happens in the clearly identifiable linguistic forms of demand and promise, in the "speech acts of duty ('thou shalt') and promise ('thou wilt')."[66] God does not express himself in any other third way. God only encounters mankind judgingly or redemptively.[67] Therefore mankind has no other path to salvation—for instance,

58. Ringleben, *Gott*, 54.
59. Korsch, *Leitidee*, 94.
60. Korsch, *Leitidee*, 215.
61. *De servo*, WA 18, 674,6–7.
62. *Römervorlesung* 1515/16, WA 56, 423,19–20.
63. Ebeling, *Luther*, 275.
64. *De servo*, WA 18, 663,14–15.
65. Ebeling, *Luther*, 275.
66. Korsch, *Leitidee*, 95.
67. Korsch, *Prinzipienfragen*, 356.

by way of free will as postulated by Erasmus:[68] "There is namely nothing else which leads to the grace of God and eternal salvation [*aeternam salutem*] as the word and work of God."[69] The differentiation of law and gospel, for which Luther criticizes Erasmus' disregard in his *Diatribe* as a fundamental error in biblical exegesis,[70] will again play a role in section 4.4 on the validity of the word of God.

4.3. The Genesis of the Word

The development of the word of God and its forms—including human language—is a theme of salvation history in Luther.[71] From creation through pre- and postlapsarian communication with the first humans, through his dealings with Israel, from the word becoming flesh in Jesus Christ to the salvation in the eschaton, God's effect can be characterized as the history of his discourse with mankind: "And as the world was created by the word, thus is it redeemed by the word . . . and thus the word in salvation has become flesh or man."[72] In this passage the stages of salvation history are illuminated under the aspect of the word.

From the creation story and the John prologue follow for Luther the verbality of all creatures as well as the un-creatureliness of the word. Here is Luther's sermon on John 1:1–14 from 1522: "If the word was for all creatures and all creatures came into being and were created through this same word, then the word must be of a different nature than creatures and therefore it neither came into being nor was created as were the creatures."[73] This means in turn for the origin of the word: "So it must be eternal and have no beginning, it was already there and cannot be grasped in time nor as a creature, but hovers over time and creatures, indeed becomes time and creatures, and begins thereby."[74]

68. Erasmus, *De libero arbitrio*, I.b.10: "In this context, by free will we understand the capacity of the human will by which means mankind is either led to eternal salvation or can turn away from it."

69. *De servo*, WA 18, 663,15–16.

70. *De servo*, WA 18, 680,23–25.

71. Ringleben, *Gott*, 108–9.

72. *Festpostille*, WA 17.2, 316,30–33.

73. *Weihnachtspostille*, WA 10.1.1, 183,1–3.

74. *Weihnachtspostille*, WA 10.1.1, 183,3–7.

The word looks beyond the beginning of time and space. That the primary cause of creation is explained with a linguistic term is, to Luther, more than just an image. The preexistent *verbum aeternum* expresses that "the redemptive force of God" consists in the "interaction between Father, Son, and Holy Spirit."[75] In his sermons Luther did not shy away from illustrative descriptions of divine monologue: "*In aeternum* God looked at himself in his eternal divine essence, formed himself and spoke of himself, who he would be: What am I then? And formed himself and designated it *filius dei, qui est deus in aeternum, nisi quod pater est* image, *sed filius. Ubi sic se* pronounced in eternity, he spoke one word, spoke and laughed, thanked *et secutum, quod fuit spiritus sanctus.*"[76]

This divine word, in which the *divina cognitio*[77] is reflected, fully contains the essence of its speaker—without being identical to him. This distinguishes it from the human word: "For any word is a sign that indicates something. But here the meaning is naturally in the sign or in the word, which is not in another sign; this is why he properly calls it an essential image or a sign of his nature."[78]

A human utterance, even when it captures the opinion of the speaker exactly, remains a series of signs. Just as the "wooden image or golden image"[79] does not contain the essence of that being portrayed, it only transports a meaning. For God's word, on the other hand, it holds that "Whoever has the word, has the entire divinity."[80] In this sermon from 1522, Luther expressly rejects the differentiation touched upon earlier between *verbum internum* and *externum* for, respectively, the uncreated word and the natural word of God[81]—this suggestion "has remained quite deep and dark, and will probably remain so."[82]

With the creation, the word of God expresses itself. Not in the fact that it generates a sign to a content of meaning, as would be conceivable within the *internum/externum* concept (Ebeling), but in the fact that

75. Lienhard, *Zeugnis*, 239.

76. *Predigten* 1532, WA 36, 412,26–32.

77. *Genesisvorlesung* 1535, WA 42, 17,26.

78. *Weihnachtspostille*, WA 10.1.1, 187,5–8.

79. *Weihnachtspostille*, WA 10.1.1, 188,11.

80. *Weihnachtspostille*, WA 10.1.1, 188,8.

81. On the earlier use of this differentiation by Luther and the reasons for his later rejection see above all Bayer, *Promissio*, 26–31 and 339–51. Otherwise Junghans, *Wort*, 171–72.

82. *Weihnachtspostille*, WA 10.1.1, 188,20–21.

the uncreated word "on its own distinguishes an outer from itself":[83] "Thus the Father spoke inwardly, and outwardly light was made and came into existence immediately. In this manner other creatures, too, were made later."[84]

God's word makes itself available in the process of creation, understood as "becoming material of sense,"[85] a reference in time and space: "the word of God is a thing, not a mere word."[86] That which is for us the sound of the voice—the sensory articulation of our discourse[87]—is for God the signified thing itself: "that which among us has the sound of a word *is* a reality with God."[88] While human speech can only signify something which exists, divine speech calls things into existence. Everything created is *vocabula Dei*.[89] God is the "author,"[90] indeed the "poet" of the world and mankind *versus . . . et carmina quae condit*.[91]

Early on Luther had seen—here more humanistically influenced than scholarly[92]—a *similitudo* in human language capability which is mentioned in Genesis 1:26 (Vulgate). Regarding one of the aphorisms of Petrus Lombardus connected to this Bible passage Luther wrote: "It could well be that man is the image of God, in imitation of God, in order to move forward and act . . . then the form of the word is God."[93] This is pointedly expressed especially in the prelapsarian exercise of human language. In the primitive state, Adam's speaking is also creative in the sense that, in Luther's interpretation of Genesis 2:19–20, Adam intuitively grasps the essence of animals and chooses appropriate names for them

83. Ringleben, *Gott*, 101.

84. *Genesisvorlesung*, WA 42, 15,22–24 [trans. Schick].

85. Ringleben, *Gott*, 102 (footnote).

86. *Genesisvorlesung*, WA 42, 17,23.

87. See Ringleben, *Gott*, 102 (footnote).

88. *Genesisvorlesung*, WA 42, 17,18.

89. *Genesisvorlesung*, WA 42, 17,19.

90. *Genesisvorlesung*, WA 42, 20,21.

91. *Genesisvorlesung*, WA 44, 572,25–27.

92. See Junghans, *Worte*, 158–63.

93. *Randbemerkungen*, WA 9, 67,15–18. See also *Vorrede auf den Psalter*, WA DB 10.1, 100,12–13: There is "no more powerful nor nobler work of man . . . than discourse, since mankind is elevated above other animals mostly by language."

according to their nature:[94] "What an ocean of knowledge and wisdom there was in this one man!"[95]

This holds true up to the fall from grace—which for Luther in many respects undergoes a linguistic interpretation which emerges from the word of God, and under this aspect even salvages the further "decline of language as the wages of sin."[96] Firstly the cause of the fall is to be described as the attempt to gain divine knowledge outside of his revealed word: "Note that it is the curiosity of Adam, who in paradise asks of God beyond the word."[97] The promise contained in the word of the serpent, "to be like God,"[98] corresponds to the rising attitude in many variants of mankind which considers human cognitive faculty superior to divine revelation. That is the "radical, capital, and truly mortal sin,"[99] which—from Luther's perspective—befalls Erasmus when he fails to distinguish between *verbum Dei* and *Deus ipse*[100] and places more trust in *propriae speculationes* than the revealed one: "Of the things that are not revealed, even though they be broken, we will understand nothing, and our own speculations above and beyond the word, inquiring of and investigating the master, are quite dangerous to ourselves."[101]

In the story of the fall from grace, Luther discovers the circumvention and disregard of the word of God in linguistic detail.[102] First of all, in Genesis 3:3 Eve diminishes the divine death threat from Genesis 2:17 (Vulgate)[103] with a *forte*: "The woman began to think: 'perhaps it is the word, and who knows, if it is the word of God?'"[104] This challenge, according to Luther, surely indicates the negation of the word of God. Secondly, Eve untruthfully adds to the divine prohibition of eating from the tree of knowledge with "and neither shall you touch."[105] For Luther this is an equally paradigmatic error in dealing with the word of God: "The

94. On this see Meinhold, *Sprachphilosophie*, 42–43.
95. *Genesisvorlesung*, WA 42, 90,39 [trans. Schick].
96. Meinhold, *Sprachphilosophie*, 43.
97. *Genesisvorlesung*, WA 43, 239,17–18.
98. Gen 3:5 Vulgate.
99. *Disputationen*, WA 39.1, 84,10.
100. See *De servo*, WA 18, 685,25–27.
101. *Disputationen*, WA 39.1, 288,12–289,1.
102. On this see also Schwarz, *Luther*, 112–14.
103. This weakening is only found in the Vulgate.
104. *Reihenpredigten 1. Mose*, WA 14, 131,19–20.
105. Gen 3:3 (Vulgate).

woman added to the word of God 'Do not touch,' which is human infidelity; adding to the word of God should be based on a higher authority."[106]

In this linguistic interpretation, the fall from grace comprises three violations of the *verbum dei* which correspond to an increasing remoteness from union with the creator:

a. total disregard for God's word in striving without discerning this,

b. its weakening by arbitrary interpretation,

c. supplement of divine discourse by human additions.

With this new self-understanding, no longer grounded in God, mankind involves the clarity and unambiguity of linguistic communication. Now human language signifies "only vaguely the essence of things."[107] The original wisdom of Adam, intuitively grasping the nature of things, gives way to a fragile knowledge built on trial and error. The decline of language as a consequence of original sin is deepened in the story of the tower of Babel.[108] The punishment of worldwide linguistic confusion touches mankind permanently since it causes conflict and wars: "This describes a horrible penalty, from which wars, bloodshed, and evils of every kind flourish all over the earth."[109]

Because mankind itself has destroyed loss-free communication with God, postlapsarian mankind perceives the speech of God in two ways. Luther proves this by language use in the Bible: In *locqui* (or also *vocare*) the word of God comes into view as speech directed at mankind, whose fulfillment does not necessarily occur—to some degree because it is not heard nor understood. By contrast it is valid for the "unopposed creating"[110] *dicere*, that which was expressed with the word necessarily occurs: "To speak" is to send and direct the word openly to someone else. "To say," however, is only to bring the word forth and to establish and determine it distinctly. . . . For whatever God said came into being and was done. . . . But quite often he also spoke many things that were not done and heard and received by men.[111]

106. *Reihenpredigten 1. Mose (Druckfassung)*, WA 14, 131,19–20.

107. Meinhold, *Sprachphilosophie*, 43.

108. On the interpretation of the yahwist prehistory as a "deconstruction of human language as a result of sin" see also Zaborowski, *Aber sprich nur*, 64–69 (here: 69).

109. *Genesisvorlesung*, WA 42, 421,35–36.

110. Ringleben, *Gott*, 107.

111. *Dictata super Psalterium*, WA 3, 280,17–281,5 [trans. Bouman].

Additionally, after the fall God allows his word to be heard exclusively through persons (or, with a view to Numbers 24, animals):[112] "Our Lord God does not speak as mankind speaks, he has no mouth, *sed loquitur per hominem*."[113] In his sermons, Luther employs a great deal of exegetical fantasy against the idea of a spontaneous divine voice. So, for example, the sentence "Where is your brother Abel?" (Gen 4:9) is directed by Adam to Cain;[114] the divine command to Noah to go into the ark (Gen 7:1) comes from the mouth of his grandfather Methuselah who died in the year of the flood.[115]

Both the partition into two manners of speaking and the indirect address change with Jesus Christ. In him both manners of speaking are merged once again.[116] The *locutio* of God is connected to his humanity, the *dictio* to his divinity.[117] The revelation of Christ is the "restoration of the original orientation, consistently demanded by God's word, of mankind to God and co-creation.[118] The word of God is taken up under the conditions of fallen creation and newly envisioned: "It all has to do with the word, what is created and written,"[119] Luther remarked concerning John 1:14. Seen from salvation history, the proclamation of Christ proves to be the identification of Christ and the eternal *verbum dei* for mankind's sake. "If one is simply 'the word,' then his being is altogether (as man and as a person) 'speaking' and his discourse is the truth of that being."[120] On the one hand, Christ is proactively the "final word . . . that determines the world,"[121] and on the other hand retrospectively the same voice which speaks in the promises of the Old Testament: "*qui meum verbum audit,*

112. *Reihenpredigten Johannes 6–8*, WA 33, 148,30–33: "Even if it were just a donkey who spoke it, as happened with Balaam, it would still be God's word."

113. *Tischreden mit dem cod. Besoldi*, WA 48, 688,4 (7098).

114. *Tischreden mit dem cod. Besoldi*, WA 48, 688,2–3 (7098). See also the embellished story in *Genesisvorlesung*, WA 42, 202,11–17.

115. *Genesisvorlesung*, WA 42, 320,12–22.

116. See also Beutel, *Anfang*, 99–100.

117. *Dictata super Psalterium*, WA 3, 281,5–6: "Hence he has spoken in the beloved Son according to his flesh."

118. Löfgren, *Theologie*, 164 (emphasis in original).

119. *Bibel- und Bucheinzeichnungen*, WA 48, 130,9–10.

120. Ringleben, *Gott*, 132.

121. *Predigten* 1523, WA 12, 598,21–22.

audit illud quod Abraham audivit, idem verbum, nisi quod alio tempore dicitur, one and the same, discourse and oral word."[122]

In contrast to the word of creation, the word of God is revealed in Jesus Christ in human language. In this way a *nova lingua*[123] is initiated and then given over to proclamation on Pentecost[124]—a new language in which no new words appear but seemingly familiar words are first understood in their actual meaning (on this see section 4.6 for more detail). In a sermon on Pentecost in 1545 Luther says the following: "Peter and others preached in different languages, not only Latin and Arabic, but others as well, saying things about not slaughtering oxen, not offering sacrifices, but because they were no longer strong enough, they preached the new kingdom of heaven and the Messiah who frees from sin and death. . . . The Holy Spirit cast out demons from the madman, understanding and preaching the truth of scripture. That made their hearts full so that they overflowed. Not only the disciples, but women as well spoke in various and new languages."[125]

At the same time, the incarnation is an "inverbation."[126] The condescension of God in "clear, unadorned, bright word and text"[127] and his condescension in the son of man are "a miracle."[128] For us is shown the complete alignment of word and deed, in which not only the life of Christ corresponds to his words, but furthermore his works themselves are divine words: from the temptation in the wilderness through the calling of the first disciples, the miracles of nature and healing, to the promises to the others being crucified.[129] "*Summa summarum: Christi officium,* work of the word."[130]

The *Verbum dei, quod Christus est praedicatus nobis*, is the medium in which the son of man "hastens, begets, nourishes, teaches, exerts, protects, preserves and triumphs in eternal life."[131] The word of God in Christ

122. *Predigten* 1529, WA 29, 130,11–131,1.

123. *De divinitate*, WA 39.2, 94,21 (Thesis 22).

124. See Streif, "*Novis linguis loqui*," 177.

125. *Predigten* 1540/45, WA 49, 753, 10–18.

126. Ebeling, *Evangelienauslegung*, 365.

127. *Vom Abendmahl*, WA 26, 404,22–23.

128. Ringleben, *Gott*, 128.

129. On this see the numerous proofs from Luther's sermons in Beutel, *Anfang*, 327–30.

130. *Predigten* 1529, WA 29, 398,4.

131. *Operationes in Psalmos*, WA 5, 477,37–38 and 478,2–3.

is not to be separated from its eschatological function: "when you hold on to the word in faith, you then receive another pair of eyes that can see through this death into the resurrection."[132] In this way, the word retains its creative power by "eschatologically altering" man and "bringing him forth as a new man."[133]

The concept of the word is Luther's key to understanding Christ, which ranges from the preexistent word through the mediator of creation to the savior. As Heinrich Bornkamm expresses it, "Christ as the abbreviated, concrete presentation of God himself cannot be outlined more accurately then by the concept of the word."[134]

The "work of the word" in salvation history is refined more precisely in the following sections, namely 4.4 under the aspect of validity, the aspect of proper usage in 4.5, and in 4.6 the aspect of the specific limit of daily colloquial language with the new meanings of the "*nova* sprach"[135] which allows us to speak "in quite heavenly German."[136]

4.4. The Validity of the Word

The creative power of the word of God is immediately connected to its absolute validity. As *creaturae verbi Dei* we stand in relationship to the word as "opposite to our origin. . . . This means: by the word of God, God sets our relationship to it."[137] The creative nature of the word remains to this extent permanent, not only because it calls mankind into existence initially in Genesis 1, but also after the fall it wishes to transform its existence, as long as mankind faithfully embraces the word: "Just as we own the word, it is necessary that the word change us."[138] The recipients do not change the content of the heard word through mental processing—the exact opposite is the case. The word sees to an earth-shaking new determination of the faithful recipient in that it creates new standards for truth

132. *Predigten* 1533/34, WA 37, 69,33.

133. Ringleben, *Gott*, 564.

134. Bornkamm, *Wort Gottes*, 159.

135. "New language," a phrase peculiar to Luther, from the *Predigten* 1532, WA 36, 647,2.

136. *Predigten* 1532, WA 36, 644,25–26.

137. Iwand, *Theologie*, 215.

138. *Römervorlesung*, WA 56, 227,4–5.

and justice: "Now the rule is similar, that we are in one who believes in the word of truth and justice."[139]

This process of the *verbum dei* obtaining for itself unconditional validity is unfolded most clearly in Luther's treatise on freedom from 1520.[140] The focus of this writing is the not to be annulled difference between the *natura corporalis* and *spiritualis*[141] of man.[142] For Christian believers[143] this ontological polarity, connected as it is to the body-soul differentiation, is reinterpreted to the polarity between the "old" and the "new man."[144] Thereby the aporia is characteristic for the "old man" not to reconcile these two natures, and thus to be able to lead to freedom.[145] The spiritual nature, as the realm in which man comes to recognize the world and his self, cannot arrive at its goal by means of "anything external"[146]—namely to define one's self as spirit and through one's self to define the body in such a way as to preserve the permanence of the former and the variability of the latter. "To call on the external world for the purpose of self-explanation indicates a confusion of multiplicity with unity,"[147] variability with permanence. To achieve unity an external quantity must be added: "Man arrives at inner unity [*spiritus*] not by active self-explanation [*caro*], but only by passive ability to embrace an absolute external acceptance of his non-identity which stands in radical disagreement to him."[148]

This is exactly what happens in the "new man" who lets himself be defined by the external word of God. This is not to be thought of as an external determination which would not be distinguishable from an external-worldly dependence, but as "a new possibility of self-definition, namely to know one's self as having been defined by God."[149] Then "the internal and the external can exist side-by-side," because they "have been

139. *Römervorlesung*, WA 56, 227,6–7.

140. *De libertate* (Latin) or *Von der Freiheit eines Christenmenschen* (German).

141. *De libertate*, WA 7, 50,7.8.

142. See on the following Korsch, *Luther-Von der Freiheit*, 83–88.

143. See Jüngel, *Freiheit*, 75: "The differentiation between the old and new man is . . . christologically conditioned."

144. *De libertate*, WA 7, 50,7.8.

145. *De libertate*, WA 7, 50,10–12.

146. *De libertate*, WA 7, 50,15.

147. Rieger, *Von der Freiheit*, 80.

148. Rieger, *Von der Freiheit*, 80.

149. Korsch, *Luther-Von der Freiheit*, 96.

transferred into a well-ordered accordance . . . as long as the internal defined by God shapes external actions."[150] In the Latin text, Luther stresses pointedly that this definition cannot be achieved with internal reflection or spiritual feelings, not with "speculation, meditation, and whatever things can be performed by the exertions of the soul."[151] It concerns the complete denial of self-righteousness and self-explanation in favor of the acceptance of a "radically alien external."[152]

Since this acceptance takes place in the inner person,[153] it can only exist in a transference of meaning or significance. And for that hardly any other means of communication are conceivable besides the medium of language. If the message should come from without, it can only be thought of in the form of an address. Consequently Luther introduces the decisive instance of the word of God as "preached by Christ."[154] In the ambiguity of subjective and objective connection, it is significant at the same time that the word of God a) was proclaimed by Christ himself and b) came about in discourse about Christ.

For this intriguing aspect of validity, it is decisive that the question of truth in this approach is shifted from an epistemological to an existential one. The form of address does not decide only the content of the linguistic statement concerning its truth, but this first comes fully into being in the encounter of message and listener. In the freedom treatise this is expressed by Luther's referring back to the word of God, both in the Latin version as well as the German version, initially as life and then as truth. In the German version an inverted rendering of John 11:25 ("I am the life and the resurrection")[155] is followed by the verse John 14:6 ("I am the way, the truth, and the resurrection").[156] The litany of qualities of the word of God in the Latin version begins with the life, followed by the truth: "But, having the word, it is rich and wants for nothing, since that is the word of life, of truth, of light, of peace, of justification, of salvation, of joy, of liberty, of wisdom, of virtue, of grace, of glory, and of

150. Korsch, *Luther-Von der Freiheit*, 88.

151. *De libertate*, WA 7, 50,32–33.

152. Rieger, *Von der Freiheit*, 97.

153. *De libertate*, WA 7, 50,15.

154. *Von der Freiheit*, WA 7, 22,5. In the Latin version the connection to mode of communication is missing.

155. *Von der Freiheit*, WA 7, 22,6.

156. *Von der Freiheit*, WA 7, 22,7.

every good thing."[157] From the basis of *vita* and *veritas* emerge the further biblical genitive attributes which characterize the word of God as the "inexhaustible ground of everything that mankind needs."[158] Whoever does not have the word of God, lacks the "basis of his existence in his sense as well as in his being."[159]

Out of the existential truth of the word follows immediately how mankind is to navigate the world with this. The only adequate reaction to this is immediate faith which is indebted solely to the evidence of the word of God and not any human work of interpretation: "For the word of God cannot be received and honored by any works, but by faith alone."[160] The faithful person "partakes of the truth, which makes him truthful."[161] "For faith alone and the efficacious use of the word of God, bring salvation."[162] The *salutaris usus* refers to the fact that faith itself contains the salvation of the "old man" promised in the word of God, which is underscored in the Latin text with three citations from Romans: 10:9, 10:4, and 1:17.

Salvation, however, completes itself in two stages, which Luther makes audible in one sentence from the German edition: "When you truly believe this, how you are sinful, then you must despair of yourself and recognize the truth of the line from Hosea: 'O Israel, in you is nothing than your own destruction, but in me is your help.'"[163] Despair and help—these experiences prefigure the differentiation presented later in the course of the text[164] of law and gospel. The comfort of the promises of help can then only unfold when mankind despairs of his own powers and recognizes the aporia of a spiritual self-determination which can only choose between an alien definition through worldly, temporal instances and a content-empty self-reflection. There is an exceptional situation in which help can come only from the speaker who opens up insight into mankind's own inadequacy in which mankind trusts and from which he hopes only for good: God "put his beloved Son Jesus Christ before you and conveys through him his living, comforting word: You should give

157. *De libertate*, WA 7, 50,2–3.

158. Rieger, *Von der Freiheit*, 104.

159. Rieger, *Von der Freiheit*, 107.

160. *De libertate*, WA 7, 51,20–21.

161. Korsch, *Luther—Von der Freiheit*, 104.

162. *De libertate*, WA 7, 51,17.

163. *Von der Freiheit*, WA 7, 22,28–31.

164. *De libertate*, WA 7, 52,25 and *Von der Freiheit*, WA 7, 23,30.

yourself over to him with firm faith and trust in him directly."[165] In this way the "new man" grounds his new, free existence on the comforting message from that Christ who arose, acted, and spoke in the name of God: "Then for the sake of this faith all your sins shall be forgiven and all your destruction overcome, and you will be just, true, at peace, righteous, and having fulfilled all commandments and been freed from all things."[166] Luther closes this train of thought in the German edition with the great statement from Romans 1:17: "As St. Paul says in Romans 1: 'A righteous Christian lives by faith alone.'"[167] With that, the process of implementing a new standard for truth and justice by the word of God has been demonstrated.

A separate look is in order for the differentiation of law and gospel within the word of God, because it is here where the aspect of its validity is further distinguished. Luther himself formulated a possible objection against the absolute validity of the *verbum dei*: What function have all the "laws, commandments, works, instructions, and regulations" prescribed in the holy scriptures when they have nothing to do with the actions of the individual?[168] How does this align with the creative effect of the word, when the laws "teach us what is good, but what they teach is not forthwith done?"[169]

The meaning of the commandments, as Luther answers the objection formulated by himself, consists not in the fulfillment of their demands but in the fact that God has demonstrated to us our obligations: "they show us what we ought to do, but do not give us the power to do it."[170] In this there are two things to consider: First is understanding the imperative of the commandments as divine address and inquiry of mankind. Do you want, what you should? Alongside this "communicative-intersubjective" aspect enters the "objective-goal oriented" aspect which is directed towards the fulfillment of the demands.[171] "It is now obvious that both of these planes . . . are of equal importance."[172] The intersub-

165. *Von der Freiheit*, WA 7, 22,32–23,1.
166. *Von der Freiheit*, WA 7, 23,1–3.
167. *Von der Freiheit*, WA 7, 23,4.
168. *Von der Freiheit*, WA 7, 23,24–26.
169. *De libertate*, WA 7, 52,25–26.
170. *De libertate*, WA 7, 52,26–27.
171. Korsch, *Luther—Von der Freiheit*, 107.
172. Korsch, *Luther—Von der Freiheit*, 107.

jective side dominates, because the demand—even in profane human everyday life—receives thereby its validity, that those who communicate about this are united in the contentual sense. If this happens, the demand is valid—independent of its satisfiability. Therefore no special rule is to be formulated for the validity of the commandments within the word of God. In the moment of their genuine, poignant adoption, their absolute validity for mankind has been implemented.

Against the background of this validity, the gospel can prove itself as promise and assurance. Mankind, who now shares the commandments of God as a justified demand, is at the same time aware that he cannot always fulfill them,[173] is made "truly humble and annihilated in their own eyes."[174] In this existential despair over the inability for self-definition the comforting divine promise touches mankind: "if you want to fulfill all the commandments . . . believe in Christ, in whom I pledge to you all grace, righteousness, peace, and freedom."[175] This promise from God fulfills everything that the commandments demand: "He alone demands, He alone fulfills."[176] It is the proclamation of Christ that guarantees the unity of the word. He fulfills the law and he preaches the gospel. "In the gospel, God himself demonstrates exactly the same love which he demands from us in his law."[177] The central concept for Jesus' proclamation of the "kingdom of God" (Mark 1:15, NRSV) has a legal component—the claim of divine will—and a promising component, "because the connection to mankind initiated by God proves itself to be fundamental and permanent, over and above its denial by the immediate self-connection of mankind."[178]

The law is connected to the gospel, and the gospel to the law. One cannot have one without the other. The Latin terms chosen by Luther *praecepta et promissa* ring out their close relationship in the triad of alliteration, equality of syllables, and homoioteleuton. Luther's characterization of the law as "Old Testament" and the gospel as "New Testament"[179]

173. Luther shows the fundamental non-fulfillment of the divine commandments by mankind in the freedom treatise through the example of lust: "'Thou shalt not covet' is a precept by which we are all convicted of sin, since no man can help coveting, whatever efforts to the contrary he may make." *De libertate*, WA 7, 52, 30-32.

174. *Von der Freiheit*, WA 7, 24,8.

175. *Von der Freiheit*, WA 7, 24,12–13.

176. *Von der Freiheit*, WA 7, 24,20.

177. Watson, *Gottheit*, 181.

178. Korsch, *Luther—Von der Freiheit*, 113.

179. *Von der Freiheit*, WA 7, 23,25–26 and 24,21. Rieger (*Von der Freiheit*, 150: translation of WA 7, 53,14) displays a difference of meaning in his translation (in

does nothing to contradict this. Here the intent is not "Old" and "New" Testaments but rather that which is connected to the "old man" and the content of the word of God which destroys him, and the self-same content which creates the "new man."[180] Even when Luther himself evokes a different impression with partially misunderstood formulations in some of his texts and sermons,[181] his differentiation, fundamental to the hermeneutics of the canon, can only be comprehended as he expressed it in the *Adventspostille* from 1522: "There is not one book in the Bible in which one does not see both, God always put them together, both of them, law and promise."[182]

We will return to law and gospel in section 4.5.2 when the focus is on the proper use of the word of God in understanding scripture and in proclamation. For the question of validity it remains to be said that *praecepta* and *promissa* claim absolute validity for themselves. To the extent that obligations ("Thou shalt") and promises ("Thou wilt")[183] are interpreted as speech acts,[184] they are to be classified directly as successful and fulfilled respectively as soon as they have been heard, understood, and believed. There exists an inner unity between the word of God in its dual form and human acceptance of the same. The acceptance of the word by mankind "does not involve external confrontation, rather acceptance arises from the word, and acceptance and word become one."[185] The soul also becomes a venue of mankind's self-definition: "united with the word, so fully and completely, that all the virtues of the word become the soul's own property, and thus through faith, the soul by the word of God becomes sacred, righteous, truthful, peaceful, free, and full of goodness, a true child of God."[186]

---

opposition to Korsch, *Von der Freiheit*, 25: translation of WA 7, 24,21) as well as with the aid of upper and lower case.

180. See Rieger, *Von der Freiheit*, 146.

181. On this see Ebeling, *Evangelische Evangelienauslegung*, 429–31, and Beutel, *Anfang*, 62–65 along with the examples cited there.

182. *Adventspostille*, WA 10.1.2, 159,7–8. Luther offers a brief survey of divine promises in the Old Testament in *Unterrichting*, WA 16, 381,7–383,8.

183. See Korsch, *Leitidee*, 95.

184. On this see in detail chapter 6 of this work.

185. Rieger, *Von der Freiheit*, 158.

186. *Von der Freiheit*, WA 7, 24,24–27.

To what extent does this truthfulness—in the Latin text *verificatio*[187]—align with truth in the classic epistemological sense? Does Luther present in some way a theory of double truth which fits well as an article of the philosophy of natural reason and consequently can be false in the theology of revelation, and vice versa?[188] In his disputation *Verbum caro factum est* from 1539 Luther speaks unequivocally of the unity of truth: "All truths are in harmony with the truth."[189] Nevertheless, according to Luther, "by no means is the same true for different sciences [*professionibus*]."[190]

How can this be? As will be demonstrated in greater detail in section 4.6, here we see a quite modern insight in the philosophy of language from Luther. Just as the different dimensions of length, volume, and weight are quantified with different units of measure, so do the sciences as well as theology and philosophy develop their own semantics.[191] Is not the same already true in the various arts?[192] How much less can it be true of philosophy and theology?[193] On account of the different word definitions, the apparent contradictions do not lie on the same plane.[194]

Of course, Luther leaves no doubt about where the most comprehensive meaning is demonstrated and where only partial aspects come up. Already in his first lecture on the Psalms, Luther states regarding Psalm 45:5: "Note, however, that truth is here put without qualification, where elsewhere truth is often called 'your' truth, which is Christ, the fulfillment of the law. But here it should be understood as referring to the same and every other truth."[195] Only in the revealed *verbum dei* itself is the absolute truth demonstrated. All human efforts, on the other hand, arrive at partial insights which in the face of totality have the effect of lies:

> Concerning the truth it can be said "that . . . through it God's truth will be glorified, . . . that I know I am a sinner, that I am a liar, and I cease to be a liar when I accept the truth that comes

187. *De libertate*, WA 7, 53,21.

188. On this concept see Großhans, *Wahrheit*, 1255.

189. *Verbum caro factum est*, WA 39.2, 3,1 (Thesis 1).

190. *Verbum caro factum est*, WA 39.2, 3,1–2 (Thesis 1).

191. *Verbum caro factum est*, WA 39.2, 5,15–18 (Thesis 30–31) and 5,31–36 (Thesis 38–40).

192. *Verbum caro factum est*, WA 39.2, 5,31–32 (Thesis 38).

193. *Verbum caro factum est*, WA 39.2, 5,33 (Thesis 39).

194. See Streif, "*Novis linguis loqui*," 112.

195. *Dictata super Psalterium*, WA 3, 263,8–10.

> from God, I accept that by this and not by my own efforts do I become truthful, that my boasting may cease and only God will be praised in me, because he alone has made me truthful or has made of me a truthful man, while my own truth in his sight is a lie."[196]

4.5. The Use of the Word

The ultimate maxim in dealing with the *verbum dei* is formulated clearly by Luther in his writing dedicated to the sacraments, *De captivitate babylonica ecclesiae* from 1520: "No violence of any kind may be done to the words of God, neither by mankind nor by an angel. On the contrary, they are to be preserved as far as possible in their simplest meaning [*in simplicissima significatione*]."[197] All of Luther's reflections on the proper use of the word lead back to this central statement—whether in the form of the holy scriptures, or the proclamation of the gospel, or in the special form of the sacraments.

Furthermore, it is characteristic for Luther's argument that a falsifying handling of the word can never be confined to the sender or the medium but only by the recipient. Those that impart, proclaim, write down, and carry out God's word can certainly behave themselves in a false and unworthy manner, but they alter nothing of the impact of the word by their behavior. That is decided by the recipient alone who faithfully accepts the word—or not. "God's word is the treasure that makes all things holy."[198] Even an unworthy servant who preaches, baptizes, and breaks bread: "Who would doubt that the gospel is also proclaimed by non-believers [*impios*]? . . . Even if . . . a non-believer baptizes, it still means that the word of promise and the sign of water over the baptized can be brought to the fore, in the same manner he can also proclaim the promise of this sacrament [communion] and reach those partaking of the bread and wine."[199]

God is able to do good through evil—that holds for his word as well. In an inverted direction of speaking, when the words of mankind ascend to him instead of descending, this does not function at all. The

196. *Römervorlesung*, WA 56, 216,18–23.

197. *De captivitate*, WA 6, 509,8–10.

198. *Deudsch Catechismus*, WA 30.1., 145,20–21.

199. *De captivitate*, WA 6, 525,35–526,7.

prayers of an impious priest, no matter how appropriate and scripturally formulated, miss their mark.[200]

The question of the proper handling of God's word can be concretized as a) the question of the appropriate interpretation of scripture as well as the proclamation based on it (section 4.5.1) and b) the question of the proper understanding of the sacraments (4.5.2).

4.5.1. Understanding Scripture without *proprius spiritus*

From Luther's postulate "that no violence of any kind may be done to the words of God"[201] follows a sacrosanct hermeneutic priority of the text vis-à-vis the recipient. The aids to understanding the holy scriptures are only to be found in the scriptures themselves—any other external rule of exegesis would subject the word of God to a human standard. The position of the readers of the Bible corresponds to that of mankind *coram deo*. Proper understanding of scriptures is not an achievement of mankind itself, but like the justification of the sinner, is a gift from God and an effect of the *sanctus spiritus*.[202] In contrast to that stands *proprius spiritus*,[203] that stubbornness in exegesis which inexorably leads to error because the conditions for understanding the word of God are contained within the word itself.

This also holds for the recourse to the church fathers—even Augustine, who is venerated by Luther—whose designs of normativity are subordinated to the word of God. If this were otherwise, an infinite regression in the understanding of the scriptures would ensue: "Who can convince us that they properly understand Augustine? Even for Augustine there must also be another interpreter [*interpres*] so that our own mind [*proprius spiritus*] does not deceive us in his books. If this must happen in this way, then it must also happen that the third needs a fourth interpreter,

200. *De captivitate*, WA 6, 526,10–20, and *De divinitate*, WA 39.2, 96,27–28: *E contra, so quis reprobus sensu etiam commode locutus fuerit ipsamque scripturam iactarit, tolerandus non est.*

201. *De captivitate*, WA 6, 509,8–10.

202. See Wabel, *Sprache*, 183.

203. *Assertio*, WA 7, 96,11 and other passages. On the history of the phrase and the sentence quoted by Luther *non licet scripturas proprio spiritu intelligere* (96,35–36) see Ebeling, *sola scriptura*, 121–22.

and the fourth needs a fifth, and so on into eternity. The danger of our own mind would force us to never learn or read anything again."[204]

So the search for a firm ultimate grounding of scriptural understanding leads to an aporia, which, according to Luther, "was undoubtedly introduced to us by Satan himself."[205] The way out for Christians consists in the *assertio*: the consistent adherence, strengthening, confession, and respect for the scriptures.[206] "Embrace the assertions and restrain Christianity."[207] Here one could suppose, with a view to modern scientific theory in Luther's concept of scripture, an axiomatic construction of biblical interpretation whose efficiency depends on the acceptance of defined axioms. But this is not what Luther means by the methodological *assertio*. Rather, for Luther, true certainty is only possible where "it has its basis not in mankind itself, its qualities and achievements, but in that which is the divine truth itself."[208] The reason for this renewed understanding is Christ: "If you embrace Christ and the scriptures, what more could you find than in these?"[209] Faith in Christ and understanding of scripture are in Luther immediately connected to one another. "Scriptural interpretation is the form for knowledge of Christ, and knowledge of Christ is the content of scriptural interpretation."[210]

With that, a *generalis scopus*[211] of scriptures is defined, and out of which the Bible attains unity—certainly in opposition to the tradition; not in the form of a "sum" of divine revelations, but as a "point at which everything comes together," as a "goal to which everything comes down."[212] The Christian canon achieves its value not as a backwards looking history book but divine promise with and given from Jesus Christ. The "point of the Bible" is therefore that "from the outset it keeps an eye on the fact that it keeps going."[213] At the same time, with the criterion derived from this, Luther gains a hermeneutical principle whether

204. *Assertio*, WA 7, 96,27–31.
205. *Assertio*, WA 7, 96,37–38.
206. See *De servo*, WA 18, 603,12–13.
207. *De servo*, WA 18, 603,28–29.
208. Ebeling, *Lutherstudien*, 2, 56–57.
209. *De servo*, WA 18, 603,29.
210. Führer, *Gottes*, 109.
211. *Predigten* 1532, WA 36, 180,11.
212. Ebeling, *Bibel*, 293.
213. Ebeling, *Bibel*, 294.

biblical texts "deal with Christ or not,"[214] from which scriptures are clear and self-explanatory: "That means that they are completely certain on their own terms, easily and completely accessible [*facillima*], completely understandable [*apertissima*], its own interpreter, scrutinizing everything about everything, judging, and enlightening."[215]

The conventional method of interpretation with its doctrine of four-fold meaning of scripture was turned on its head by Luther. Since all biblical texts *ad literam* point toward Jesus Christ, Luther combines the literal meaning with the tropological and arrives at a christological meaning. As Gerhard Ebeling has demonstrated, this approach emerges in Luther's first lectures on the Psalms.[216] In Luther's focus on the situation of mankind *coram deo* and his new understanding of existence demonstrated through Jesus Christ, the (in a narrower sense) allegorical[217] as well as the anagogic-eschatological sense[218] each lose their independent meaning.[219] It all boils down to one thing: "In this way all four senses of scripture flow together into one very large stream."[220]

Luther's emphasis of the tropological sense[221] may not, of course, be understood in the moral sense, that proper understanding of the Bible with handling instructions aims at the behavior of mankind. Rather, Luther understands the tropological sense as the healing and altering intervention of God into human existence.[222] Mankind need only believe and allow—which likewise is not his own work but the act of the Spirit combined with the word: "For no one can stand properly before God or God's word except by means of the Holy Spirit. No one can have anything of the Holy Spirit other than that he experiences it, strives toward it, and feels it:

214. *Vorrede auf die Epistel*, WA DB 7, 385,27.

215. *Assertio*, WA 7, 97,27–29.

216. Ebeling, *Anfänge*, especially 58–61.

217. See Luther's polemic against Origen in *De captivitate*, WA 6, 509,12–15 and in *Wider die himmlischen Propheten*, WA 18, 180,21–27.

218. See Ebeling, *Anfänge*, 62: "But when the actual *intention* of the word is not to communicate something about the future but towards the future, and in such a way that one then understands himself from the *futura*, then the actual scopus of the *sensus anagogicus*, but only in the *sensus tropologicus*, comes into its own."

219. On this see also Korsch, *Luther*, 48–50.

220. *Dictata super Psalterium*, WA 3, 46,28–29 [trans. Bouman].

221. *Dictata super Psalterium*, WA 3, 335,21–22: "And therefore the final tropological sense and principal intent of scripture."

222. See Ebeling, *Anfänge*, 64–68.

and in the same experience the Holy Spirit teaches as in its own school, outside of which nothing is taught but the illusory word and claptrap."[223]

Luther's position is distinguished by the fact that he binds the impact of the Spirit tightly with the external word. Luke 1:41–42 (NRSV),[224] Mary's visit with Elizabeth, describes paradigmatically for Luther how the word precedes the receiving of the Spirit and faith: "Here is depicted for us how it must go when we ought to be pious, namely that faith cannot rise up except by the Holy Spirit, and in the same way not without the external word. . . . Therefore one must hear the external word in advance and not scoff at it, as many do."[225]

The binding of the Spirit effect to the word ensures that the divine discourse is a quantity which remains *extra nos*, and not—as with the fanatics and spiritualists—placed within the randomness of human feeling.[226] Just as the papist church incarnated the spiritual in the authority of its supreme leader, the adherents of Andreas Karlstadt have made spiritual "what God as corporal and external" has given.[227] The *sola scriptura* is directed against the papist church, and against the fanatics the principle of the external nature of the word of God must be broadened and refined.[228] Everything "which is praised without such a word and sacrament from the Spirit is the devil."[229]

In Augustine's terminology, Luther's understanding of the Spirit lends itself to being described as the power which effects from the external impulse of the *verbum externum* and originates in the believer the inner result of the *verbum internum*.[230] In contrast to Augustine, though, it does not concern a transformation in the disparity of significance but a doubly divine effect in the word and Spirit: "Firstly God gives us the word

223. *Das Magnificat*, WA 7, 546,24–29.

224. "When Elizabeth heard Mary's greeting, the child leaped in her womb. And Elizabeth was filled with the Holy Spirit and exclaimed with a loud cry, 'Blessed are you among women, and blessed is the fruit of your womb.'"

225. *Festpostille*, WA 17.2, 459,35–37 and 460,1–2.

226. See Iwand, *Theologie*, 213 and zur Mühlen, *Nos extra nos*, 229.

227. *Wider die himmlischen Propheten*, WA 18, 181,33–34.

228. See Wabel, *Sprache als Grenze*, 282–83.

229. *Schmalkaldische Artikel*, WA 50, 246,28–29.

230. See Krause, *Studien*, 240–241: "Faith is the view of unity which listens in on and understands the *spiritus sanctus* (*verbum internum*) in the *verbum externum*." Bornkamm also undertakes an equivalence of Augustine's *verbum intimum* and Luther's spirit (*Wort Gottes*, 160.)

in order to enlighten us, and afterwards the Holy Spirit which works in us and ignites the faith."[231] The Spirit remains bound to language—it concerns understanding, not feeling: "The word must precede or be spoken beforehand, and afterwards the Holy Spirit works through it, thus, that one does not invert it and dream of a Holy Spirit which works without the word and before the word, but with and through the word comes and goes no further than the word goes."[232]

Against the temporality of linguistic mediations, the Spirit cares for a "lasting vibrancy" of the divine word:[233] "The word can condemn and go away, the Holy Spirit speaks vain flames in our hearts and remains there."[234] To this extent, God's word as such is first demonstrated through the Spirit because it overcomes spatial and temporal distance, and as the "gatekeeper"[235]makes possible the "co-present communication of God with us."[236]

In the direct opposition of that which is spoken and that which is heard, language has, and the word has, its own venue: "The word is between the speaker and the hearer."[237] Out of this comes the pre-eminence of the spoken word over and against the written word in Luther. The voice first gives the word its soul.[238] Only in the "aggregate situation of spoken language" can the word, all the more the word of God, "with the ultimate obligation, penetrate to be heard as such."[239] For the holy scriptures, this means: "The gospel is essentially not the written, but spoken word, which the scriptures allow to be heard as Christ and the apostles preached it. This is why Christ himself wrote nothing, but spoke, and his doctrine is not written, but is called the gospel, the good news or proclamation, which should be presented not with the pen, but with the mouth."[240]

231. *Predigten* 1519–1521, WA 9, 632,32–34.

232. *Crucigers Sommerpostille*, WA 21, 469,7–11.

233. Ringleben, *Gott*, 523.

234. *Predigten* 1529, WA 29, 365,20–21.

235. *Weihnachtspostille*, WA 10.1.1., 17,1.

236. Dalferth, *Jenseits*, 254.

237. *Vorlesungen*, WA 13, 601,14.

238. *Operationes in Psalmos*, WA 5, 379,5–8: *non scripturam dei, sed eloquia potissimum casta vacat. Non enim tantum nocet aut prodest scriptura quantum eloquium, com vox sit anima verbi.*

239. Beutel, *Anfang*, 194 (emphasis in original).

240. *Weihnachtspostille*, WA 10.1.1., 17,7–12.

In contrast to the law, which also can be imparted in spoken language "according to the letter,"[241] the divine promises are "a good message, a good story, good news, good noise, about which one can sing, speak, and be happy."[242] The law remains dead letter because it is for the most part not attainable and "no life can follow out of it."[243] The gospel, on the other hand, promises a new understanding of existence, and to that extent gives life—and "this spirit cannot be grasped by anyone in letters, it cannot be written down with ink, in stone, or in books, . . . but it will be written on the heart, it is a living document of the Holy Spirit, without any mediation."[244]

Luther does not wish to legitimate a hermeneutic program surreptitiously "by which a literal exegesis could be superseded in this manner by a spiritual exegesis, that on this second plane, the reality of salvation can first be demonstrated."[245] Rather, here it is about the effect of the gospel on humanity, which surpasses the semantic meaning of the promises. Here the word of God is again and again understood as a renewed language event which effects changes in the lives of believers. The liberating message evokes "a voice which resounds throughout the entire world and shouts out publicly so that people everywhere hear it."[246] In this way the holy scriptures continue seamlessly in their proclamation. Out of the "word read" comes the "word lived."[247]

For Luther, therefore, the criterion for the effect of the proclaimed word is whether or not God is the sender. Mankind's role as medium is assigned only as *ius verbi*, since the language event's total effect on mankind, the *ius executionis*, is still reserved for God himself:[248] "One can certainly preach the word to me, but no one but God can give it to me in my heart, he must speak into the heart, otherwise nothing will come of it. For when God remains silent, the word is not spoken."[249] But when God is not silent, then we can hear God himself talking to us, from whatever human mouth it may sound forth: "Better to let this be a treasure which

241. *Reihenpredigten 1. Petrus*, WA 12, 275,8.

242. *Vorrhede auff das Newe Testament*, WA DB 6,2,23–25.

243. *Antwort auf Emser*, WA 7, 654,34–35.

244. *Antwort auf Emser*, WA 7, 654,9–12.

245. Schwarz, *Luther*, 42.

246. *Reihenpredigten 1. Petrus*, WA 12, 259,12–13.

247. *Psalmenauslegungen* 1529/32, WA 31.1, 67,25.

248. *Predigten* 1522, WA 10.3, 15,10.

249. *Roths Sommerpostille*, WA 10.1.2, 335,34–36.

God has spoken to you in your corporeal ear. . . . For I hear the sermon well, but who is talking? The pastor? No, you are not hearing the pastor. The voice is fine, but the word that was previously whispered or spoken, that is spoken by my God."[250]

4.5.2 The Correct Understanding of the Sacraments

In comparison to Augustine and his intensive engagement with the allegorical nature of the word, it appears rather startling that for Luther, sign is only a theme worth mentioning in the context of his doctrine of the sacraments. As will be demonstrated in the next section, from a theological perspective Luther is not interested in the signification process but in the hermeneutic process. While Augustine looks at the word analytically in order to understand the semiosis, Luther has a synthetic perspective. His theme in the philosophy of language is the contextuality and the effect of the word.

However, in Luther's understanding the sacrament is constitutive of the external sign since it marks the difference with the pure word of God: "A sacrament has three things which one must recognize. The first is the sacrament or sign itself. The second is the meaning of this sacrament. The third is the faith in both of these. So there must be these three elements in every sacrament: the sacrament must be external and visible in its corporeal form or shape. The meaning must be internal and spiritual in the spirit of man. Faith must bring both together in their effect and utilization."[251]

Luther's use of language is not entirely unambiguous, but in the nature of things, transparent. In the cited passage from the sermon of 1519 the sacrament is, in the narrower sense, the external sign. By contrast, in *De captivitate babylonica ecclesiae,* which appeared one year later, the sacrament appears in the even narrower sense as the divine address itself, the word of God: "Before anything else I must protest the number of seven sacraments and for the moment present only three: baptism, confession, and communion. . . . Of course, when I wish to orient myself to the

250. *Reihenpredigten Johannes 3–4*, WA 47, 229,28–33. See also *Hauspostille*, WA 52, 454,1-3.

251. *Sermon von dem Sakrament des Leibes Christi*, WA 2, 742,6–14.

language usage of the scriptures, only one sacrament is left, just like the three sacramental signs [*signa sacramentalia*]—but more on that later."[252]

Luther never returns to this promise in the text. Only confession—strictly speaking[253]—is excluded from the circle of sacraments on account of this missing external sign, so in the end only two sacraments remain.[254] The "only sacrament" of which Luther speaks can only be the divine promise itself which underlies all the sacraments.[255] The apparent contradiction with the communion sermon is thus easy to resolve. The word of God is the *genus proximum* of the sacrament concept, the sign is the *differentia specifica*. Luther expresses this unmistakably in his sermon on the New Testament from 1520:

> The words are a divine promise, an assurance, and a testament; the signs are the sacrament, and therefore holy signs. Just as the testament matters more than the sacrament, so the words matter more than the signs. For the signs also could not give it, but nevertheless mankind would have the words and would be blessed without the sacrament but not without the testament. . . . So we see that the best and greatest element of all the sacraments . . . are God's words and promises, without which the sacraments are dead and nothing.[256]

The basically dispensable signs are a concession of God to weak faith which hungers for approval.[257] The strongest, most efficacious assurance of the faith occurs in the sacrament of communion, which, in contrast to one-off baptism, is "a practice for one's entire life."[258] The word which forms the basis of this sacrament—the communion paradosis—one can designate, with Joachim Ringleben, as "the language event per se."[259] "Our text 'this is my body' etc. is not from man, but from God himself, spoken from his own mouth with those letters and set down by

252. *De captivitate*, WA 6, 501,33–38.

253. *De captivitate*, WA 6, 571,12.

254. *De captivitate*, WA 6, 501,15–17.

255. See *Predigten* 1519–1521, WA 9, 440,9–10: "So the words of Christ are a sacrament, for they are the works of our lives."

256. *Sermon von dem neuen Testament*, WA 6, 363,4–13.

257. *Sermon von dem neuen Testament*, WA 6, 358,25–27.

258. *Sermon von dem neuen Testament*, WA 6, 354.

259. Ringleben, *Gott*, 149. In a similar vein Hilgenfeld, *Mittelalterlich-traditionelle Elemente*, 60.

him."[260] From this it follows—as always, provided that one has attentive listeners—that in these words there can be no imprecision or vagueness of meaning. As the words express it, that is how it is: "as soon as Christ says 'this is my body,' his body is there by the word and the Holy Spirit. If the word is not there, then it is stale bread; but if the word should come, it brings along the means by which it sounds."[261]

Just as Christ's salvific significance in its being-in-itself is translated by the word in its being-for-us and comes to mankind,[262] the incarnation unfolds its effect only as an inverbation,[263] in this way the Christ grasped in the word transmits himself conversely in the selection of the natural element: "He composes himself in the word, and by the word he composes himself in the bread as well."[264]

This transmission is completed not as a transformation of earthly material but as a language event which creates a new plane of significance: "As the word of the creator in the mouth of Christ reshapes the created natural elements, and elevates them without disposing of them into a new word-reality which is Christ's own, . . . the original language of the created world—perverted and forfeited by sin—is vicariously reinstated in principle by the cosmic elements of water, bread, and wine."[265]

Seen from this perspective, it becomes clear just how indispensable the (taken literally) *est* of the words of institution is for Luther. If the bread and wine were only referring to Christ's body and blood, the original language plane would not be abandoned, but finally used in the figurative sense in order to express something inexpressible in a different way. The words of institution would remain totally and completely on this side of human language, their interpretation would be subordinated to "subjective meaning and finite reflection,"[266] they would be "peculiarly

260. *Vom Abendmahl*, WA 26, 446,1–3.

261. *Sermon von dem Sakrament des Leibes und Blutes Christi*, WA 19, 491,13–16.

262. See *Wider die himmlischen Propheten*, WA 18, 202,38–203,2: "For if Christ were given up and crucified for us a thousand times, it would all be in vain if the word of God had not come and was imparted and gifted to me and spoken, this shall be yours, take it and have your portion."

263. See Ebeling, *Evangelische Evangelienauslegung*, 365.

264. *Sermon von dem Sakrament des Leibes und Blutes Christi*, WA 19, 493,21–22.

265. Ringleben, *Gott*, 156.

266. Ringleben, *Gott*, 157.

opaque" and "pedantic."[267] Whoever gives up the *est* in its literal meaning as a statement of identity, conjures away the word of God in the end.

What exactly happens now on this new language plane constituted by the *est*? According to Luther, the typical element of divine discourse shows itself, that a familiar word can be placed in a new context and thereby find its true essence for the first time, for which the old word from now on is just an allegory. In his dense text *Vom Abendmahl*, Luther explains this using the example of the holy scriptures: "Now God created all ways in which the meaning or allegory occurred previously, and afterwards followed the correct essence and fulfillment. Then the Old Testament goes before as an allegory and the New Testament follows after it as the correct essence. Just like this, when a *tropos* or a new word is created, it takes the old word which is an allegory and gives it a new meaning, which is the correct essence."[268]

In the case of the words of institution, it is not the word "bread" to which accrues a new, metaphorical meaning (as in the position of Huldrych Zwingli), but the "body" which in the new understanding arrives at its correct essence: "The word 'body' according to its old meaning is the natural body of Christ. But according to the new meaning it must be called an entirely new body of Christ, compared to which his natural body is an allegory."[269] Here we see the "ontological relevance" of the figurative manner of speaking as described by Eberhard Jüngel. Its creative potential consists directly in the fact that the recipient takes it "literally in metaphorical statements."[270]

Luther illustrates this "innovative exploiting of new realms of meaning"[271] with the language creations "fleshbread or bodybread" and "bloodwine."[272] The phrase "this is my body" is to be understood as a synecdoche in which a *pars* (body) stands for the actually intended *totum* (bodybread = new body of Christ).[273] Therefore it is not about a new sig-

267. *Vom Abendmahl*, WA 26, 269,2–3.

268. *Vom Abendmahl*, WA 26, 382,26–383,3.

269. *Vom Abendmahl*, WA 26, 382,8–10.

270. Jüngel, *Wahrheit*, 103.

271. Jüngel, *Zur Bedeutung*, 36.

272. *Vom Abendmahl*, WA 26, 445,11.14.

273. *Vom Abendmahl*, WA 26, 443,8–444,20. Zwingli by contrast speaks of an "alloeosis" in the words of institution because they "speak of the one [divine] nature in Christ while they are breaking the other [human nature] in his name." (*Über D. Martin Luthers Buch*, 127–28.) The words of institution become an "improper statement"

nification relation between "bread" and "body" and "wine" and "blood," but it is about a relation oriented on the *communicatio idiomatum*: "The original meanings of the commonly predicated terms 'bread' and 'body' become permeable for one another."[274] The statement "this is my body" is analogous to the statement "God is man." Just as in Christ human and divine nature are merged in one person and all predications of the person are connected to both natures,[275] this also applies for body and bread: "for if both body and bread are two different natures, each unto itself, and where they are separated from one another, obviously neither is the other. But where they come together and become a new, complete essence, they lose their difference to the extent that it relates to a new essence unto itself, and as they become a thing and are, then one calls and speaks of them as one thing."[276]

The identity relationship, which the word of God establishes in the words of institution, permits "no reflection on anything which lies behind the sign."[277] In the divine promise the *signa* is the *res*—"Luther's great hermeneutic discovery."[278] "In a philosophical sign the note is missing, in a theological sign the note is present."[279] Talking and creating, word and deed, are not to be separated in divine discourse. "In this identity . . . Luther's uncompromising adherence to the literal sense of the *est* has its root in verbal reasoning: *dictum est factum*."[280] It is almost the distinctive mark of the divine word that it creates something new and does not merely confirm something extant. In the next section this function will be defined more precisely.

4.6. "*Nova sprach*": God's Word and Man's Word

From his understanding of God to his concept of the sacraments, Luther remains true to the thought that God reveals himself to us completely in

without ontological correlation (Hilgenfeld, *Mittelalterlich-traditionelle Elemente*, 348).

274. Wabel, *Sprache*, 251.

275. On this see *De divinitate*, WA 39.2, 93,4–7.

276. *Vom Abendmahl*, WA 26, 445,2–7.

277. Metzke, *Sakrament*, 177.

278. Bayer, *Schöpfung*, 37.

279. *Tischreden* WA TR 4, 666,8–9.

280. Beutel, *Anfang*, 327.

his word. The *verbum divinum* appears without loss in human language. It is really the paradigm of language because it demonstrates to mankind in a perfect way what is possible with linguistic means. No one speaks "more clearly or more strikingly"[281] than God himself: "The word of God cannot be understood in the creations of God by speaking, but I believe they feel the word of man in things alien to speech."[282] In the human communication medium, destroyed in its transparency by the fall from grace and the Babylonian confusion of languages, the word of God appears as a focal point for what language can create. It is the basis for a "new language,"[283] a "new grammar,"[284] and a "new rhetoric."[285]

The point of departure for this [*in*]*novatio*[286] of language is the statement about Christ noted biblically in the prologue to John, then later as a confession in the Nicaeno-Konstantinopolitanum and the Athanasian Creed: "Christ is true God and true man."[287] Luther dedicates himself intently to the consequences of this statement in both disputations *Verbum caro factum est*[288] from 1539 and *De divinitate et humanitate Christi* from 1540.[289] One can read the second series of theses as a continuation of the first. In *Verbum caro factum est* Luther argues that the truths of the faith cannot be presented in the language of philosophy: "We would do better if we left dialectics and philosophy in their sphere and learned to speak in a new language [*loqui novis linguis*] in the realm of faith outside that other sphere."[290]

De divinitate takes up these ideas and designates as the reason for the new language the communication of idioms from the confession of Christ: "that which belongs to mankind is rightly from God, and on the

281. *Rationis Latomianae*, WA 8, 118,5.

282. *Rationis Latomianae*, WA 8, 118,6–7.

283. *De divinitate*, WA 39.2, 94,21 (Thesis 22).

284. *Genesisvorlesung*, WA 42, 195,21.

285. *Ennarratio Psalmi*, WA 40.3, 487.2.

286. See *Rationis Latomianae*, WA 8, 84,9. On the *novatio* as the crucial term in Luther's understanding of figurative speech, see Hilgenfeld, *Mittelalterlich-traditionelle Elemente*, 169–71.

287. See *De divinitate*, WA 39.2, 93,2–3 (Thesis 1) and *Verbum caro factum est*, WA 39.2, 3,5–6.

288. WA 39.2, 1–5.

289. WA 39.2, 92–96.

290. *Verbum caro factum est*, WA 39.2, 5,3–4 (Thesis 40). *Novis linguis loquis* is a play on words from verse 17 of the canonical conclusion of Mark's gospel.

other hand, that what belongs to God, is said by mankind."[291] That has far-reaching consequences. In the *nova lingua* the following statements, for example, hold true: "This man [Christ] created the world" and "This God suffered, died, and was buried."[292] Now it is important to see that the truth of these articles do not evolve from any metaphoric use of language. *Deus est homo* is not to be compared semantically with the figurative expression "Achilles is a lion."[293] The predication "X is a lion" does not alter its fundamental meaning by the *significatio metaphora*, with that no new language is initiated. By contrast the statement "God is man" creates something new because the same *res* is equipped with a new *significatio* which in this *nova lingua* presents a *significatio simplex* (not *metaphora*!): "It is certain that all words [*vocabula*] take on a new meaning [*novam significationem*] in Christ when the same thing [*eadam re*] is indicated. . . . So it necessarily follows that the words man, mankind, suffered, etc. and everything said about Christ are new words [*nova vocabula*]."[294]

For example, if "creature" in the *vetus lingua* means "a thing which is separated from the divinity for all eternity," in the *nova lingua* it means "a thing which is inseparably bound in the same person with the divinity."[295] Through Christ, "God and man" are connected to one another "in a common process of meaning" so that one may speak "of God in human terms and of man in divine terms."[296] With the use of these new words the speaker emerges as a new man who by faith in Christ has acquired a new understanding of existence and may now speak "of God in no other way as in connection to mankind, and of mankind in no other way than in relation to God."[297]

Whoever does not have this new understanding of existence and persists in using, in his old language, terms such as "creature" and "man" in connection with Christ, is guilty of an equivocal use of language[298]—so argues Luther against the position of the radical spiritualist Caspar Schwenckfeld that Christ in his human nature was never a creature, as

291. *De divinitate*, WA 39.2, 93,6–7 (Thesis 3).

292. *De divinitate*, WA 39.2, 93,8–9 (Thesis 4).

293. On this classic example see Aristotle, *Rhetoric*, III, 4, 1406b.

294. *De divinitate*, WA 39.2, 94,17–18 and 23–24 (Theses 20 and 23).

295. *De divinitate*, WA 39.2, 94,19–22 (Theses 21 and 22).

296. See Korsch, *Luther*, 62.

297. Korsch, *Luther*, 63.

298. *De divinitate*, WA 39.2, 94,29–30 (Thesis 26).

well as against the Arian interpretation that Christ was utterly a creature.[299] The fuzzy interpretation of the terms is not the cause of this equivocation, but its use in a false play on words. In both the old and new language, the words, correctly used and in each case unequivocal, express univocity of being.[300]

The guide from the old to the new language is the holy scriptures and the orthodox church fathers. The "manner of speech in scriptures and the orthodox fathers"[301] renders the "grammar of the Holy Spirit"[302] recognizable and opens us up to the understanding for the *novatio* of the word of man by the word of God. An example of this understanding of language is provided by the discussion of the concept of sin in Luther's response to the criticism of his theses on indulgences by Jacobus Latomus.[303] Latomus had fashioned four different meanings of *peccatum* in the canon in order to, among other things, dull the effect of such verses in which sins are connected to Christ (such as 2 Cor 5:21). Here Latomus differentiates sin intended as "sacrifice and oblation for sin" from sin as guilt of humanity.[304] In contrast, Luther insists that *peccatum* in the scriptures can only have one meaning: "Sin can be nothing other than that which does not accord with the law of God."[305] This definition assumes that we can differentiate between *contra legem* and *secundum legem*. That, however, is only possible for mankind by the power of the word of God in his new understanding of existence as *homo spiritualis* which is no longer grounded in himself—and thereby plainly in sin.[306] Therefore the application of *peccatum* ascribed to Christ is to be counted as mandatory for the fundamental meaning of the word and not as a metaphorical figure of speech to be translated into another expression:

> As Christ was sacrificed for us, he is metaphorically made to be sin [*factus est peccatum metaphorice*] so that he became in all respects similar to a sinner: damned, forsaken, come to naught, so that nothing differentiated him from a true sinner, except for

299. *De divinitate*, WA 39.2, 94,27–38 (Theses 25–30).

300. On this see Saarinen, *Sprachphilosophie*, 34–38.

301. *De divinitate*, WA 39.2, 94,7–8 (Thesis 15).

302. *De divinitate*, WA 39.2, 104,32–33: *Ergo Spiritus sanctus habet suam grammaticam.*

303. *Rationes Latomianae*, WA 8, 82,19–99,24.

304. Latomus, *Articulorum doctrinae*, 8v.

305. *Rationes Latomianae*, WA 8, 83,28–29.

306. On this see Maurer, *Mensch*, 260–261.

> the fact that the guilt and sin which he bore was not his own doing. . . . And whatever was transferred [*transferuntur*], was transferred in the same measure by the equal form, otherwise it would not be a transfer at all. . . . And in this translation [*translatione*] there is not only a metaphoric of words, but also of things [*non solum est verborum, sed et rerum metaphora*].[307]

The term *metaphoricus* is used here by Luther, for his part, metaphorically, "and certainly not to make an improper manner of speaking even more improper, but to show the christological-soteriological metaphor to be a proper manner of speaking by the power of ontological reduplication—and in such a way, that a transference of being in the past in its corresponding translation of the word comes up for discussion."[308]

So, what was at first glance the unsettling transference of sin onto Christ prepares the understanding of its true meaning. The "sins are recognized *sub contraria specie*, and precisely in this, the essence of sin comes to the fore."[309]

We also have to concern ourselves with a "precise hiddenness"[310] of divine revelation on the language plane, which can be recognized and understood by mankind. This communicates an "absolute hiddenness" of divine discourse to which we have no access: "When God speaks in the language of his majesty, no man can hear it and live."[311] We are referred to the mediator, Christ, who "whispers in our language"[312] and imparts to us the word of God "in a friendly way"[313] but without loss of meaning.[314] For many humans, the new language remains, nevertheless, a hidden one with "concealed words."[315] It is almost a "structurally inherent peculiarity in the word of God"[316] that the "plentiful promises in plain

307. *Rationes Latomianae*, WA 8, 86,31–34 and 87,3–8.

308. Jüngel, *Bedeutung*, 38–39.

309. Maurer, *Mensch*, 261.

310. Jüngel, *Quae supra nos*, 239. See section 4.2.

311. *Predigten* 1540/45, WA 49, 737,8–9.

312. *Predigten* 1540/45, WA 49, 282,33–34.

313. *Reihenpredigten Johannes* 3–4, WA 47, 37,31.

314. *Tischreden*, WA TR 5, 48,21–24 (5294): "Whoever hears Christ, he hears God himself; whoever hears St. Peter or a preacher, he hears Christ and God himself talking to us. As he says: *Qui vos audit, me audit.* And *Paulus ad Galathas: Accepistis verbum meum ut verbum Dei. Sicut re vera est.*"

315. *Predigten* 1540/45, WA 49, 256,21–22.

316. Beutel, *Anfang*, 338.

words"[317] can be grasped—in an inconspicuous, seemingly powerless form which only the believer recognizes. But whoever underestimates language—according to the Satanic motto "*Suum verbum* must be the most wretched"[318]—not only has he misunderstood the word of God, but he has misunderstood the power of the word altogether.[319]

Luther describes the interdependence of the word of God and language quite strikingly in his writing *An die Ratsherren aller Städte deutschen Lands*:

> And let us say that we will not receive the gospel very well without languages. Languages are the scabbards into which the sword of the Spirit is inserted. They are the cabinet in which we carry our jewels. They are the vessel in which one savors the drink. They are the dining room in which the food sits. And as the gospel itself shows, they are the basket in which one holds the bread, fish, and crumbs. Surely if we were ever to mistakenly (as God foresees) abandon languages, so would we not only lose the gospel but would also revert to confusion, since we would not know how to speak or read proper Latin or German.[320]

The divine self-communication in human language sanctifies this. Entirely immediate, according to Luther, this holds for the original tongues of the holy scriptures, Hebrew and Greek, in which God first spoke through mankind.[321] By careful translation this sanctity can be transferred to other languages.[322] Birgit Stolt has demonstrated in impressive fashion the care Luther himself took for the task of translating the Bible into German, along with his combination of an astonishingly modern interdisciplinary-scientific approach with emotive genius.[323] In Stolt's studies it is also clear how greatly Luther was concerned with the depiction of the "*nova* sprach." Stolt speaks of a "sacral language"[324] which is recognizable by certain text markers, Hebraisms, and Grecisms.[325] That

317. See *Vorlesung über Jesaja*, WA 25, 369,17.

318. *Predigten* 1533/34, WA 37, 258,12.

319. See *Predigten* 1538, WA 46, 253,2–4: "If a country should founder, then one would not only live wildly and boldly but also despise the word."

320. *An die Ratsherren*, WA 15, 38,7–15.

321. *Predigten* 1533/34, WA 37, 258,117–19.

322. *An die Ratsherren*, WA 15, 38,5–6.

323. Stolt, *Rhetorik*, 84–85, 88, 90 and especially 98–103.

324. Stolt, *Rhetorik*, 169.

325. Stolt, *Rhetorik*, 169–72 and Stolt's articles mentioned on page 177.

Luther looked the German people "in the mouth"[326] is only one side of the truth. The other side is that he stylistically supported the Christian *innovatio* of language with a consciously inserted alienation effect. His rhetorical means may be compared "with the voices of an instrument": "The person being addressed should comprehend with all of his senses that it concerns an existential question, the totally other."[327]

4.7. Summary

Unlike Augustine, Luther never left behind a work in which he dealt systematically with language. Therefore, many of his individual insights fit seamlessly into a comprehensive theory of language.[328] For Luther, language capability is the *differentia specifica* of humankind[329]—that which separates us from other life forms and makes us in the image of God.[330] Without the divine gift of language mankind has no access to self-interpretation or interpretation of the world, as Luther shows in several of his sermons on the example of Jesus' healing of the deaf-mute. The single word "Hefata" from Mark 7:34 opens the pathway for the sick from existence to essence: "And he said: 'Be opened.' One word opens language, heart, and not in vain the gospel to the Hebrews. It sounds like a thunderclap. When 'open' is said, in that moment occurs man's illumination, man recognizes all things: himself, Satan, and God."[331]

By the fall from grace, human language forfeited effect. While the prelapsarian Adam is able to give animals their names according to their essence,[332] postlapsarian the worldwide confusion of language leads to catastrophe and war.[333] Nevertheless human language did not lose its mediality for the word of God. Quite the contrary—precisely its incompleteness is the surface, under the *sub contrario*, the word of God as the

326. *Sendbrief vom Dolmetschen*, WA 30.2, 637,21.

327. Stolt, *Rhetorik*, 171.

328. See Endermann, *Anmerkungen*, 281.

329. See Beutel, *Sprache*, 253.

330. See *Randbemerkungen*, WA 9, 67,15–18 and *Vorrede auf den Psalter*, WA DB 10.1, 100,12–13.

331. *Predigten* 1525, WA 17.1, 408,27–30. For further sermons on this pericope see WA 29, 511–20; WA 34.2, 146–56; WA 37, 506–20.

332. See *Genesisvorlesung*, WA 42, 90,35–91,4.

333. *Predigten* 1525, WA 17.1, 421,35–36.

only manner of divine revelation, efficacious and targeted, which can encounter the individual person.[334]

The word of God reaches mankind as address, more accurately as a call to a new self-determination through God, which is fulfilled by the open, impartial acceptance of the word. Thereby the sermon of Christ, in the double meaning of the sermon on Christ and Jesus' words, is also accepted. Then, concurrently, the divine claim to fulfillment of the commandments (law) and the promise of forgiveness of sins (gospel) prove to be true. Out of the "old man" a "new man" has emerged.[335] The *innovatio* enabled by Christ expresses itself in his "work of the word"[336] primarily in language. Once again it is the two named sources from which the new aspect feeds itself: Jesus' word itself and the proclamation about Jesus. Paradigmatic for the first case are the words of institution which in the capacity of a synecdoche opens up a new reality in linguistic terms (section 4.5.2). In the second case it is the sentence "God is man," out of which, in the communication of idioms, the concepts of the *vetus lingua* are transferred into those of the *nova lingua* (section 4.6). With this gain in competence with metaphors, a new language of faith comes into being which corresponds to the new understanding of existence.

With these reflections, Luther solved the old problem of Augustine—How can a deficient signification system mirror the perfection of the word of God? It is not the frail connection of *res* and *signa* that piques Luther's interest but the entire context which was first established by God's word. These are not new things which the new language defines, but the new language opens up a new vista in which it defines known things in a new way—with divine authority.[337] The question of which *res* is hiding behind the *signa* is, strictly speaking, no longer raised.[338] The *res* of the *nova signa* proves itself in the use of the language of faith, for the word of God creates whereof it speaks: "If you only have the word, you can surely grasp it and have it and then say: Here I have you, just as you

334. See Kinder, *Was bedeutet "Wort Gottes?"* 20–24, where theocentrism, intentionality, *Efficacia*, and hiddenness are named as "concerns of the reformatorical emphasis on the 'word of God.'"

335. On this see the reconstruction of the argument from *De libertate* in section 4.5.3.

336. *Predigten* 1529, WA 29, 398,4.

337. See *De divinitate*, WA 39.2, 94,25–26 (Thesis 24): *Non quod novam seu aliam rem, sed nova et aliter significant, nisi id quoque novam rem dicere velis.*

338. See Bayer, *Schöpfung*, 37.

said."[339] The word of God takes place "in, with, and under"[340] human discourse. As Ulrich Körtner said about Luther's understanding of language, "God's word and man's word [cannot] be separated from one another but still are not simply identical." The point is "that God's word and human discourse can no longer be immediately identified."[341]

From the viewpoint of the philosophy of language this calls to mind the late philosophy of Ludwig Wittgenstein in two-fold regard.[342] On the one hand, his *Philosophische Untersuchungen* can be read as the most convincing contradiction of a conception of language as a system of correspondence of things and signs. On the other hand, Wittgenstein developed a strong explanation model in his late work for the generation of new and transcendent meanings. Section 6.2 in chapter 6 will interface with the first point, dedicated to a linguistic-analytic solution to the problem of signification—along with Augustine's theme. The second point is the focus of section 6.3, where Luther's greatest achievement in the philosophy of language—the description of formation mechanisms for a language of faith—will be thought forward by means of modern philosophy of language. Prior to this, though, yet another theological concept shall be analyzed, one which takes a closer look at the moments of action in the word of God, which Luther laid out with his differentiation of law (obligation) and gospel (promise).

339. *Daß diese Worte Christi*, WA 26, 436,22–23.

340. See *Konkordienformel*, SD, VII, 133 (BKSL, 434).

341. Körtner, *Theologie*, 145. Emphasis in original.

342. See Bayer, *Theologie*, 452: "If theology wants to hold fast . . . to the reformatorical hermeneutics of Luther, convinced of its truth, then it will consider its case in time-related formulation more in relation to language analysis, especially the late Wittgenstein and Austin, than on the basis of existential analysis." Acting on this suggestion, for example, is Thomas Wabel with his study *Sprache als Grenze*, which however did not unearth all the parallels between Luther and Wittgenstein.

5

The Word of God in Karl Barth

5.1. Introduction

Even though the theology of Karl Barth first achieved its complete shape in the *Kirchliche Dogmatik* (*KD*) as a theology of the word of God "in its totality as well as in the details,"[1] the crucial stages of thought toward this result were already clearly apparent early on. In the Aarauer lecture *Die Gerechtigkeit Gottes* from 1916 "that momentous change in perspective"[2] from an anthropocentric to a theocentric approach was apparent, which Trutz Rentdorff later characterized as a "new Enlightenment" in the service of the "radical autonomy of God."[3] Against the background of political misuse of religion in the First World War, Barth demanded: "Above all we must concern ourselves in general with recognizing God, once again, as God. In a nutshell—acknowledge God. But that is child's play, when compared to all the cultural, social, and patriotic tasks before us."[4]

The contemplation of God as totally other[5] naturally raises the question of to what degree one can talk responsibly about this God without once more falling back into the old models of human projections. How

1. Korsch, *Aufgabe*, 276.

2. Anzinger, *Glaube*, 123.

3. Rentdorff, *Autonomie*, 164.

4. *Gerechtigkeit*, 242.

5. *Totaliter aliter*, a key concept in the theology of Barth and Rudolf Bultmann. See *Brief an Eduard Thurneysen* 1919, cited in Busch, *Lebenslauf*, 121.

can we communicate about anyone who "encounters us as the totally other, as the holy one with his No, in such an inescapable manner?"[6] Certainly the most famous formulation of this problem was delivered by Barth in his Elgersburger lecture from October 1922: "As theologians we ought to speak of God. But we are also humans and as such cannot speak of God. We should know both, our ought-to and our not-able-to, and just because of that give God the glory. That is our predicament. Everything else is child's play by comparison."[7]

This fundamental question of the possibility of theological communication, indeed—as will be shown—the possibility of any human communication with connection to the one reality, is a *basso continuo* of Barth's work. It turns out to be the most comprehensive theological approach to the phenomenon of language in the twentieth century.

To this extent the term "word of God" plays the decisive role because it is introduced by Barth as an almost purely formal answer to the fundamental theological question of how to talk responsibly about God. God comes up for discussion when God himself speaks.[8] Just how the "divine self-word"[9] can be concretized further in terms of content, ontologically and empirically, will be unfolded in sections 5.3 to 5.8.

That the "fundamental communicative sense" of the word of God[10] is to be understood linguistically was recently refuted in an attempt by Joachim Ringleben in his study with the climactic title *Sprachloses Wort*. In contrast to Luther's real presence of the *verbum divinum* in human language, Barth's word of God is "principally without connection to the human word, which is to say, with language."[11] Ringleben accuses Barth (unlike Luther) of not having completed the "intertwined thought of God's word and man's word," which is why in the *KD* "no word of God in its direct actual sense" comes to be seen.[12] On the face of it, Ringleben has the (superficial) argument on his side, that Barth devotes himself explicitly in only a few passages of the *KD* to human language.[13]

6. *Römerbrief, zweite Fassung*, 66.

7. *Wort Gottes*, 151.

8. See *Wort Gottes*, 171.

9. *KD* 1/1:52.

10. Korsch, *Kommunikation*, 1045.

11. Ringleben, *Sprachloses*, 152.

12. Ringleben, *Gott*, 54 (footnote).

13. The keyword index of the *KD* evinces only four references to the word "language"—and none in the relevant passages for the doctrine of the word of God §§ 4 to 6. On this see also Fischer, *Glaubensaussage*, 13.

But when Ringleben speaks of a "consistent avoidance of the topic of language"[14] by Barth, he seems to have in his mind's eye a traditionally concentrated image of language built on inflexible structures under the neglect of the language event.[15] Such a simplification, which disregards the active character, was cultivated in the philosophy of language well into the twentieth century. It is precisely that which Barth did not take on, but he focuses always on language as event, or as he himself said, as "saying."[16]

Therefore the thesis is made quite strongly here, in direct opposition to Ringleben's argument, that the fleeting and fragmentary connection of God's word and man's word in Barth reflects a modern insight into the essence of linguistic communication. The insight, namely, that a successful communication event is not exclusively bound to linguistic structures and impressionable factors.

In order to make this plausible, the following presentation inverts Barth's argument in the *KD*. Section 5.3 describes the communication situation of God—Man as the primordial model of every language event. Section 5.4 explains Barth's equivalence of the one word of God with Jesus Christ on the basis of §69 of the *KD*. Sections 5.5 and 5.6 deal with the recognizability and essence of the word of God (§§6 and 5), and finally section 5.7 discusses the three-fold shape of the word of God, with which the *KD* begins (§4). In this movement of thought from the abstract to concrete phenomena, the consistent linguistic alignment of the word of God with Barth's implicit language theory[17] becomes especially clear. Prior to all that, section 5.2 brings partially into view the lines of development between Luther and Barth, which are of interest with regard to the cognition-inducing theme here.

14. Ringleben, *Sprachloses*, 7.

15. In the author's opinion, a similar misinterpretation lies at the basis of the critique of Graham Ward. He criticizes Barth for creating no connection between "divine and human representation" (*Barth, Derrida* 240) and "word and Word," man's word and God's word, have not been transparently connected to one another (*Barth, Derrida* 40). For Barth, the word of God is certainly not formulated in its own divine language, but shows itself in eventful fashion only in human language. The conditions for this event are specified rather precisely by Barth in §4 of *KD*, as will be shown in section 5.7.

16. *KD* 2/2:104.

17. Korsch, *Religionsbegriff*, 200.

5.2. Martin Luther and Karl Barth

As the decisive linguistic innovation which emerges from Luther's reflections on the word of God, the fourth chapter of this work has emphasized the innovative power which encompasses in a *nova lingua* a new level of meaning. The new language of faith leads to a renewed understanding of existence. This idea is now radicalized ontologically by Barth. Barth allows the *omnia vocabula*, which according to Luther is gained in *Christo novam significationem*,[18] "to take on not only a new but its actual meaning . . . which then in a reverse twist helps to divulge its customary meaning within and without theology in its abstractness, preliminal character, and ambivalent inauthenticity."[19]

For Barth, it is a salvation act of God that creates a "real reality"[20] in Jesus Christ, from which derives all being in the theological and non-theological realm. God and mankind, being and time, "can only be discussed in their actual sense from the central event of the death and resurrection of Jesus Christ."[21] For Barth there are not two kingdoms. All concepts developed in the wake of the Christ event have their "prototypical meaning for both language contexts" in the theological and the non-theological context.[22]

Ingolf Dalferth calls this approach "eschatological realism,"[23] while Bruce McCormack speaks of "critical realism,"[24] which certainly causes confusion with the philosophical position of the same name (on this see section 6.5.2), but it nevertheless touches an important point in comparison to Luther. The capability of human language, to testify to the revelation of reality, "comes from without—it is grace and not nature."[25] The unveiling is an inaccessible event whose conditions of entry do not lie in human power and therefore remain "critical." "I was and am a customary theologian" wrote Barth in his *Christliche Dogmatik* (*CD*), the prequel to

18. Luther, *De divinitate*, WA 39.2, 94,17–18.

19. Dalferth, *Realismus*, 417.

20. *Römerbrief, erste Fassung*, 88, 161, and 227.

21. Dalferth, *Realismus*, 417.

22. Dalferth, *Realismus*, 418.

23. Dalferth, *Realismus*, 407.

24. McCormack, *Dialektik*, 385–87.

25. McCormack, *Ort*, 32.

the *KD*, "who stands not at the disposal of the word of God, but at best a 'doctrine of the word of God.'"[26]

It is this "Yes, but . . ." with which Barth again and again agrees thoroughly with Luther and then distances himself just a bit. This double step is found explicitly in the word of God lecture from Elgersburg[27] and in the article written one year later on Luther's understanding of communion:

> Reformed doctrine will gladly go along the entire way that Luther goes, here and in any other fashion, in order to, when the final word falls, thwart the Lutheran Yes by the Reformed not No but rather But, to expand, to explain, in remembrance, that when this word does fall, the circle of that way closes, and the point has been reached again from which Luther set out, where the equation becomes a simile, where the critical question must be revived again, so that the divine answer may be truth and remain so.[28]

Obviously the Barthian inversion of Luther's word of God differentiation must be seen under this aspect: "It marks that the dialectic of law and gospel for its part must be placed on the horizon of the gospel,"[29] since only by doing so would this do justice to its essence as an address of God to mankind. "The word of God proves its unity in the fact that it is always grace, that is, free, no balance due, unearned divine goodness, mercy, and condescension, when it is spoken to us and when we are allowed to hear it. . . . That God talks to us, that is under all circumstances truly grace in itself."[30]

Luther would hardly have lodged a veto against this accentuation.[31] With this clarification, Barth is reacting to the historical relativization

26. *CD*, 8.

27. *Wort Gottes*, 175. "I have a duty as a Reformed Christian—and in my opinion not only as that—to the Lutheran *est* just as I do to the Lutheran certainty of salvation, to keep a safe distance."

28. *Ansatz und Absicht*, 305. The extent to which this article does justice to Luther will not be the subject of this work. It is still astonishing that Luther's innovative interpretation of the words of institution as a synecdoche (see section 4.5.2) serves for Barth only as a "purposeful impediment" to understanding communion (*Ansatz und Absicht*, 304).

29. Dalferth, *Realismus*, 418.

30. *Evangelium und Gesetz*, 2–3.

31. See Luther, *Predigten* 1532, WA 36, 19,32–20,22: "Learn, that not only the law is given by God, but an even higher word, which is the gospel. When they wrestle with one another, the law and the gospel, . . . then I will follow the gospel and say: Goodbye, law, it is better to not know the law than to abandon the gospel."

of the—undoubtedly constant for Luther—concept of the law in the post-Reformation era. This relativization threatened to turn into a time-dependent "adaptation" of the gospel. It is no coincidence that Barth held the lecture *Evangelium und Gesetz* on his last trip to Nazi Germany in 1935.[32] The lecture did not concern settling the differentiation of the law and the gospel with any of its "soteriological self-potentiation of mankind's defensive relevance," but rather to place both quantities, while acknowledging their difference, "in the one word of God, in Jesus Christ."[33] This aligns with Luther's conception to the extent that for him Christ is also "no longer the righteous one before whom the sinner must flee, but the righteous one to whom the sinner can flee."[34]

In his momentous analysis of the relationship between Luther and Barth, Gerhard Ebeling placed emphasis on the fact that with the former, the unity of the revelation is completed in the eschaton, while for fallen mankind the gospel becomes "irrelevant" without the "adversarial experience of the hidden God."[35]

In the following sections these aspects will be expanded upon. First of all, the concern here is no longer Ebeling's assessment that word of God theology from Luther to Barth experiences a "profound tectonic shift,"[36] but rather an intellectual specification which rests on a more exact understanding which takes into account the event character of successful communication. Finally, it will be about "nothing other than the word of God"[37] for both thinkers.

5.3. Mankind before God: The Linguistic Situation

"The task of theology is the word of God."[38] This programmatic sentence of Barth's "word" is not intended metaphorically as an isolated, stationary quantity, isolated and apart, but as a linguistic component of a real, empirical communication process. Thereby the actual object of theology

32. See Korsch, *Barth*, 1143–44.

33. Demut, *Evangelium*, 339. Demut's work earmarks this fundamental idea as formative for Barth's entire public ministry (see Demut, *Evangelium*, 338–52).

34. Iwand, *Barmer*, 229.

35. Ebeling, *Ringen*, 571.

36. Ebeling, *Ringen*, 573.

37. Bayer, *Theologie*, 379.

38. *Wort Gottes*, 173.

can be refined down to a particular interaction situation. As a result it wins its case "that without being tempted to go astray to the right or the left, every contact—all contact of God with mankind in which it comes to contact of mankind with God—tries to see, to understand, and to engage in conversation."[39]

In both lectures from 1922, *Not und Verheißung der Verkündigung* and *Das Wort Gottes als Aufgabe der Theologie*, Barth described quite precisely this prototypical communication situation. Out of concern for his own existence, mankind successfully answers a number of questions himself. Still, these questions stand in a bracket before which stands, like "a minus," the "question of all questions": "a great What? Why? Whence? Whither?"[40] It is the fundamental question of mankind itself: its essence, its destiny, its origin, its goal. In this universality it can only be answered with mankind itself: "For if mankind itself is the question, then the answer must be the question, it must be itself, but only as an answer, as an answered question."[41]

People certainly know that "they themselves cannot provide the answer to this question." Such attempts remain particular and subjective. Nevertheless, when people entrust others with this question, they do so in the expectation of an answer.[42] For this answer would have to possess "genuine transcendence" in order to "solve the riddle of immanence."[43]

In *Not und Verheißung der Verkündigung*, Barth further sharpens his focus on human striving for knowledge—here as a narratively designed expectation of Sunday church-goers—as he designs some conceivable gateways to transcendence. Observation of nature, appreciation of art, realization of freedom and righteousness, successful work—all these moments of a life fulfilled could be runway lights guiding us to immanence. Still, the crucial answer goes beyond "a cherry blossom in bloom," "Beethoven's Ninth Symphony," "the state," and "our and others' noble daily work."[44] When people pose these questions to themselves, "then they have put behind themselves, whether they know it or not,

39. *Menschlichkeit*, 19.
40. *Wort Gottes*, 151.
41. *Wort Gottes*, 154.
42. *Wort Gottes*, 152.
43. *Wort Gottes*, 161.
44. *Not und Verheißung*, 75.

cherry blossom, symphony, state, daily work, and still other concepts as somehow exhausted possibilities."[45]

> The answer: God is present, which is undoubtedly given one way or another in all these possibilities, the truthfulness of these things, their testimony to a meaning of life, has obviously become once more dubious, the great riddles of existence: the unfathomable muteness of that so-called nature which surrounds us, the randomness and darkness of all that which is distinct and in time, sorrow, the fate of nations and individuals, radical evil, death, they are there again and they speak, louder than all of that which would like to assure us that God is present. No, the question cannot be suppressed any longer, it is burning hot: If it is, then, also true?[46]

Put in a nutshell, one can formulate the question of all questions in this way: Is it then true that God is present? Here are the three decisive elements:

a. the question of essence, origin, destiny, and goal of existence (*God*—firstly as a placeholder for a final determination)
b. the question of the validity of any such final determination (*is it then true?*)
c. the question of relevance directed at the individual person (*present*).

The question, and thus the certainty, that God is present can only be answered one way: by God himself. And he does so while revealing that one sentence with which the question of all questions is answered: "God becomes man"[47] or even more briefly "Jesus Christ."[48] The sentence fulfills the function of an answer only when he is expressed "as God's word."[49] Because God himself does not speak person to person to humanity, it only remains "the possibility that God himself speaks where he is being spoken of."[50] But this is not a language event predictable from humanity's angle. It can only take place where the most

45. *Not und Verheißung*, 75.
46. *Not und Verheißung*, 75–76. Emphasis in original.
47. *Wort Gottes*, 160.
48. *Wort Gottes*, 175.
49. *Wort Gottes*, 160. Emphasis in original.
50. *Wort Gottes*, 171.

promising way to speak of God is broken off.[51] This set of circumstances will be taken up in section 5.7.

The next section will concern itself with defining more precisely God's word "Jesus Christ" as an answer to the fundamental human question. With a view to the prototypical communication situation God-Man, the subject will be expanded here to include a discussion of the reference to Christ in Barth's argument as a sharpening of the fundamental question and the usual relation between question and answer is inverted. The question "if it is, then, also true?" is posed, according to biblical tradition by Jesus himself on the cross, in incomparable form: My God, My God, why have you forsaken me?"[52] The "human life question" is thereby "translated into a question after God."[53] Then again, one can only pose the question if one already hears the answer. Dietrich Korsch comments on these ideas of Barth: "The question after God is the critique of every possible human horizon of experience. . . . God encounters mankind only in such a way that mankind learns to ask after him precisely—and this question emerges out of God's answer given in advance. God must have already come in order to question after his presence, and questioning his presence is the proper way of dealing with his presence."[54]

In questioning doubt the Yes shows itself because God's Yes first induced the question after his presence. This is what is meant by Barth's paradoxical formulation: "The question is the answer."[55] In communication with God, man always enters as the one spoken to, the addressee.[56]

5.4. Jesus Christ as the One Word of God

The analysis of the primordial linguistic situation between God and man has shown that the fundamental question of humanity corresponds exactly to an answer from God: "God has become man" or "Jesus Christ." With that, in principal, the crucial thing has been said about God and God's word. As Eberhard Jüngel states: "God is completely defined by the event of

51. *Wort Gottes*, 166–67 and 171.

52. See *Not und Verheißung*, 85, with regard to Mark 15:34 (NRSV).

53. *Not und Verheißung*, 86.

54. Korsch, *Barth*, 1113.

55. *Not und Verheißung*, 87.

56. At least to this point, Barth's approach is thoroughly comparable to that of Martin Buber. See Brinkschmidt, *Buber*, 32–36 and 163.

his identity with one man to the benefit of all mankind. By this realization, the entire dogmatics of Barth in its inner context is opened up."[57]

From this perspective, if one follows Jüngel's recommendation, one paragraph of the *KD* gains initial and central significance. It is not counted among those passages in the introductory "Doctrine of the Word of God (*KD* 1)" but in Barth's doctrine of reconciliation (*KD* 4): Barth's reflections on the prophetic office of Christ in §69. The paragraph with the superscript "The Glory of the Mediator" is prefixed by Barth to the first thesis of the *Barmer Theologische Erklärung* (*Barmen Declaration*): "Jesus Christ, as he is attested for us in holy scripture, is the one word of God which we have to hear and which we have to trust and obey in life and in death."[58] This sentence fits seamlessly with the essay discussed in the final section of this study, *Das Wort Gottes als Aufgabe der Theologie*, which concludes with a reference to Christ.[59]

Therefore Barth's reflections on the word of God in the *KD* shall be reconstructed in an inversion of his own depiction: from the analysis of the *one* word of God in Jesus Christ through the questions of the recognizability and essence all the way to the concrete manifestations in three-fold form. This inverse process also avoids the otherwise possibly arising impression that Barth moves from a sensory-empirical starting point on a course of increasingly dogmatic constriction. It is inappropriate to apply Barth's own biographical self-assessment of his thought as an increasingly "christological concentration"[60] to the line of argument of the *KD* itself.[61] The doctrine of the word of God in *KD* 1 is christologically designed throughout. Otherwise it would not be at all comprehensible. It is precisely this characteristic of *KD* that here it is not the logos of which the John prologue speaks, containing a "peculiarly meaningful significance"[62] which then—like so many times in the theological tradition—is placed in a context with Jesus Christ. Instead, the ὁ λόγος in John 1:1 is "seen semantically, a placeholder for Jesus of Nazareth."[63]

57. Jüngel, *Barth-Studien*, 339.

58. *KD* 4/3:1. See *Barmer Theologische Erklärung*, 296 [trans. pcusa.org].

59. See *Wort Gottes*, 174–75.

60. *How my mind*, 186.

61. As for example Stoevesandt, *Dogmatikvorlesung*, 84, and Jüngel, *Barth-Studien*, 276–77.

62. Korsch, *Dialektische Theologie*, 88.

63. Korsch, *Dialektische Theologie*, 88. See *KD* 2/2:103: "ὁ λόγος is unmistakably substituted for: Jesus."

The revelation in Jesus Christ is primarily the reason that we find any way at all to speak of God, the totally other. In this revelation God communicates with us, it is "a transient, a communicative event"[64] which is not bound to any period in time but occurs again and again, always new. The Christ testified to in the Bible "lives,"[65] he is doubly present as true man and true God: "in the manner of God . . . in absolute freedom and power," "in the manner of man . . . in the relative dependence of the individual member in the natural and historical context of the created world."[66] Jesus' existence is therefore concurrently an *act*, namely the "creative realization of being," and a *deed*, the deed of a person.[67] In the God intended for mankind in Jesus Christ, every person lives in this connection to God. Every attempt at self-determination, every "I" of mankind, redounds to this bond: "When any of us says I and in his attempt at life uses the freedom given by the fact that he is I and not It, he declares that in some sense he belongs to the territory in which Another, this One, is Lord and Servant—to the sphere in which God himself says I in this Other, and as man makes effective and not merely tentative use of his divine freedom."[68]

Jesus Christ is the reason why there is no "God there" and "man here," but only God as the "God of man" and man as the "man of God."[69] The individual self-determination of man can only succeed when man recognizes himself as recognized by God. That is possible in turn because the recognition by God (his confirming word) precedes the reciprocal recognition of man (his faith).[70] The word of God encounters man as a pure source and shows itself as exactly that when it becomes the basis of his individuation.[71]

Connected with this is, for Barth, the "necessity of granting to christological thinking this unconditional supremacy, this function in the strictest sense of foundational thought."[72] Barth calls "christological" that

64. *KD* 4/3:7.

65. *KD* 4/3:41.

66. *KD* 4/3:41.

67. *KD* 4/3:41–42.

68. *KD* 4/3:43 [trans. Bromiley].

69. *KD* 4/3:45.

70. *KD* 4/3:48.

71 For this emerges the curious correspondence of essence and recognizability of the word of God in the *analogia fidei* (section 5.5).

72. *KD* 4/3:200.

which is "thinking in perceiving and comprehending, in understanding and in acknowledgment of the reality testified to in the holy scriptures of the living person Jesus Christ himself, in the awareness of the scope and significance of his existence, in the openness with regard to his self-revelation, in the consistency of the obedience to which he is entitled."[73]

Because the discussion here is about a "living person," and thus a man testified to in history, "christological" does not mean the deduction from a "Christ principle."[74] Jesus Christ is not an axiom but a fact,[75] in Kantian terms, a synthetic statement a posteriori. Nevertheless one should expect a proof of the fundamental sentence that Jesus Christ is the one word of God, as Barth makes plain. That would mean "that we are beholden to Feuerbach while trying to resist him!"[76] A classification of the word of God in human contexts of reasoning would immediately disqualify it as an answer to the fundamental question of essence, origin, destiny, and goal. We are searching for a "word that is predominantly spoken to us, that we do not speak to ourselves, but are only just able to hear and repeat."[77]

Barth highlights four qualities of the *one* word of God from which follows its uniqueness:[78]

1. *Sufficiency.* With the one word of God, God said everything both about himself and about mankind. It is concurrently the doctrine of God and anthropology, ontology and ethics: "What he is for us and wants with us—but also what we are for him, what we intended to be in relation to him, to want and to do, that is revealed to us in Jesus Christ as the one word of God exhaustively without qualification and remainder."[79]

2. *Exclusivity.* The word of God stands under no pressure to justify itself against a competing statement, doubts on its authority, or problematized inquiry. These challenges can only come from God

73. *KD* 4/3:199.

74. *KD* 4/3:199.

75. Korsch, *Dialektische Theologie*, 172, speaks of a "principally (singular) fact."

76. *KD* 4/3:79.

77. *KD* 4/3:79.

78. On the summarized concepts see Korsch, *Dialektische Theologie*, 171.

79. *KD* 4/3:110.

himself. But because God reveals himself completely in his word, there is no room left for a *deus absconditus*.[80]

3. *Nonderivative nature*. The word of God cannot be combined with any other ideas—"even if they were the most enlightening, the most urgent, and the best!" Any blending with other religious ideas or philosophical principles disempowers the word. "For the person who dares such things, Jesus Christ . . . [ceases] to be, who he is."[81] Notwithstanding this, the word of God can, of course, be combined with human words—indeed, it relies on humans to witness to the word. They were the biblical prophets and apostles, but they could also be "humans outside of the biblical-ecclesiastical sphere."[82]
4. *Unparalleled status*. The one word of God in Jesus Christ is finally not to be surpassed in its content, its profundity, its urgency, and its benevolence. It contains "everything worth knowing, understood correctly," it commends itself compellingly to mankind in the cognitive sense ("profundity") and existential sense ("urgency"), and is the most comprehensive consolation which is possible in linguistic communication.[83]

One could read these four qualities as a utopia of linguistic communication that knows no misunderstandings nor ambiguities, no inquiries nor alternatives. The word of God is, however, concurrently so strong that it survives unscathed even from these upheavals of the language event of fallen creation. It actualizes itself anew, again and again, with regard to human incompleteness. The one word is "grasped in a continuous self-completion—not in looking at it as if it were not complete and sufficient, but rather in looking at the profound need for completion of all our hearing."[84]

Now what exactly is the content of this one word? On this Barth referred to the life of Jesus Christ as an historical event in human history: "His life . . . is his existence as the true Son of God, who as such is also the true son of man."[85] This life encompasses, on the one hand, the

80. *KD* 4/3:111.
81. *KD* 4/3:112.
82. *KD* 4/3:112.
83. *KD* 4/3:114.
84. *KD* 4/3:110.
85. *KD* 4/3:117.

life of God "as the incomprehensible source, . . . the incomprehensible goal, . . . the eternal good," and on the other hand the life of man "in this profundity, this abyss, even in this wistful crying out . . . to God."[86] The life of Christ encompasses these poles and reconciles them: "It is the life of the completely humiliated God and of man elevated to God by just this humiliation."[87] In Jesus Christ, God speaks the word "that enlightens mankind about the conditions of his existence," and this word is, at the same time, that which "with God himself brings his existence to consciousness."[88] To this extent it is appropriate to speak of this life of Jesus Christ as the content of the word of God, because this life "talks": "It talks . . . to all mankind. Now it also talks to us. Sometimes it says, other times it calls, sometimes this life cries out: it is about us. It becomes and is for us (*pro nobis*), lived for you and me (*pro te et me*), in this life God is with us (Immanuel, *dominus nobiscum*), with each and every one of us."[89]

In §69 of the *KD*, Barth translated in two brief pages and in all linguistic facets, just how this life of Jesus Christ "speaks for itself"[90] and for us:[91]

1. The *sign* of this one word of God is the name Jesus Christ, "which marks him and separates him from all else that there is, with which he is to be described and under which he is to be addressed." He is not chosen capriciously, but is made aware of himself, because "with his naming," he expresses "his inner self."[92]
2. The *semantic content* of the word is the "history attested in scripture" of Jesus Christ.[93] All verifications of derived articles and all interpretations must refer to this content.
3. The *validity* of the word arises from the fact that, in the moment of its understanding, it must inevitably be acknowledged: "It carries the necessity of its recognition and acknowledgment not only in itself, so that it can break forth from it, to a certain degree before

86. *KD* 4/3:117.
87. *KD* 4/3:118.
88. Hafstad, *Wort*, 124.
89. *KD* 4/3:118.
90. *KD* 4/3:49.
91. *KD* 4/3:49–51.
92. *KD* 4/3:49.
93. *KD* 4/3:50.

itself, into mankind, to whom it is addressed, for whom it happens, so that for them its disregard or even denial, can only be enforceable in the form of a lie."[94] Any contradiction of the word of God is virtually unthinkable, since one such could never claim the same authority. Counterarguments are only proof of misunderstanding.

4. The word of God is a *language act*, a "divine and human deed,"[95] which triggers a reaction within a communication situation. It issues a call for "a correct decision," namely from whom "the Yes spoken in the deed" was addressed to, and they must answer with their own Yes.[96]

5. The *effect* of the word is knowledge of reality in a comprehensive sense. Barth speaks of the "light of life," the essence and significance of Jesus Christ "is first made visible to mankind, . . . but also of mankind itself as well as the world."[97]

This framework of theses requires further elaboration, which will be carried out in the following sections. These five theses proceed obliquely to further argumentation. They are equally to be considered under the aspects of recognizability, essence, and the empirical shape of the word of God.

The function of the word that opens up reality has a consequence that reality experienced in this way can itself, in turn, produce an effect that broadens recognition. If the only road to recognition of reality goes through Jesus Christ, then "there is no profanity cut adrift from him nor confiscated from his decree."[98] Or, in the light imagery typical of Barth, "Should there be some sort of—which certainly is not to be automatically disputed—really shining lights of life out there, giving the true word of God, so is this word solely out there, so those lights also shine out there, because and while there is also—nothing other than his light, shining."[99]

For the question which interests us here, it is truly of decisive significance that this truth of other words of Barth is derived likewise from the one word of God—and indeed with the aid of parables from the New

94. *KD* 4/3:50.
95. *KD* 4/3:50.
96. *KD* 4/3:51.
97. *KD* 4/3:49.
98. *KD* 4/3:139.
99. *KD* 4/3:107.

Testament. These are "something like the primordial image of order, in which there can be, alongside the one word of God, created and defined by this, corresponding to it exactly, serving it completely, and therefore in its power and authority, other true words of God."[100]

These parables are almost "pronouncements,"[101] insofar as they reflect—mostly weird—events from the human sphere of everyday life, and yet, in the capacity of metaphoric language application, aim for another plane of meaning—the kingdom of God. They are in addition more than pronouncements while they are authorized by the Son of God himself and therefore are to be understood as "unveiled and veiled revelation."[102]

Parables are to this extent comparable to the incarnation because in both God "allows some of his creatures or an event, in the space and time of the world created by him, to speak for him."[103] According to Christian Link, parables are "interpretations of the sentence from John 1:14 in the space of human history."[104] When, however, the parables are connected to the only "real reality,"[105] God's kingdom, then only reality is discussed in this graphic discourse. Formulated differently: by the allegorical word of God, human language first achieves its reference, its connection to reality.[106] The one word of Jesus Christ gets the world to speak. Everything can become a parable and in this linguistic structure first experiences its reality.

In the following, further facets of this basic structure will be considered. In this section, it should have become clear that the christological basis of the word of God in Barth is through and through linguistically designed, the "christological concentration" remains true to the basic communication-oriented approach of Barth—man before God.

5.5. The Recognizability of the Word of God

It lies in the essence of the term "word" that it is recognizable to others—not for everyone, not always and everywhere, but in certain situations.

100. *KD* 4/3:126.
101. *KD* 4/3:125.
102. *KD* 4/3:125.
103. *KD* 2/1:50.
104. Link, *Verständnis*, 371.
105. *Römerbrief, erste Fassung*, 97.
106. See Hunsinger, *Karl Barth lesen*, 243.

This also holds true especially for the word of God:[107] "People can recognize the word of God, because and to the extent that God wishes that they should recognize it, because and to the extent that against the will of God there is only disobedience, and because and to the extent that it is a revelation of the will of God in his word, in which precisely this impotence of disobedience is abolished."[108]

From the principle precedence of the divine word it follows that its recognizability cannot be found in a special human capability, but that "this ability is granted by the word itself."[109] A closer look at this event shows that here Barth conceptually joins three aspects of his epistemology: a) the linguistic nature of the divine word, b) a concept of self-definition inspired by Immanuel Kant, and c) an "experience" understood in Hegelian terms.[110]

a. The word of God comes as a "call" to mankind, as a "founding of connection,"[111] as a language event which demands a reaction. The reception of the word is therefore not a passive process but an "act," the "hearing [is a] decision,"[112] that, in the best case, is followed by recognition.

b. Barth defines this recognition "as that testing of human knowledge of an object through which its veracity becomes a determination of existence of the discerning person."[113] It is the process by which something of "clarity and certainty" is gained, which then becomes evident in the fact that the self-determination of the autonomous, discerning subject is adopted and then confirmed as "real reality."[114]

c. The concept of experience is introduced by Barth as a result of the cognitive process, as the "determination of existence of the discerning person."[115] Cognition in this sense goes beyond perceiving—in linguistic terms: hearing or reading. What is discerned serves a

107. *KD* 1/1:195.

108. *KD* 1/1:204.

109. *KD* 1/1:204.

110. See Korsch, *Barth*, 1203.

111. Korsch, *Dialektische Theologie*, 125.

112. *KD* 1/1:209.

113. *KD* 1/1:206. See *KD* 1/1:195. On Kant's concept of autonomy see especially his *Grundlegung*, 63–75.

114. *KD* 1/1:195.

115. *KD* 1/1:206. See Hegel's concept of experience in his *Phänomenologie*, 38–39.

definitive purpose in consciousness.[116] Accordingly, experience of the word of God means this for mankind: "the certainty of their existence as people by the word of God."[117]

Characteristic for Barth's reconstruction is the causal priority of God's determination over self-determination. The knowledge of having been spoken to by God first makes possible the determination of existence of mankind. The "anthropological venue," where this determination of existence takes place as experience of the divine word, is explicitly left open by Barth. Will, conscience, feeling, intellect—all are possible.[118] Any limitation would abet incorrect thinking; there would be no disposition to religious experience grounded in mankind.[119] But the reverse holds true. No one is "religiously unmusical," to take up an oft-quoted phrase from Max Weber.[120]

Barth's approach is at bottom strictly empirical. It is not the free "I" observation of experiences from without—as in René Descartes—that constitutes human self-determination, but rather the accidental, contingent experience. Barth firmly sets a boundary from subjectivism of Cartesian imprint[121] using a neo-Kantian argument:[122] "Man does not exist abstractly, but concretely, which is to say in experiences, in determinations of his existence through objects, through an external world differentiated from him."[123] The effect of the word of God is to grasp a "specified self-determination of mankind"[124] to the extent that we rediscover that we are determined by God. Thereby it is not about a restriction of human possibilities, for this God whom we acknowledge as the final instance of validity, has determined himself for us—as Barth explains in the doctrine of election in the *KD*.[125] Consequently, this idea express-

116. *KD* 1/1:207.

117. *KD* 1/1:207.

118. *KD* 1/1:210–211.

119. *KD* 1/1:201.

120. Weber, *Briefe*, 65: Weber to Ferdinand Tönnies, 19 Feb 1909.

121. See *KD* 1/1:203: "In theology . . . one cannot think in Cartesian terms."

122. See Lohmann, *Barth*, 377. This anti-subjective epistemology is, as far as this study is concerned, the only neo-Kantian constant in Barth's thought from the *Römerbrief* to the *KD* (see Lohmann, *Barth*, 402).

123. *KD* 1/1:206.

124. Korsch, *Dialektische Theologie*, 125.

125. *KD* 2/2:101.

es just the opposite of "the highest degree of freedom."[126] Every other instance would lead us into dependency.

The experience of the word of God takes place in the form of an "acknowledgment."[127] With this is expressed the fact that this self-determination is not created by the self but occurs in acceptance of the "authority of another."[128] In recognition of the word of God lies the experience of being spoken to, of being addressed and along with that the experience of one's own acknowledgment. To this extent we may say: The experience of the word of God means the acknowledgment of my being acknowledged before God.[129] This experience is constitutive for all other experiences[130]—it is a "disclosure event"[131] for self-relation, world-relation, and God-relation. Or, to use a well-known dictum from Eberhard Jüngel, "experience with the experience."[132]

Barth's reasoning allows for acceptance of a totally comprehensive determination of mankind originating from God without leaving behind the plane of experience. The word of God is not experienced as a supranatural event, but as a contingent communication situation. The word of God becomes a transcendent phenomenon by its earth-shattering effect which differentiates it (not only quantitatively) from other conceivable anchor points of human self-determination. The experience of the word of God is so radical that it allows all other experiences to appear in a new light—not only current, but past experiences as well.[133] "Because it takes place as experience, it ceases to be experience."[134] This self-determination by and toward God contains its wide-ranging effect and validity for us

126. Korsch, *Religionsbegriff*, 209.

127. *KD* 1/1:214.

128. *KD* 1/1:217.

129. *KD* 1/1:217.

130. See Korsch, *Dialektische Theologie*, 125.

131. Ian Ramsey introduced the term "disclosure" into the theological debate at the end of the 1950s (*Models*, 9–10). The German translation "*Erschließungsgeschehen*" was coined by Eilert Herms in his lecture *Offenbarung und Wahrheit* (1984) in reference to Ramsey.

132. Jüngel, *Gott als Geheimnis*, 70. See also Richard Schaeffler, *Erfahrung als Dialog mit der Wirklichkeit*.

133. See Dalferth's reflections on "radical transcendence" of "sense-events" (*Ereignis*, 498–99).

134. *KD* 1/1:218.

not by any comprehensible reason, but by a "miracle"—the faith.[135] Only in the "security of faith . . . does mankind have and know and confirm *this* possibility of knowledge of the word of God: the possibility that laid in the word of God itself, which came to him in the word, and which is present to him in the word."[136]

Faith understood in this way has an almost transcendental function for the recognition of the word of God in Barth. "The faith . . . is the enabling of this recognition, taking place in the real recognition of the word of God."[137] But as distinguished from the transcendental categories of Kant, the faith is not a possibility lying at the disposal of mankind, it comes out of the word of God. The "act of acknowledgment" which mankind completes as a reaction to the word of God is "not as such [yet] acknowledgment of the word of God."[138] We may accept many statements, for example those about the historical person Jesus of Nazareth. But these facts will by no means have anything to do with determination of existence. Not every "accept as true" is faith in the existential sense. Faith emerges where *the word "gives* subject matter"[139] to faith. These two movements—the acknowledgment emerging from mankind and the giving-itself-as-subject matter emerging from the word—meet in the "becoming one with that which is believed, thus with Jesus Christ."[140] This becoming one "combines the actuality of the consummation of determination with the externality of the source of determination."[141]

From a linguistic perspective, two results of Barth's analysis of the process of recognition are crucial:

a. The *truth of the word of God* is evident in the sense that it opens itself independently of all experience over and above. This experience of opening itself up is, of course, an individual and contingent event, actual and inaccessible as it occurs in time and space. That separates the word of God from necessary truths in the sense of modern logic.

b. The *effect of the word of God* is to this extent peculiar as the recognition of a language act as the word of God, which has as a consequence

135. *KD* 1/1:234.

136. *KD* 1/1:236. Emphasis in original.

137. *KD* 1/1:239.

138. *KD* 1/1:242.

139. *KD* 1/1:242. Emphasis from author.

140. *KD* 1/1:253. Emphasis in original.

141. Korsch, *Barth*, 1204.

> for all mankind a comprehensive alteration (or confirmation) of his self-determination—the recipients become one with he who communicates linguistically.

In the "oneness of the divine and human *logos*," the word is recognized by mankind.[142] Recognition aligns with the one recognized. Barth calls this the *analogia fidei.*[143] "While God is present at the venue of faith, namely the self-determination of mankind, the being of mankind aligns with the being of God."[144] Therefore Barth can speak of the "God-conformity"[145] of mankind in faith. The *analogia fidei* guarantees that what is recognized as the word of God actually corresponds to the manner and essence of the word of God.[146] In recognizing the word of God, the "real reality"[147] which determines everything is demonstrated to us.

5.6. The Essence of the Word of God

The intellectual separation of the aspects "recognizability" and "essence" is surely the most significant difference between Barth's analysis of the word of God in the *KD* in contrast to his attempt five years later in the *CD*.[148] As a result, the reasoning became both more unequivocal[149] and more stringent.[150] The significance of the word for mankind, to whom it is addressed, and the provenance of the word from God are cleanly separated methodically in the *KD*. While in the *CD* the conversation is about the "reality of the word of God,"[151] in the *KD* this is "not directly thematicized but is dodged, with paraphrases of essence and recognizability."[152]

142. *KD* 1/1:255.

143. *KD* 1/1:257.

144. Korsch, *Dialektische Theologie*, 127.

145. *KD* 1/1:251.

146. *KD* 1/1:257.

147. *KD* 1/1:195.

148. See Meckenstock, *Prolegomena*, 301.

149. On this see Barth's own explanation of an existential misapprehension of the *CD* in Meckenstock, *Prolegomena*, 128–36.

150. On the methodological superiority of this distinction in comparison to the approaches of Rudolf Bultmann, Gerhard Ebeling, and Wolfhart Pannenberg, see Goebel, *Wort Gottes*, 279–81.

151. *CD*, 33 and 123–42.

152. Korsch, *Dialektische Theologie*, 124.

In our inverse presentation of Barth's analysis, this section does not correspondingly link up immediately to reflections of the preceding, but to a description of the primordial communication situation between God and man in section 5.3. This origin is decisive for possible statements on the essence of the word—not its recognizability, on whose basis only anthropological constants would be absolutized. The word of God is to be determined purely from itself outward. The motto of §5 of the *KD* contains the three inferable characteristics of the essence: "The word of God is . . . God's discourse with mankind. That is why it happens, holds, and impacts in the act of God to mankind. Just such a thing happens in the fashions of God, different from all other events, this is to say, in the mystery of God."[153]

The word of God is God's discourse, God's act, and God's mystery. With the definition of "God's discourse," the term "word" is first and foremost taken seriously. Barth explicitly shifts against a symbolic understanding: "We have . . . no occasion not to take the term 'word of God' primarily literally."[154] The three definitions are then themselves unfolded in ternary fashion by Barth.

a. To begin with, it follows from the essence property "discourse" that the word of God is of a spiritual nature—a "rational happening" in which the "reason of reason, person of the person" communicates."[155] For its communication to "us, persons of a spiritual-natural essence," the word necessarily assumes a physical, real form—it becomes a sign. It is characteristic for the word of God that this signification process—in contrast to other words—changes nothing of its form. Only in the word of God do the (spiritual) truth, thus the will of God,[156] and (natural) reality, thus the factual situation of mankind, meet one another, while "for every other word . . . the physics of its limitations [indicate] concurrently the betrayal of the impotence of its spirituality. Every other word lacks sometimes truth, other times reality, and therefore surely both."[157] In taking the word of God

153. *KD* 1/1:128.

154. *KD* 1/1:137.

155. *KD* 1/1:139.

156. On the definition of the word of God as the will of God, see *Evangelium und Gesetz*, 9.

157. *KD* 1/1:140.

seriously, "frantic idealism" and "frantic realism" are overcome.[158] In completely linguistic communication, the physical nature shows itself without loss of significance in the rational. That is, however, always an event, not a result. If the word of God is interpreted as such arbitrarily by mankind, it loses its truth. Divine truth and human reality meet one another in the word of God always in the manner of an event as *reality*.[159]

b. Alongside rationality, from the definition of the essence of the word of God as discourse, follows its personality. What this means, is that in his discourse, God shows himself as a person. Every topic of his discourse is connected to him and not to be abstracted from him. "God's word means—the speaking God."[160] Every other definition outside of his revelation in Jesus Christ would add something human to the divine. Therefore the equivalence holds: "God's word is God's Son."[161] The "personality of the word of God" does not mean "its de-wording," but it does remind us that this literality may not be depersonalized in order to be used "for construction of a human system."[162] God's word does not show itself on an abstract plane but always *concretissimum*, it cannot be separated from its sender nor from the concrete language situation.[163] Otherwise—somewhat as a general transmission of information without a personal sender—the word of God could make no contribution to the formation of human subjectivity.

c. It is precisely that which the third characteristic of discourse as understood word of God emphasizes, namely its "deliberateness,"[164] its intentionality. As *concretissimum* the word of God cannot be separated from its sender nor from its recipient. It wishes "to say to every person again and again something exceptional, expectant, directly to him and only to him."[165] It is the new, the unique, the unique

158. *KD* 1/1:140.

159. See *Evangelium und Gesetz*, 28, and Korsch, *Barth*, 1146.

160. *KD* 1/1:141.

161. *KD* 1/1:142.

162. *KD* 1/1:143.

163. *KD* 1/1:141.

164. *KD* 1/1:144.

165. *KD* 1/1:145.

which touches every individual in their existence, which stands out from the crowd of human words.[166]

The second definition of the essence of the word of God after discourse is its character as act, by which both aspects belong inseparably together. The word "happens, holds, and impacts"[167]—it is a language event.[168] Barth expresses the act character along three main lines:

a. "Contingent contemporaneousness."[169] The address which takes place in divine discourse actualizes itself over and over again as new, in that it can show itself in proclamation to mankind, occurring and transmitted in writing, *illic et tunc* and *hic et tunc*.[170] Indeed, this happens solely by the language event itself, not by any "hermeneutic art."[171]

2. "Power to rule."[172] Under this rubric Barth describes the immediate reality of the word of God, "as promise, claim, judgment, and blessing,"[173] independent of any other factors and unconditional. The promise "God with us" is fulfilled in the moment in which it is given. At the same time, listening man places himself before the divine address, he becomes "one who has been called for by God."[174] In the wake of God's judgment, he lives as a new man who stands under his "favor and protection."[175]

3. "Decision."[176] The word is not a coincidental event, but an intentional one, a "choice taking place."[177] What reads initially as a matter of course—in the end the word of God is an act of discourse—unveils itself at closer examination as a momentous insight. In the word of God, spoken in freedom, God shows himself as "real reality"[178]

166. *KD* 1/1:146.

167. *KD* 1/1:128.

168. On this see also Meyer zu Hörste-Bührer, *Gott und Menschen*, 238–39.

169. *KD* 1/1:150 [trans. Bromiley].

170. *KD* 1/1:155.

171. *KD* 1/1:153.

172. *KD* 1/1:155 [trans. Bromiley].

173. *KD* 1/1:159 [trans. Bromiley].

174. *KD* 1/1:158.

175. *KD* 1/1:158.

176. *KD* 1/1:162.

177. *KD* 1/1:163 [trans. Bromiley].

178. *KD* 1/1:195.

which differentiates itself as "uncreated reality" from the humanly perceptible creation by the fact that it is "not generally available or ascertainable."[179] It becomes merely occasional, *suo modo, sua libertate, sua misericordia*, "reality in our reality."[180]

That leads us to Barth's final definition of the essence, the description of the word of God as mystery. It shields the previous reflections from being interpreted as rigid structural features of special language acts. The qualities named are not criteria, but indices—"only signals, alarm signals."[181] The word of God is not comparable to the axioms of mathematics,[182] which together with logical rules of inference, comprise the whole system. If it acted in this way, the word of God would be at the mercy of human availability and convenience. It could then no longer function as an external basis of human self-determination which leads out from pure connectedness to the self into mankind's actuality and contingency.

Barth describes the inaccessibility of the word of God under the rubric "mystery" in three respects:[183]

a. The "worldliness" of the word means that the divine discourse encounters us in created reality and comes to consciousness solely by means of "our fallen reason."[184] It follows from both that the word of God can never mark itself off "from the rest of what happens" and therefore can always "be interpreted as a part of this other happening."[185]

b. The "one-sidedness" of the word consists in the fact that we are always only able to recognize one side of the whole from a parallax view at the moment, but never both sides simultaneously. We either perceive "the worldly form without the divine content" or the divine content "without the worldly form."[186] In analogy to the

179. *KD* 1/1:195.

180. *KD* 1/1:164.

181. *KD* 1/1:170.

182. On this see *KD* 1/1:163, and on the demarcation of theological from mathematical axioms *Das erste Gebot*, 209–10.

183. *KD* 1/1:168–94.

184. *KD* 1/1:172.

185. *KD* 1/1:171 [trans. Bromiley].

186. *KD* 1/1:182 [trans. Bromiley].

wave-particle-duality of physics, one could speak here of a content-form-duality. As soon as we analyze the one, the other fades away from us and vice versa. This trait bears the reality-constitutive function of communication reckoning. Reality is created with language; language is simultaneously part of this reality. To think of them both in one moment of observation exceeds our command of complexity. "We are able to think realistically or idealistically, but not in a Christian sense."[187]

c. The "spirituality" of the word first makes it possible for us, in faith made effective by the Spirit, "to hear the divine content of the word of God, although unfortunately only its worldly form is visible to us" and "to hear the worldly form of the word of God, although only its divine content is insightful."[188] This as well is not a "synthesis" of both manners of observation[189] because this would be to understand it as a conscious act controlled by us. It is, instead, a "justification and sanctification . . . of our thinking" that we are not able to create ourselves.[190]

In summary, from the three characteristics of the essence—discourse, act, and mystery—emerges the definition of the word of God as a communication event that expresses itself 1. linguistically, and thus symbolically, 2. always achieves its intended effect, and 3. is by necessity inexplicable in its efficacy.

The following overview is oriented on the content of the explanations in this section, so it does not consistently follow Barth's terminology. In recognizing that the mysterious character of the word is its inaccessible core, the three characteristics are arranged as overlapping concentric circles.

187. *KD* 1/1:182 [trans. Bromiley].

188. *KD* 1/1:183. See *KD* 1/1:189–90.

189. *KD* 1/1:182.

190. *KD* 1/1:183.

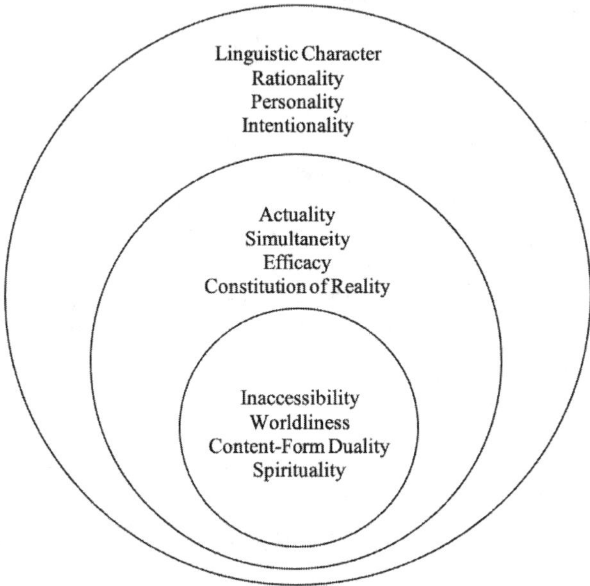

Figure 5: The Essence of the Word of God according to Karl Barth

5.7. The Threefold Form of the Word of God

With the inverse reading of the *KD*, the systematic venue of Barth's analysis of the threefold form of the word of God becomes especially significant. It presents itself as the concretization of the threefold description of the essence under the perspective of human recognizability and experienceability. The *proclaimed word* of God accentuates its linguistic nature in the reality of human discourse. The *written word* of God corresponds, to this extent, to the act character, since it records the tangible effects of divine discourse in the form of canonically fixed "testimonies." Finally, in the *revealed word* of God is shown its typical dialectic of concealment and disclosure, which turns it into a mystery.[191]

Just as the three essence aspects are inconceivable separated from one another, so does the threefold form construct a unity. The increasing emphasis of this idea can be read from Barth's terminology. In his first

191. See Meckenstock, *Prolegomena*, 301.

lecture on dogmatics from 1924, *Unterricht in der christlichen Religion*,[192] the discussion is about the "three salutations" of the word,[193] in the *CD* Barth speaks of the "three forms,"[194] and finally in the *KD* he speaks singularly of the "threefold form."[195] The three aspects establish "directly in the ineluctable differentiation"[196] the unity of the word of God. They stand, on the one hand, in a genetic and logical context of justification. The revealed word has a "constitutive significance" for the written word[197] that for its part enables and legitimizes the proclaimed word.[198]

On the other hand, the aspects stand in an inverse context of recognition. Only the proclaimed word can be experienced humanly, to the extent that it rests on the written word and, in there, the revealed word is shown.[199] This double relational structure certainly allows for an ordinal relationship, but "no differentiation of level or value."[200] There is "no *prius* or *posterius*, no *maius* or *minus*."[201]

The differentiation of the word permits a more precise analysis of the three linguistic aspects of communication between God and mankind. With the proclaimed and written word, orality and scribality stand in focus, while the revealed word shifts the focus to the event character of the language event.

5.7.1 The Proclaimed Word

Proclamation is a "region of human discourse,"[202] which occurs with a specific claim and is stamped with specific expectations.[203] This holds true for many language acts—but what is special about this language act is that its

192. On this title inspired by John Calvin's *Institutio*, see Reiffen, *Vorwort*, VII-VIII.

193. See *Unterricht* 1, 18–19.

194. *CD*, 58.

195. *KD* 1/1:89. Admittedly this is only valid for the heading. In the text Barth speaks further on of the "three forms" (see for example *KD* 1/1:124).

196. Korsch, *Barth*, 1201.

197. *KD* 1/1:105.

198. *KD* 1/1:103.

199. *KD* 1/1:124.

200. *KD* 1/1:124.

201. *Unterricht* 1, 19.

202. *KD* 1/1:94.

203. *KD* 1/1:89.

success is tied to conditions which lie beyond those speaking. It does not extend to wanting or supposing proclamation—proclamation occurs while the word of God gains an object. Barth compares this event with the sacramental consecration. No convention lends earthly things a new meaning, but it is God's actual activity which brings about a "new form."[204]

Barth describes the specific features of the communication act of proclamation with the aid of four conditions which he describes as "concentric circles"[205] from outside going inside. Proclamation is

1. assigned and not initiated by those speaking (occasion)
2. issue-related and not based on feeling (object)
3. true, but not irreducible (judgment)
4. contingent and not causally enforceable (event).[206]

On 1. Since proclamation becomes "real proclamation,"[207] its motivation may not be solely communication of facts, convictions, or moral value judgments. Only "God's positive commission"[208] is decisive "which we can only simply receive and in the act of receiving, have, which simply touches us and the whole world of our motivations from outside, it cancels and provides."[209]

Here, the discussion of "commission" is misleading to this extent because we can do no other than comply with the divine order within the framework of our possibilities, as soon as we "believe to have heard it"[210] as such. As a result, Barth avoids all terms which take the perspective of mankind and thus could have him appear as the subject of the activity. That does not mean, however, that this perspective does not exist at all. Here one could speak of "emotion" in the sense of an experience of self-transcendence[211] without making the passive role of mankind any stronger, as Barth intended.

204. *KD* 1/1:90.
205. *KD* 1/1:90.
206. See *KD* 1/1:90–97, and Korsch, *Barth*, 1200.
207. *KD* 1/1:90.
208. *KD* 1/1:91.
209. *KD* 1/1:92.
210. *KD* 1/1:92.
211. On this see Joas, *Braucht der Mensch Religion?* 17.

On 2. The object of proclamation, God's word, is not an object of human contemplation, but it must be graphic in its proclamation. All contents which lend themselves to be said in other ways—for instance in the form of scientific sentences, artistic objects, or political speeches—withdraw in favor of proclamation. It is not about proofs, aesthetic forms of expression, or weighing arguments. God's word as an object of proclamation manifests itself in promises, indeed in "promise of future revelation on the basis of revelation that has already taken place."[212]

On 3. The third circle includes the question of validity of proclamation, the judgment as to whether it is true or false. In this short and dense paragraph Barth discusses the epistemological status of the word of God and simultaneously makes known his understanding of language. The truth of sentences does not depend only on "the essence of their object," but "also on the situation and concerns of the one speaking."[213] For the 1930s, this is an unusually modern rejection of an understanding of language as reflection of extralinguistic reality. Here truth is described as successful communication.

In the case of proclamation of the word of God we have to do, in slang terms, with a teammate in the communication event about whose "situation" and "concerns" we have no information. As a consequence, the proof for the truth of proclamation with human criteria must remain principally incomplete. The verdict on this stems from a "fundamental from-elsewhere."[214] The truth of the proclaimed word can only be evident to us without proof—and "while we acknowledge it as the word of God."[215]

On 4. Finally, in the central fourth circle, the word of God is described as the event that makes proclamation ultimately into a "real proclamation" in the presence of all other conditions.[216] This cannot be achieved from the human side alone, it is "God's own doing," an inexplicable "miracle."[217] Naturally not in the form that "naked, divine reality" would bring into a "gap" in human reality.[218] True proclamation is rather

212. *KD* 1/1:93 [trans. Bromiley].

213. *KD* 1/1:94.

214. *KD* 1/1:94.

215. *KD* 1/1:94.

216. *KD* 1/1:95.

217. *KD* 1/1:95.

218. *KD* 1/1:96.

to be understood as analogous to the incarnation. The "divine desire and achievement" occurs as a "human event."[219] The result is entirely divine and entirely human at the same time: "human discourse before God, in which and through which God speaks about himself."[220]

As Barth's image insinuates, with its four concentric circles, the four aspects of the connection between the word of God and its proclamation cannot be separated. The word of God, then, is not a timelessly valid series of signs detachable from an historical event—like, for example, mathematical truths—but a contingent communication event which has an occasion, a content, and an effect. It can realize itself in an oral language event—proclamation—if certain conditions are satisfied. Some of these have been discussed in this section. In his further reasoning, Barth expands and concretizes this approach.

5.7.2. The Written Word

Barth's reflections on the written word start off with the object definition of proclamation as promise of present revelation in remembrance of past revelation.[221] This section concerns itself with the essence of the remembrance intended here.

Firstly, Barth retires a Platonically understood anamnesis, an explanation of "recollection" as "actualization of an immanent revelation germinal to the existence of every human being."[222] God is not revealed to man immanently—and also not in hidden or forgotten form.[223] Barth concedes that this possibility definitely persists. The human "relationship to the eternal and absolute" is the "most central and momentous part of that, of the timeless, essential state of man himself."[224]

Here Barth comes surprisingly close to Friedrich Schleiermacher's "sense and taste for the eternal,"[225] as well as to the classic authors of the

219. *KD* 1/1:96.

220. *KD* 1/1:97.

221. *KD* 1/1:93.

222. *KD* 1/1:101.

223. *KD* 1/1:102.

224. *KD* 1/1:102 [trans. Bromiley].

225. See Schleiermacher, *Über die Religion*, 212.

theology of religious experience like William James[226] and Rudolf Otto.[227] Then comes the U-turn in Barth's reasoning. The free God has made no use of this—empirically given—possibility, but "it has pleased God" to reveal himself "otherwise than in pure immanence,"[228] namely in concrete historical events. The canon of holy scriptures reports on these in the form of testimonies. This concept is central to Barth's understanding of canon and language. Following the line of reasoning in the *KD*, the uniqueness of this "testimony" as articulation of a transcendent experience will be expanded upon in the following section on the revealed word. At this point it should be noted for the record: Testimony is the linguistically formulated remembrance of God's revelation.[229]

With the acknowledgment of the attested revelations in the Bible as *κανών*, as standard, ecclesiastical proclamation commits itself to specific, non-interchangeable contents. These can also not be reduced in their form or, by the smoothing over of supposed contradictions, to general theological principles. The preachers of the present day stand at the end of a series founded by "Jeremiah and Paul," a prophetic-apostolic succession of preachers all with the same "work assignment."[230] The canonicity of holy scriptures is not legitimized by its originator or its provenance (it is "a human document like any other"),[231] but by its function in the communication event between God and mankind. It witnesses to the word of God in the language of mankind, who has "longed for it, awaited it, and hoped for it and finally, in Jesus Christ, saw it, heard it, and touched it."[232] Thereby it enables the actualization of the divine answer to questioning mankind:[233] "Immanuel! God with us!"[234]

226. See James, *Vielfalt*, 89.

227. See Otto, *Das Heilige*, 11.

228. *KD* 1/1:103.

229. *KD* 1/1:114.

230. *KD* 1/1:104.

231. *Biblische Fragen*, 674.

232. *KD* 1/1:110.

233. On this see *Biblische Fragen*, 671–73.

234. *KD* 1/1:110.

The process of constant interaction with the "self-imposing,"[235] and thus self-prevailing canon[236] can only remain vivid if it is set in writing: "Insofar as it has pleased God to make the unwritten, intellectual-oral tradition into the canon of his church, then there would be so little to differentiate the canon from the life of the church, just as we are able to differentiate some of the blood of our forefathers coursing through our veins from our own blood."[237] The connection to something unchanging of higher "originality"[238] prevents the church from becoming a monologue in proclamation.

At least with regard to the New Testament, this description of the perpetual correction function of the historically evolved canon is a thoroughly modern interpretation of Protestant *sola scriptura*. The "principle that underlies its origin," as Jens Schröter writes on the New Testament, "does not consist in defining a theological norm by means of which Scripture will be judged, but by the combination of the apostolic testimonies to faith and its demarcation from later 'falsifications' in order to preserve the connection of Christian faith to its origins."[239] In the same fashion Jörg Lauster stresses: "The articulation executions [in the biblical writings] contain the special formative power . . . by their historical anchoring. From the viewpoint of future generations, they present the first fixed written expressions of transcendental experiences which are formative for Christianity."[240]

Naturally, the transition from oral to written transmission was in no way as distinct[241] as Barth obviously thought it was in the 1930s, and as the Nestle-Aland edition of the Greek New Testament conveys, with its

235. Wolf Krötke supposes correctly that the famous U-turn has a model in Johann Wolfgang Goethe's *Italienische Reise* (Körtner, *Schriftwerdung*, 126)—not within a description of Rome, of course, but the amphitheater in Verona (Goethe, *Italienische Reise*, 40).

236. *KD* 1/1:110.

237. *KD* 1/1:107.

238. *KD* 1/2:600

239. Schröter, *Jesus*, 275. In Schröter's view this changes nothing about the discussion of the New Testament Apocrypha. The extracanonical Jesus traditions—inclusive of the Gospel of Thomas!—lead back to "controversies of the second and third centuries" (Schröter, *Jesus*, 277) although here, of course, even older traditions would have been accepted.

240. Lauster, *Prinzip*, 451.

241. Schröter, *Jesus*, 294.

ideal of an historical *Urtext*.[242] Rather, one must go out from the synchronous coexistence of different narrative traditions and text versions in the first two centuries, which nevertheless indicate a coherence of content and language.[243] The "productive tension"[244] between the diversity of early Christian "closer to the source"[245] memoirs and the evolution of *one* standard theology proved itself strong enough to exclude, for example, the docetic, gnostic, and montanist alternatives of interpretation.[246] Right in its formation process, that later canon consolidated itself for the early Christian faith communities into an effective means of "repression of variance" of interpretation and against "loss of meaning by entropy," as Jan Assmann describes the genesis of the main medium.[247]

The precondition for a productive dialogue between canon and proclamation, according to Barth, is free exegesis. The interpretation of biblical texts is "to be deregulated from all sides"—no theological nor ecclesiastical instance may intrude here, not on account of freedom of thought, but freedom of the Bible.[248] Barth's skepticism is expressed in this demand as to whether or not scientific exegesis can supply in any way an essential contribution to the understanding of scripture: "The canonical text already, as text, has the character of a free power and the church need not do anything about any exegesis, and if it were the best at making the difference between text and commentary clear anew, the text to speak anew impartially, in order to experience the sovereignty of this free power."[249] What goes for the proclaimed word goes also for the written word. Its becoming-God's-word is to be understood as an event whose occurrence does not lie in our power. We do not reach for the Bible, the Bible reaches for us.[250]

This idea of methodologically untethered interpretation earned Barth a great deal of criticism, especially in connection with his own

242. On this see also Aland/Aland, *Text*, 284: "Only one reading can be the original, even though many variants may have existed in one place." On criticism of this position see Parker, *Living Text*.

243. See Schröter, *Jesus*, 294.

244. Schröter, *Jesus*, 376.

245. On the term "closer to the source," see Lauster, *Entzauberung*, 50–54.

246. See Schröter, *Jesus*, 366–67. In a similar vein Theißen, *Religion*, 367.

247. Assmann, *Gedächtnis*, 123.

248. *KD* 1/1:109.

249. *KD* 1/1:110.

250. *KD* 1/1:112.

exegesis practice in the *KD*. The accusations range from a selective and faulty use of exegetical methods[251] through a "free-floating re-narrative handling of the Bible"[252] to the verdict that Barth pursued[253] the "reversion to dogmatic, pre-critical Bible exegesis in the realm of systematic theology."[254] In view of the abundance of advances in historical-critical methodology in the *KD*,[255] this last criticism is certainly unjustified. As Hans-Joachim Kraus, with a view to acknowledging the digested secondary literature on Barth, writes: "One can only name one single dogmatics in which historical-critical research with its exegetical benefits experienced such an empathetic effect and that is Barth's."[256]

Barth is not concerned with the holy scriptures as an historical witness to Near Eastern or Anatolian culture, but with the object which makes scripture into a canon: the testimonies of successful communication between God and mankind. In its "form of the human word"[257] the Bible must obviously be explained and interpreted[258]—but "as the word of God it needs, of course, no explanation."[259] "The Holy Spirit surely knows what it said to the prophets and apostles and what it wants to say to us through them. This clarity, which Scripture as God's word has in itself, its objective *perspicuitas*, falls under no human responsibility or effort. . . . All explanation of Scripture for which we are responsible can only be undertaken subsequently to ensure that Scripture as the word of God is clear in itself."[260]

Since Barth sees only the object which makes the Bible into a canon—the divine word—he demands a "priority of exegesis over methodology."[261] He turns against "an approach to the texts that has noth-

251. See for example Bächli, *Das Alte Testament*, 175 and 235.

252. Lauster, *Entzauberung*, 94.

253. A survey of the reception of Barth's exegesis is offered by Bergner, *Um der Sache willen*, 319–20. Also eye-opening is the repartee between Wolf Krötke and Michael Trowitzsch in Beintker/Link/Trowitzsch, *Karl Barth*, 471–74.

254. Ulrich Barth, *Protestantismus*, 198.

255. See the meritorious list of Gerhard Bergner in his *Um der Sache willen*, 322–26.

256. Kraus, *Vorwort*, 8.

257. *KD* 1/2:799.

258. *KD* 1/2:798.

259. *KD* 1/2:798–99.

260. *KD* 1/2:799.

261. Smend, *Barth*, 245.

ing to do with them"[262] and employs indifferent methods. In this way his famous dictum is to be understood: "The historical-critical school must be more critical of me!"[263] Scientific exegesis has a predominantly heuristic function for contemporary proclamation of the divine word. The *sensus* must serve the *usus*, "the meaning of the *explicatio* is the *applicatio*."[264] Communication does not succeed when the contents are dissected, but succeeds when the speech act is understood as a whole.

If we are unable to recognize God in conversation with ourselves, in inward contemplation, in the "homecoming to ourselves,"[265] we are referred to an external impulse—"God's word." This impulse can appear to us most clearly in linguistically communicated form where other people are discussing similar impulses: in the books of the Old and New Testaments. The model for all revelation is the certainty of "God with us," whose strongest image is Jesus Christ. How this transference of happening revelation to happened revelation is to be grasped conceptually forms the theme of the following section.

5.7.3. The Revealed Word

In Barth, the central concept which conflates divine revelation and human language is "bearing witness." On the one hand, it is the hinge between biblical writings and the experiences they describe, and on the other hand it is the bridge from historical revelations to present and future revelations. Here we will consider the first aspect.

The Bible is not "itself and in itself God's . . . revelation," but "witnessed" revelation. "Witness means: to point in a particular direction beyond oneself to another. Witness is therefore service to this other, in which the witness vouches for the truth of this other, service which consists in reference to this other."[266] Barth stresses in many variants this reference function to the other and impressively describes Matthias Grünewald's painting of the crucifixion with the long pointer finger of John indicating

262. Trowitzsch, *Hermeneutik*, 163.

263. *Römerbrief, zweite Fassung*, 14.

264. *KD* 1/2:989.

265. *KD* 1/1:111.

266. *KD* 1/1:114.

the crucified one,[267] a reproduction of which hung in Barth's study.[268] The actual solution of the phrase "bearing witness" threatens to stay, however, in the shadows. When one comprehends "bearing witness" as a language act and inquires after its essential rules, one can state:

1. Precondition for bearing witness is a particular experience that was witnessed. Whoever makes a statement about something not experienced and calls this "bearing witness," that person witnessed nothing, and lies. One must discern a *false* witness—for example, based on a fallacious memory.
2. In bearing witness an experience is formulated linguistically. More so: through linguistic articulation a particular group of events in the stream of sensory data is first generated as a singular experience, communicable and—that is as a rule the overriding meaning of bearing witness—made comparable with other textually worded observations.
3. As distinguished from "claiming," the witness vouches for the truth of their statement with their entire credibility.[269] As Paul Ricœur formulated it, in "bearing witness" certainty and conscience interface to the highest "epistemic instance."[270] Between witness and proof "a categorical difference cannot be kept up."[271]

When one, with Barth, comprehends the biblical writings as bearing witness to divine effects, these observations may be interpreted as follows:

1. The canon does not confront mankind with abstract reflections, but tells of concrete observations which were experienced as God's actions.
2. This experience constitutes itself first in its formulation. As Barth emphasizes, there are no "facts standing somewhere *behind* the texts," in the biblical writings "form and content" are not to be separated.[272]

267. *KD* 1/1:115.

268. See Busch, *Leidenschaft*, 15.

269. See *KD* 1/2:913–14. On the difference between "claiming" and "bearing witness" in religious discourse see also Fischer, *Behaupten*, especially 237–38.

270. See Ricœur, *Selbst*, 33–34.

271. Reichel, *Theologie*, 281.

272. *KD* 1/2:545.

3. Whoever formulates such an experience as "bearing witness" expresses thereby the unconditional and (by any other observation) unshakable significance which he attributes to this experience, and thereby to the interpretation of this observation.

Understood in this way, the Barthian concept of bearing witness explains the religious content of the holy scriptures, similarly transparent like the experiential-theological concept of interpretation as it was brought into the theological discussion by Alfred Ritschl,[273] unfolded by Matthias Jung,[274] and has presently been taken up by, for example, Ulrich Barth,[275] Dietrich Korsch,[276] and Jörg Lauster.[277] The notion that there is a pure religious experience without interpretation from which one could cut away, as it were, linguistic or other forms of articulation, in the capacity of analysis, is labeled by Jung as "experiential positivism."[278] An experience is always an experience *of* someone—and this subjective participation arises through the expression of affective moods and observations in a system of signs.[279]

Jörg Lauster writes that "experience is always interpreted processing of observation."[280] Only then can an observation become a religious experience, when it is comprehended as such linguistically or symbolically with the aid of appropriate offers of interpretation.[281] For this, the canon of the Bible provides "sediments of earlier executions of articulation,"[282] with whose help new experiences can be prefigured in the same language game. God is not to be had without the word of God—and this word "is not a symbol"[283] but a phenomenon of human language.

273. See Ulrich Barth, *Theoriedimensionen*, 40.

274. Jung, *Erfahrung*.

275. See Ulrich Barth, *Theoriedimensionen*.

276. See Korsch, *Religionsbegriff*, 219–62.

277. See Lauster, *Entzauberung* as well as his *Prinzip* and his *Religion*.

278. Jung, *Erfahrung*, 306.

279. It is possible that this is the more profound insight which underlies the, at first glance, contradictory descriptions of the perceptions of Paul's companions at his Christophany in Acts 9:7 (they see nothing) and 22:9 (they hear nothing). If only one of them has it, whether it is the observation (see) or the system of signs (hear), then he experiences nothing.

280. Lauster, *Religion*, 24.

281. On this see as a whole Lauster, *Religion*, 23–25.

282. Jung, *Erfahrung*, 263.

283. *KD* 1/1:137.

Religious testimonies or interpretations differentiate themselves from others by the fact that they "interpret the finite connotations of life according to their unconditional meaning."[284] This aligns with thesis 3 above. Those bearing witness, those interpreting, "have no choice but to evaluate and interpret what they experience as something extrasensory, infinite, and transcendent."[285]

The understanding of this "have no other choice"—logically equivalent to "must"—is the point at which the Barthian "bearing witness" and the modern, experiential-theological "interpret," in certain circumstances, separate again. Is this "must" explicable principally anthropologically and without connection to a reason which lies beyond mankind—or is it to be understood with Barth in the sense of 1 Corinthians 9:16 (NRSV): "If I proclaim the gospel, this gives me no ground for boasting, for an obligation is laid on me?"[286] Posed differently: is the connection to the transcendent finally a potential which dwells within man, a sort of "religious apriori"[287]—or do such interpretations come forth because they are "demanded by another?"[288]

Barth's approach to the word of God here can only lead to the option of "genuine transcendence,"[289] which owes nothing to anthropological constants. Nevertheless his vote for the divine revelation in the word of man is in no way a "violent infantilization of the concept of God,"[290] but differentiates itself from a naïve positivism of revelation precisely in the fact that "the revelation is comprehended as a semiotic process" which God, present only as one absent, allows to be.[291] Revelation is "linguistically structured as good news," that is, "God sees to it that his word is presented in the abiding form of testimonies and is readable for us."[292] This idea is thoroughly compatible with a modern understanding of language and religion.

284. Ulrich Barth, *Theoriedimensionen*, 76.

285. Lauster, *Entzauberung*, 34.

286. *KD* 1/1:114.

287. In *KD* 1/1:201, Barth takes a different position to this term introduced by Ernst Troeltsch (see Korsch, *Apriori*).

288. *KD* 1/1:115.

289. *Wort Gottes*, 161.

290. Lauster, *Entzauberung*, 22.

291. Moxter, *Kultur*, 269.

292. Reichel, *Theologie*, 243.

This also holds especially for the second aspect of the term "bearing witness," the bridging from happening to happened revelation. If one considers that "all being revealed is becoming revealed,"[293] that the word of God is then only actually realized, then this also holds for the revelation in the written word, that it is not conserved in this form for all time, but occurs always anew in the reception. "What happens in the sphere of time and visibility, happens in concrete life . . . that becoming observed of the presence of the word of God as a human word of the prophets and apostles, that is indeed to be understood as a repetition, a secondary renewal and continuation of the unique and primary event of the revelation itself."[294] This repetition makes us "contemporaries of Jesus Christ, with closed or open or squinting eyes, whether passive or active," we are "immediate witnesses of his activity."[295] In no way, then, is the Bible itself revelation—contrary to the "mechanical doctrine of verbal inspiration" of "hyperorthodoxy"[296]—but can only contingently become revelation in an act of divine grace.[297]

With "repetition," Barth did not intend at most an authentic recreation of the experiences witnessed to in Scripture, consummated in the imagination of readers—that would be, in the end, not a "continuation" of the revelation event. It is, rather, the contribution of the recipients to the understanding of the text, to which the situational dependence of the revelation also contributes. Barth invites us to "knock on the gate of the biblical texts desiring entry" and not "to sit across from them lazily."[298] In this context, "revelation" means that the attempt of acquisition of the text does not lead to a compelling result—in this sense always remaining inaccessible. In the end, for Barth it is the text which opens itself "from within" to the knocking of the readers. But what is opened up in this moment is a religious option of interpretation for the individual living environment of the recipients, in Barth's words: the "presence of the word of God *in our own presence*!"[299] The content of the word of God is a *concretissimum*, it has "something unique to say to every person, again and

293. *KD* 1/1:122.

294. *KD* 1/2:593.

295. *KD* 4/3:419.

296. *KD* 1/1:115.

297. *KD* 1/1:116.

298. *KD* 1/2:593.

299. *KD* 1/2:592. Author's emphasis.

again, directly to him and thus concerns only him."[300] "What is said by God to me is, what is also said from somebody to somebody else, that I cannot place in a row with others, not even in first place in the row. Otherwise it is just not from *God*, not to *me*, not *said*."[301]

The process in which the written word becomes the revealed word is consequently one initiated by mankind itself, and its successful conclusion, of course, an existential being-spoken-to through the accompanying "call,"[302] cannot be guaranteed by him.[303] Ulrich Körtner reports that "the inspiration of Scripture," this "pioneering approach" to the reformulation of the scriptural principle, "is first completed in the act of reading."[304]

The productive role of readers for understanding the text, which is implied by Barth's remarks, coincides with the insights of reception aesthetics as it was developed by Wolfgang Iser in the 1990s[305] and was made fruitful by Lauster for experiential-theological hermeneutics.[306] Just as Barth excluded "facts standing *behind* the texts" in biblical writings,[307] so Iser turns against all treatments which look for "the supposed message *behind* the texts."[308] According to Iser, "interpretations of literary texts are generated first and foremost in the process of reading. They are the product of interaction between the text and the reader."[309] In the "constant stream of images," which the sensory perception of the text in consciousness sets in motion, the reader registers his "attitudes, expectations, and anticipations" and thereby constitutes the "meaning."[310] This process is not capricious but is inspired by linguistic, textual, and formal impulses in the text. The result is cooperation between text and recipient in such a way, that "the reception of the text in the imagination of the reader provides forms of expression and symbolic models of interpretation which

300. *KD* 1/1:145.

301. *Menschenwort*, 435.

302. *KD* 1/1:209.

303. In Lauster's critique of Barth's doctrine of the written word (see *Prinzip*, 275) the part of the readers is seen as too passive (also in Bergner, *Sache*, 60).

304. Körtner, *Schriftwerdung*, 119.

305. See above all Iser, *Akt*.

306. See Lauster, *Prinzip*, 423–25 and Lauster, *Religion*, 74–75.

307. *KD* 1/2:545. Emphasis in original.

308. Lauster, *Prinzip*, 424. Emphasis in original.

309. Iser, *Appellstruktur*, 229.

310. "*Sinngestalt*." Iser, *Lesevorgang*, 260 and 264–65.

first allow him to interpret his own environmental observations and experience in their meaning."[311]

Transferred to the canon of biblical writings, it follows that the "past forms of expression of transcendent experiences" preserved therein by reading "become applicable to one's own environment" and thus "constitute religious experience."[312] Or, to speak again as Barth might, it enables "the presence of the word of God in our own presence"[313] to be opened. At this point the dimension of personality with which Barth characterized the linguistic nature of the word of God proves itself (see section 5.6). It singles out that the formation of human subjectivity is always grounded on personally transmitted communication, and not in some way on processes of standardized transmission of information.

One could make the objection to this parallelization of experiential-theological and revelatory-theological interpretation that in the first case, despite similar forms of expression, individual interpretations could turn out to be quite different, while Barth knows only *one* revelation. Also, under "future revelation," there is "no other to be understood . . . as the one which occurred once and for all time."[314] Still, the content of the revelation, to Barth, is not a specific statement, not a "general truth,"[315] but an existential guarantee of the fundamental question of mankind (see section 5.3): the assurance "God with us,"[316] which is tangible in Jesus Christ. The canon of the New Testament bears witness to this—and this "witness to God's revelation" is the sole reason for its authority.[317] In Lauster the same idea reads as so: "A theological significance belongs to the Bible insofar as it is able to make present the person Jesus Christ, not on account of itself."[318]

From this reflection forward, Barth accentuates the *simultaneity* with Jesus Christ differently than Søren Kierkegaard,[319] to whom this

311. Lauster, *Prinzip*, 452.

312. Lauster, *Prinzip*, 453.

313. *KD* 1/2:592.

314. *KD* 1/1:123.

315. *KD* 1/1:145.

316. *KD* 1/1:123.

317. *KD* 1/2:506.

318. Lauster, *Entzauberung*, 30.

319. Kierkegaard, *Philosophische Brosamen*, 84–85, and the classifying presentation in Hofmann, *Søren Kierkegaard*, 68–77.

term is traced back.[320] *Christus pro nobis praesens*[321] dissolves all limits of time because he embodies the *timelessly valid* "God with us." It is not about the "historicizing of the eternal" and the "eternalizing of the historical," as it is in Kierkegaard's *Philosophische Brosamen*,[322] but the "completely divine actuality," which means the "relativization of all other time."[323] Kairos conquers chronos;[324] "in the stream of becoming . . . in the middle of the ocean of incompleteness, the fulfilled time" appears as a "self-contained event."[325]

What the perpetuated event character of revelation means for the proclaimed and written word, Barth explains as a three-fold dissolution. Proclamation and Scripture are *distinguished* from the divine act in their interpretation, *limited* in their effect by their insufficiency as human works, and finally *preserved* in their validity.[326] The written and proclaimed word are God's word to the extent that they *become* it in Kairos by the revelation, while the revealed word of God becomes a linguistic (and thus humanly communicated) word of God, because it *is* revelation.[327] The "revealed word of God" is therefore actually a pleonasm while in the "written" and "proclaimed word of God" the same must first be recognized as concordance of human language and content of reality. This remains an individual event because it is only completed when the word becomes the reason for human self-determination (see section 5.4).

This event, this "unveiling of the veiled,"[328] is in its entirety a divine act which nevertheless functions by human communication and therefore as "indirect communication":[329] synchronically in oral proclamation,

320. Lauster's critique of "simultaneity" in *Religion*, 103 would therefore be differentiated.

321. *KD* 4/1:321.

322. Kierkegaard, *Philosophische Brosamen*, 75. The way in which Kierkegaard understands the simultaneity with Jesus Christ in concrete historical terms is shown by his examples in *Einübung*, 51–99.

323. *KD* 1/1:119.

324. See Mark 1:15: "The time is fulfilled, and the kingdom of God has come near."

325. *KD* 1/1:119.

326. *KD* 1/1:121.

327. *KD* 1/1:121.

328. *KD* 1/1:122.

329. On this term see Kierkegaard, *Einübung*, 147–48. Barth uses the expression for the first time in *Römerbrief, zweite Fassung*, 15, and is central to his *Unterricht* 1:177, 185–86, and 197.

diachronically in written testimony. As Barth says in his first lecture on dogmatics, "the shining light of revelation makes the medium transparent. But it remains the medium."[330]

5.8. Summary

Barth's enormously diverse analysis of the word God is based on two assumptions: a) theology is the formation of theories about religious communication,[331] and b) religious communication succeeds where an all-determining—in Barth's words "true"[332] or "real"[333]—reality articulates itself.[334] The point of contact of reality and (human) linguistic nature is to be understood as the word of God. As such, the word of God is an element of both realms. On the one hand, linguistically, meaning for mankind always tangible in the sense of an event in a concrete language event. On the other hand, it is a component part of reality, meaning of constitutive—existential—significance for world-relation and self-relation.

In one aspect, the equivalence of linguistic nature and reality remains, in Barth, not a theoretical postulate, but is totally and concretely named. Jesus Christ is the one word of God—in fact as the name "Jesus—Christ" expresses the relationship between God and mankind in exactly the same fashion as that message which is verifiable by the testimonies to the historical Jesus of Nazareth. Jesus is the Christ, God has become man, God is with us. The word of God is a proper name[335] and at the same time "the announcement in which God makes himself known to us."[336]

Seen in linguistic terms, this is a stroke of genius from Barth, since by this a "relationship of determination" becomes a "paradigm of

330. *Unterricht* 2, 20.

331. See *Menschlichkeit*, 19. On this see also Korsch, *Aufgabe*, 279.

332. *KD* 1/1:195.

333. *Römerbrief, erste Fassung*, 88 and throughout.

334. *KD* 1/1:48–49.

335. See *KD* 2/2:102, where Barth speaks with reference to Rev 19:13 of a "designation" at which point "something or someone completely other ought to become visible." See also *KD* 4/1:3: "It may be instructive to take into account that this 'God with us' is the translation of the strange name Immanuel, which appears three times [in] Isaiah 7:14, 8:8, and 8:10, in order then, according to Matt 1:21–22, to find its 'fulfillment' in the name of Jesus."

336. *KD* 2/2:104.

theological discourse generally."[337] The old problem of Augustine as to how do linguistic signs and meaning correlate, is resolved christologically. The word of God refers, on the one hand, to the bearer of the name as proper name, and on the other hand is understood as a language event which places mankind in true reality, namely God's presence. For "God with us" includes the "Us with God"[338] as our "most real being."[339] The word of God enables us to create a relationship to God, to the world, and to one another in its linguistic nature and its constitution of reality.[340] Here the word of God achieves the function of a "principle (singular) fact"[341]—a fact that turns out to be a particular language event.

If we grasp the statement of the proper name as a performative language event, as a name-giving, then the word of God is to be understood as a double language act in which "naming" and "promising" (of God's presence) generate exactly both of the quantities whose intersection is the word of God itself—language and reality. The creative power of divine discourse—but also the function of language—cannot be conceived as anything greater. Consequently, Barth recommends as the most reasonable translation of John 1:1a: "In the beginning was the saying."[342]

From this point forward the word of God permeates all communication, all linguistic regions. The words of our language "are not ours, but its property."[343] Only when we take the loan of language and "apply [it] to God" is it "led back to its original substance and thereby its truth."[344] It follows that "it could and must be so" that "all human discourse . . . is discourse about God."[345] All linguistic understanding would refer back to this—if the coming-up-for-conversation were a human affair: "Among us humans how does it come to a communication of this 'God with us?' That is the question which we could answer while we say the entirety now again, concretely as it is said in the midst of the Christian message. Right on its concrete expression as such depends everything here: the

337. Maurer, *Sprache*, 166.

338. *KD* 4/1:13.

339. *KD* 4/1:14.

340. See Korsch, *Einführung*, 31: "*To have language* and *to live in relationships* belong intuitively together. Language is precisely this: establishing relationships."

341. Korsch, *Dialektische Theologie*, 172.

342. *KD* 2/2:104.

343. *KD* 2/1:259.

344. *KD* 2/1:259.

345. *KD* 1/1:47.

entire truth and reality of its narrative and thus also the whole mystery of communication of this fact."[346]

In other words, this reality-creating "God with us" must again and again be formulated concretely anew and as an address of mankind. This occurs in the effective radius which Barth described as the "three-fold form of the word of God." Here is placed a third language act alongside the initial language acts of "naming" and "promising," which creates the connection to the human world of experience: "bearing witness." Since therein remains "God the agent," despite human speaking, the light of knowledge of reality—Luther's "*nova sprach*"—appears only as an event.

How close Barth came to linguistic analytical philosophy, which he himself did not notice,[347] will be shown in chapter 6, in which the innovative language insights of the three Christian theologians dealt with here will collectively be connected to recent philosophy of language.

346. *KD* 4/1:16.

347. In his archived library, whose contents can be viewed at http://aleph.unibas.ch/ (search by keyword "KBA"), none of the works of philosophy of language pertinent to that time are to be found. The only reference to "Bertrand Russell" leads to the pamphlet "Into the tenth decade" which deals with Russell's pacifism, not with his theory of language (telephone call on 1 December 2017).

6

Systematic Results

6.1. Preliminary Remarks

If the "word of God" should be more than an age-old metaphor that sometimes illustrates this aspect and sometimes that aspect, it must be possible to present, in systematic form, the linguistic character of divine revelation expressed therein. Even a cursory review of biblical word of God concepts reveals a contentual cohesiveness (see chapter 2). The five approaches identified showed different accentuation of an interpretation of reality that is of existential significance for the recipients of the word. If God is "the reality that determines everything,"[1] his word in our language gives us the key to assimilation of this reality.

This general statement can be grasped much more precisely. Augustine, Luther, and Barth illuminated expanding horizons of problems in linguisticality. While the bishop of Hippo thought through the signification process, we are indebted to Luther for important insights into the religious interpretation potential of language, as well as to Barth for his analysis of the concrete language event in which the divine word is passed on by mankind. These three approaches, which embrace semiotics, semantics, and pragmatics, carry the present chapter forward in dialogue with modern philosophy of language. The objective of this is to describe in greater detail the productivity of the word of God for human assimilation of reality.

1. Bultmann, *Welchen Sinn*, 26.

In each case, the sections are constructed the same: a recapitulation of the essential ideas followed by the reconstruction and finally the summary. The original themes are mildly transformed by the reconstruction. Thinking further with Augustine and semiotics leads to a normative, attitude-changing aspect of every language event (section 6.2), thinking further with Luther and religious semantics leads to the question of how mankind brings God into language (section 6.3), and thinking further with Barth and pragmatics culminates in the question of where God himself comes up in discussion (6.4). The final section summarizes the results as a look back at theological paths of thought and a look forward at the actual relevance of the word of God for human communication in religious and secular contexts.

6.2. Augustine's Theme: The Word as Sign

6.2.1. Recapitulation

Chapter 3 attempted to trace the development Augustine underwent in his posing of the question of how the divine word can be expressed in principally deficient human language. The impression of deficiency is grounded on Augustine's starting point from a picture theory of language, which in its briefest form sounds like this: words are signs for things. In that sense they are merely placeholders, they cannot teach us anything, but only refer us to reality in which they warn us to keep our eyes open. Already in *De magistro* in this *admonitio* is heard a *vocatio*. Just this warning makes itself evident in the voice of the inner teacher—Jesus Christ—who commands mankind to learn from him.[2] In other words: without signs, no knowledge of God, no matter how inadequate these signifiers may be.

In *De trinitate* Augustine abandons the picture theory and allows words to be references, but only to the point that they indicate their own referencing—while it initially remains open as to exactly what they are referring. The semiotic triangle of real reference, mental interpretation, and sensory signs no longer explains the functioning of language (as in *De magistro*), but the "self-reference of the mind consummated in love."[3] This *verbum intimum* spoken with the heart can be better under-

2. See section 3.4.2.

3. See Augustine, *De trinitate*, IX 10,15: *Verbum est igitur . . . cum amore notitia.*

stood by the hearers the greater their commitment to and readiness for understanding. What the sign character of linguistic signifiers amounts to is only to be determined from their function within successful communication.[4] Expressed in modern terms: the significance of signs is their use in normative language behavior.

In order to highlight the context of these reflections on the word of God, the starting point and objective of Augustine's reasoning should be remembered. The linguist left behind the picture theory because no *res*, no object of reference can be found for the concept of the divine Trinity. And in the end, with the *verbum intimum*, he gained that human word "through whose similarity of any kind will see the word of God only from afar, as in a riddle."[5]

Augustine's reasoning is noteworthy in that, while setting out from a structural question, he taps into an ethical component of language. As a component part of successful communication and as it relates to the *verbum divinum*, the *verbum intimum* is by necessity true and precedes every good human act.[6]

6.2.2. Reconstruction: From Picture to Form of Life

The recapitulation of chapter 3 above consciously emphasizes the ideas which demonstrate a partially astonishing parallelism to a philosopher of language born 1,500 years later—Ludwig Wittgenstein. His understanding of language also emerged from a strict picture theory and transformed over the course of time. Up to the beginning of the 1950s, the theses posed by Wittgenstein in his *Tractatus logico-philosophicus* in 1918 remained definitive for all of linguistic-analytic philosophy: "The proposition is a picture of reality."[7] And: "The totality of propositions is the language."[8] Testimony to facts would unequivocally align with this picture theory, possibly in the form of an "elementary proposition" whose uniqueness consists in the fact that "no elementary proposition can contradict it."[9] For every event in "reality" there is definitely an adequate

4. See section 3.5.
5. Augustine, *De trinitate*, XV 11,20.
6. Augustine, *De trinitate*, XV 11,20.
7. Wittgenstein, *Tractatus* 4.01 [trans. Ogden].
8. Wittgenstein, *Tractatus* 4.001 [trans. Ogden].
9. Wittgenstein, *Tractatus*, 4.21 and 4.211.

explanation—and conversely every proper description refers definitely to an event.[10]

The simple picture model of language failed for several reasons. Most of them were enumerated by Wittgenstein himself in his *Philosophische Untersuchungen* written between 1937 and 1949. (That he continually cites Augustine as the source of the discarded idea, without mentioning his development,[11] may be traced back to the fact that Wittgenstein was only familiar with his *Confessiones* but not *De trinitate*.)[12] Three reasons are given here for the failure of picture theory, of which the first is to some extent comparable to Augustine's motivation.

1. Linguistic concepts are not unambiguous designations of non-linguistic realities. (Even Augustine found no real equivalent for "Trinity.") On the contrary, words and sentences are products of a cultural process. We are unable to separate their meaning from their contingent etiology. "To imagine a language means to imagine a form of life."[13] The meaning of a word "is its use in the language"[14] and defies any fixed rule. Example: "A root has two definitions, like 'pain.' The one is used with visible injuries and is connected to nursing, sympathy, etc. The other is used with stomach pains, for example, and it coalesces with amusement over the sufferer."[15] It is conceivable, according to Wittgenstein, that this root cannot convey the similarity we feel in both "pain" definitions because perhaps this similarity is unimportant to him and therefore he has no description for it. "I would like to say: a totally different education than ours could be the basis of completely different definitions."[16]

2. The vagueness of word meanings is not only conditioned by cultural and genetic factors, but as a matter of principle. As Willard V. O. Quine has shown, following Wittgenstein,[17] different meanings

10. On the problem of empirical and particularly singular elementary or protocol propositions see Hofmann, *Radikal-empirische Wahrheitstheorie*, 69–83.

11. Wittgenstein, *Philosophische Untersuchungen*, 1–3 and 15–17.

12. On Augustine citations in Wittgenstein see Hintikka/Hintikka, *Untersuchungen*, 231.

13. Wittgenstein, *Philosophische Untersuchungen*, 19 [trans. Anscombe].

14. Wittgenstein, *Philosophische Untersuchungen*, 43 [trans. Anscombe].

15. Wittgenstein, *Zettel*, 380.

16. Wittgenstein, *Zettel*, 387.

17. Quine, *Wort*, 143 (footnote).

could be empirically equivalent in isolated observation and can be differentiated from one another in the holistic structure of a theory. Example:[18] a German-speaking field linguist is researching the foreign language Arunta. Every time a rabbit runs by, the natives say the word "gavagai." With the same empirical evidence with which the researcher concluded "gavagai = rabbit," he could translate the expression as "temporary rabbit-ness" or "contiguous parts of a rabbit." Without additional hypotheses on the ontology of the speakers, the choice here remains capricious. Strictly speaking, this fuzziness exists between members of the same language community.

3. The idea that lies at the foundation of simple picture theory, that the composite "reality" can be analyzed in exactly one way into "simple facts,"[19] is untenable. To what the terms "simple" and "composite" are connected is always dependent on the context. Example: "But isn't a chessboard, for instance, obviously, and absolutely composite? You're probably thinking of its being composed of thirty-two white and thirty-two black squares. But could we not also say, for instance, that it was composed of the colors black and white and the schema of squares?"[20]

Wittgenstein's new approach to the clarification of the relationship between language and world in *Philosophische Untersuchungen* abandons the metaphysical claim of the *Tractatus*, which puts forth a theory according to which must be the manner in which language functions,[21] and instead concentrates on a "hermeneutics of forms of our environmental access to reality."[22] In place of the "metaphysical 'must'" comes the "phenomenological 'look.'"[23] The central concept for this approach is the "language game."[24] Wittgenstein creates this term following his observation of games: "Consider, for example, the activities that we call 'games.' I mean board-games, card-games, ball-games, athletic games, and so on.

18. In the style of Quine, *Wort*, 59–147.

19. Whether this is to be understood ontologically—as in logical atomism—or empirically—as in logical empiricism as sensory data is irrelevant to this argument.

20. Wittgenstein, *Philosophische Untersuchungen*, 47 [trans. Anscombe].

21. See Hunziker, *Ludwig Wittgensteins Hermeneutik*, 444.

22. Hunziker, *Wagnis*, 7.

23. Hunziker, *Andere*, 193.

24. Wittgenstein, *Philosophische Untersuchungen*, 7 and throughout [trans. Anscombe].

What is common to them all? Don't say: 'They must have something in common, or they would not be called 'games,' but look and see whether there is anything common to all. For if you look at them, you won't see something that is common to all, but similarities, affinities, and a whole series of them at that."[25] Neither is the object of all games to win, nor are all fun, require cleverness, or dependent on chance or on a chosen strategy. There are no selective criteria, but "we see a complicated network of similarities" as with members of a family.[26]

Wittgenstein does not assert that language is a game, but that we can compare language with games to the extent that specific sub-areas of language follow specific rules and these sub-areas are similar to one another in respective variable features.[27] "Language game" is thus a "functional category of observation" which permits us "the limitation to a reasonable extract of a shielded use of language in its totality of every regimentation."[28] So, just as the discussion of a game is only sensible, as a rule, when it is actually being played, language games are also not figments of the imagination; "The word 'language game' is used here to emphasize the fact that the speaking of language is part of an activity, or of a form of life."[29] Forms of life are those which are "additive, given"[30] and form "in the epistemological sense . . . the borders of all justification."[31] Within a form of life we learn language—and surely not by "explanation," but by "training"[32]—by demonstration and imitation, trial and error. Although language "does not proceed from reasoning,"[33] still, in its sub-areas it is rule-governed and authoritative.[34] Thereby the picture theory of language—in contrast to the formerly standard interpretation of Wittgenstein's work[35]—is not completely abandoned but decisively modified. Language games are reflections of our forms of life which certainly could

25. Wittgenstein, *Philosophische Untersuchungen*, 66 [trans. Anscombe].

26. Wittgenstein, *Philosophische Untersuchungen*, 66 and 67 [trans. Anscombe].

27. See Wittgenstein, *Philosophische Grammatik*, 63.

28. Laube, *Im Bann*, 373.

29. Wittgenstein, *Philosophische Untersuchungen*, 23 [trans. Anscombe].

30. Laube, *Im Bann*, 537.

31. Krämer, *Sprache*. 121.

32. Wittgenstein, *Philosophische Untersuchungen*, 5 [trans. Anscombe].

33. Wittgenstein, *Über Gewißheit*, 475.

34. Wittgenstein, *Über Gewißheit*, 509.

35. See Hintikka/Hintikka, *Untersuchungen*, 273–75. This study which appeared in 1986 marks the turning point in Wittgenstein reception.

have unfolded quite differently. Language games are not photographs of reality but rather "genre pictures," presenting isomorphs, which nevertheless do not afford us a view of an object seemingly behind language.[36] A picture tells me *something*, "a picture tells me itself."[37]

It would be fascinating to delve deeper into these thoughts by taking an epistemological turn into Ernst Cassirer's symbol-based transcendental philosophy. Both philosophers were significantly influenced by Heinrich Hertz's *Prinzipien der Mechanik* from 1894.[38] Cassirer also parallelized the process of human way of life with the process of symbol formation[39] to which belong—not only, but in prominent fashion[40]—language signs. The symbol function which determines the synthesis of the human mind as "fulfillment of meaning of the sensory"[41] creates the pictorial worlds in which "we . . . possess . . . what we call 'reality': for the supreme objective truth which opens itself up to the mind is, in the end, the form of its own action." So that this may become distinct, the "last semblance of any mediated or unmediated identity between reality and symbol . . . [must be] expunged" and the "tension between both . . . ratcheted up to the breaking point."[42] If the reasoning below follows Wittgenstein again, and no longer Cassirer, this is because a) this approach enables a clearer reconstruction of religious language (on this see section 6.3) and b) a further appreciation of Cassirer's thought would require a clarification of his partially blurred terminology,[43] which would go beyond the scope of this study.

With Wittgenstein's reduction of linguistic significance to a form of life, a normative component comes into play which brings to mind Augustine's *verbum intimum*. When solely the attitude of mankind determines the meaning of language, then communicatively successful use of language is bound immediately to the following of rules. These do not have to be observed in absolutely every individual case, but certainly in most. Therefore Eike von Savigny suggests a different term than "rule:"

36. Wittgenstein, *Philosophische Untersuchungen*, 522 [trans. Anscombe].
37. Wittgenstein, *Philosophische Untersuchungen*, 523 [trans. Anscombe].
38. Neumann, *Cassirer*, 120.
39. Cassirer, *Philosophie* I, 51.
40. See Meyer-Blanck, *Symbolbegriff*, 92.
41. Cassirer, *Philosophie* III, 109.
42. Cassirer, *Philosophie* I, 137.
43. On this see also Richter, *Symbol*.

"Signs have a meaning only insofar as there is a custom to comply with them."[44] This situation is adapted somewhat more precisely by Herbert Hart. In a group ($a_1, a_2, a_3, \ldots a_n$) one is engaged in a linguistically triggered situation S to attitude A, if a_x

1. in S seldom deviates from A
2. in the case of a deviation sanctions of other a_y obtain
3. these sanctions are generally accepted.[45]

In the language concept of late Wittgenstein, not only are central motifs of Augustine's reasoning recognizable, but also two ideas of Barth's,[46] which are helpful in identifying the connection between language games and the word of God. On the one hand, there is the precedence of the phenomenological view ahead of analytical reflection which also became decisive for Barth's book on Anselm, *Fides quaerens intellectum* from 1931, which introduced a theological "movement of thought":[47] "*Intellegere* comes about by contemplation of the pre-said and pre-confirmed *Credo*."[48]

On the other hand is the inseparability of form and content, which is characteristic for Barth's "revealed word." The "God with Us" testimonies are not to be separated from their linguistic form, they could "nowhere else than through the medium of this testimony, nor in any sort of per se, come before our eyes."[49]

When Barth mentions John as the paradigm of a biblical witness, strikingly pointing to Jesus in the Isenheim Altarpiece of Matthias Grünewald,[50] this suggests the misapprehension that one could possibly differentiate between the event and the witness, between the revelation and its linguistic expression. Consequently Barth makes plain on four tightly packed pages:[51] "The idea from which we must protect ourselves is that . . .

44. Savigny, *Sprache*, 28. Emphasis of the author.

45. See Hart, *Begriff*, 67–79.

46. On this see also Maurer, *Biblisches*, 72–75.

47. Barth, *Fides*, 6.

48. Barth, *Fides*, 26. Emphasis in original.

49. Barth, *KD* 1/2:545.

50. Barth, *KD* 1/1:115: "Can one point away from one's self more emphatically and more completely? And can one more emphatically and more tangibly point to the subject than happens there?"

51. Barth, *KD* 1/2:545–48.

which has become endemic in theology, that reading, understanding, and interpreting the Bible serve to discover facts somewhere *behind* the biblical texts in order then to recognize in these facts the revelation (in their reality, of course, standing independent of the texts!).[52]

The revelation "is the object of biblical witness. . . . And it aligns with the nature of this object that it is united with its witnesses, or rather its testimony, *in a fashion which can never again be dissolved*."[53] In other words: revelation is bound to its linguistic articulation which construes it as revelation. That gets to the heart of the term "word of God." How this interpretation can be linguistically fulfilled stands at the core of the following section (6.3) on Martin Luther's approach and the language of faith.

6.2.3. Summary

Language cannot be analyzed by thinking of individual component parts of the signification process as isolated and then putting them back together. The dynamic interpretation of linguistic unities—from the word to the text—emerges from the attitude of those who use them. To this extent a communication community with the same language rests on a common form of life which is determined by rules.

The interdependency of form of life and language game can now be seen in both directions. Not only can a change in the form of life influence linguistic communication, but also conversely, language influences form of life. In principle, every actually expressed proposition of a communication community alters the meaning of the words in that it adds one aspect. The vivid picture of a "bundle" originates with Jacques Derrida for the loosely held together sense lines which span between signifiers and signified and whose number and composition is constantly changing.[54]

For the word of God this means initially that it owes nothing to a particular significate—no concrete object, no abstraction. It is the linguistic articulation of an interpreted experience as address from God or of God's presence which blends into a language game—and primarily this, then, in consequence can change the attitude of the communicator and finally the rules of the form of life. The more creative the articulation, and the more use is made of it, the greater the effect. For example, one may think

52. Barth, *KD* 1/2:545–46. Emphasis in original.

53. Barth, *KD* 1/2:545. Author's emphasis.

54. Derrida, *differánce*, 111.

of Christian communion, on whose historical origins coalesced experiences and certain innovative word meanings, which in turn created an expanding ritual and found its expression in liturgical rules.

Of course, this process holds true for all linguistic utterances. The specific nature of the word of God comes at all events into view when one wished to evaluate the normative results of the changes in attitude triggered thereby. That is a theme which blows up the language-theoretic approach pursued here. The fascinating linguistic and theological question is now: how does it come to an interpretation of an experience as divine address? And how is such an articulation received into the language game?

6.3. Luther's Theme: The Language of Faith

6.3.1. Recapitulation

In contrast to Augustine, there is no question for Luther as to how the word of God can show itself in human language. For him, language itself is, in the end, a divine gift and the only pathway of mankind to its self-relation, world-relation, and God-relation. Certainly the fall from grace destroyed the original purity of language, its unambiguous orientation to God and creation, but in the revelation of Christ its power to disclose reality is restored (see section 4.3).

From a language-theoretical view there are three central statements of Luther to be thought of together for this "word act of Christ":[55]

1. Divine address orients mankind completely to God. It is an earth-shaking experience which "causes us to become the opposite of that which we are."[56] As an external point of reference, it creates the possibility of a total self-determination which overcomes the abyss between corporeal and spiritual nature.
2. God's word only shows itself in the language acts of "promise" (gospel) and "obligation" (law).

55. See Luther, *Predigten* 1529, WA 29, 398,4.

56. Ebeling, *Luther*, 275.

3. God's word establishes a *nova lingua*,[57] which takes as its starting point the sentence *Christus verus deus et homo est*.[58] In this new language, the conversation can only be about God in connection with mankind, and mankind in connection to God. In this new context, the *signa* reveals that *res* which constitutes the true, divine reality (see section 4.7). The suitability of this reasoning, which rests on a later formation of doctrine, leads Luther back to the eucharist paradosis (see section 4.5.2).

On the basis of what we have worked through earlier in this study, the word of God lends itself to being seen as the foundation of a new language game—in any event one that is highlighted in extraordinary fashion. The language game concept is therefore an appropriate reconstruction method because it takes as its starting point the consummated renewal of the word through Christ and not from an extra-linguistic point of reference. It is the "final word . . . that determines the world."[59] The incarnation of the eternal word is an "inverbation."[60] The divine shows itself in human language. In the following it will be proven the extent to which Wittgenstein's approach allows for the possibility, using empirical means, of separating such a language game from other profane language games.

6.3.2. Reconstruction: From Language Game to Accessibility Situation

Wittgenstein's language game concept has been rewardingly embraced by some thinkers for theological discourse.[61] Most of these advancements place in the foreground that religious discourse as language game needs no further justification as long as it is anchored in a form of life. All systems of signs based on rule-governed human behavior are appropriate and coherent in themselves. For example, one could speak of mistakes *within* a language game,[62] according to D. Z. Phillips, the highest profile rep-

57. Luther, *De divinitate*, WA 39.2, 94,21 (thesis 22).

58. Luther, *De divinitate*, WA 39.2, 93,2–3 (thesis 1) and Luther, *Verbum caro factum est*, WA 39.2, 3,5–6 (thesis 3).

59. Luther, *Predigten* 1523, WA 12, 598,21–22.

60. Ebeling, *Evangelische Evangelienauslegung*, 365.

61. See the survey in Dalferth, *Einführung*, 48–51, and in Laube, *Im Bann*, 395.

62. Phillips, *Glaube*, 254.

resentative[63] of "Wittgensteinian fideism."[64] With this self-determination against every critique (except that it lacks coherence), theological reflection on religious discourse naturally forsakes rational discourse. Additionally, Wittgenstein's *methodological* concept of the language game for an *epistemic* safeguard of religion is misused here. The language game concept helps in describing the origin and insular regularity of language, but it is of no help in clarifying claims of validity.

Wittgenstein himself commented on religious language, especially in his *Vortrag über Ethik*. Using as an example the proposition "I am amazed at the existence of the world" as an expression of awe before the wonder of creation, he shows that:

a. "being amazed" does not have the common meaning here (because one can only "be amazed" at something in the literal sense, which could *not* be the case here, like a giant dog),[65] but

b. precisely this (at first glance ridiculous) manner of speaking is constitutive for religious forms of expression: "I see now that these nonsensical expressions were not nonsensical because I had not yet found the proper expressions, but that their nonsensicality constitutes their actual essence. I wanted to use them exactly for that in order to progress beyond the world—and that means: beyond sensical language."[66]

This "nonsensical" is in no way pejorative or intended as "irrational"[67] in meaning. Our impulse "to run up against the limits of language," to penetrate "the walls of our cage," is "totally and absolutely futile."[68] But, as Wittgenstein says further, "it is a testimony to this impulse in human consciousness that I for my part can do no other than venerate it and would not at any price make it look ridiculous."[69] Not least because we can obviously understand the proposition of "being amazed" without too much trouble, despite the "nonsensical" manner of speaking—whether or not we believe in a creation or not. Whoever engages in religious

63. See Laube, *Im Bann*, 396.

64. Dalferth, *Einführung*, 49.

65. Wittgenstein, *Vortrag über Ethik*, 15.

66. Wittgenstein, *Vortrag über Ethik*, 18.

67. See Wittgenstein, *Vorlesungen*, 81.

68. Wittgenstein, *Vortrag über Ethik*, 18–19.

69. Wittgenstein, *Vortrag über Ethik*, 19.

discourse moves in the sphere of language "like a tightrope walker . . . his territory is the most slender that can be conceived, but nevertheless he really walks on it."[70]

Based on Wittgenstein, Ian Ramsey developed a model in the late 1950s that tried to describe these religious acrobatics of articulation in the border area of language.[71] Unfortunately his approach did not find due consideration, primarily for the reason that Ramsey's second step, in which he attempts to reconstruct a logic of religious concepts, turns out to be too formalistic and therefore was heavily criticized.[72] However, his first step is still worthy of consideration. He identifies two characteristics for religious disclosure situations: the odd discernment as it is expressed in linguistic formulation, and the total commitment to the whole universe, with which this insight is associated.[73]

By odd discernment, Ramsey intends insight or knowledge with empirical indication whose content, however, can only be expressed in an indirect manner which bursts traditional semantics and creates a new language game. To the simplest forms of this manner of speaking belong "The penny drops," "I got it," and "It clicked."[74] Here, in the Wittgensteinian sense, we run up against the "limits of language" in order to describe the effect of a "disclosure" situation, the difference between the world view before and after. The imagery helps us to communicate about that which is otherwise unsayable. Examples from the Christian language of faith are "son of God," "our Father in heaven," "eternal life," and *creatio ex nihilo*.[75] Paul Ricœur adopted Ramsey's approach and spoke of "border expressions," defined as "consummated forms of the allegory or saying, by the concentrated use of exorbitance, hyperbole, and paradox."[76]

As Gerhard Sellin says, we earn for ourselves "semantic disturbances" in order to illuminate "a new level of meaning."[77] We obviously do this, in successful cases, so that on the one hand, the manner of speaking is innovative, and on the other hand can still be consummated by sufficient

70. Wittgenstein, *Vermischte Bemerkungen*, 554.

71. Ramsey, *Religious Language*. In connection to Wittgenstein see especially p. 12.

72. See for example Dalferth, *Religiöse Rede*, 320–21 and Track, *Sprachkritische Untersuchungen*, 244–45.

73. Ramsey, *Religious Language*, 41–42.

74. Ramsey, *Religious Language*, 18–19 and 55.

75. Ramsey, *Religious Language*, 49–80.

76. Ricœur, *Gott*, 173. In connection to Ramsey see also 178–79.

77. Sellin, *Allegorie*, 212–13 and 244–45.

amounts of members of the language community. We exceed the rules of language usage, but only so far that one can still reconstruct the breach of the rules.[78] While this is valid for every form of metaphorical manner of speaking, for religious forms of articulation a second feature is typical.

The *total commitment to the whole universe*, which according to Ramsey highlights religious insights, is to be circumscribed in two ways.[79] One is the partial commitment as, for example, with vegetarianism. This decision only touches the environmental sub-area of nutrition and not the entire self-understanding. The other is the *total commitment to a part of the universe*, as for example love for another person. Ramsey's total commitment to the whole universe brings to mind the "acknowledgment of a new self-understanding" which in section 5.5 described the recognition of the word of God in Karl Barth's terminology.[80] And the odd discernment is then that "Yes in No"[81] which makes possible, in a situation almost incomprehensible linguistically, the articulation of an experience.

Ramsey's recommendation is therefore predominantly interesting for the examination of religious language innovations since their origin is rooted in disclosure situations.[82] Ramsey combines the empirical foundation of religious experience with its linguistic creativity. We experience something that comprehensively alters our "orientation to existence and action"[83] and by the particular fashion of linguistic processing becomes a religious experience.

The process is comparable to the formation of a "metaphor," as Paul Ricœur has described it: understood as an "outrageous predication"[84] and as "that strategy of discourse through which language carries out its usual function in order to serve the extraordinary function of the new description."[85] Here the term "metaphor" is intended not in the Aristotelian

78. Shortly after Ramsey, a similar theory was developed by Donald Evans with his "onlooks" behind which the confessional statement stands: "I look on x as y" (see Evans, *Logic*, 124–40).

79. See Ramsey, *Religious Language*, 35–39.

80. A still more differentiated boundary of daily and religious disclosure situations is found in Herms, *Offenbarung*, 180–82 (explicit connection to Ramsey's model: 176 [footnote]).

81. Barth, *Not und Verheißung*, 246.

82. On this see also de Pater, *Erschließungssituationen*, 206–8.

83. Track, *Untersuchungen*, 217.

84. Ricœur, *Metapher*, VI.

85. Ricœur, *Stellung*, 53.

sense as retranslated analogy formation,[86] but in the sense of Hans Blumenberg as "absolute metaphor" which makes something as something comprehensible in the first place[87]—to a certain extent "a difference-preserving process of differentiation and a contingency-preserving process of contingency."[88] To this extent Ricœur is very near to Luther's *nova lingua* when he attributes an ontological relevance to metaphorical significance. The transferred reference creates "a pre-objective world in which we find ourselves from birth forward and in which we nevertheless design our own possibilities."[89] Precisely because "the limits of my language . . . mean the limits of my world,"[90] the creative use of signs enables the shifting of the boundaries of knowledge. Alongside "semantic innovation," the metaphor acquires a "heuristic function"[91] for the disclosure of reality: "Must one not say that the metaphor only dissolves order so it can invent another? That the mixing-up of categories is only the flip side of the logic of discovery? If one thinks this suggestion through to the end, then one must say that the metaphor has content of information because it 'describes reality anew.' The mixing-up of categories would then be the deconstructive interplay of describing and newly describing."[92]

Admittedly the stronger one valorizes the metaphor in general epistemological regard, the more difficult it becomes to describe the specific role of religious metaphors. And the reverse holds: the more constrained the metaphor is to its religious meaning, the more complicated becomes the boundary of this application from the profane. One can see this danger with Christian Danz in Paul Tillich's concept of symbol.[93] There the inauthentic manner of speaking helps to circumvent the "eternal paradox" of the unconditional[94]—and thus the contradiction that on the one hand Kant provides no pathway to the conditional, and on the other hand the absolute is taken with every act of meaning which aims for fulfillment

86. See Aristotle, *Poetics*, chapter 21.

87. Blumenberg, *Paradigmen*, 11.

88. Stoellger, *Sinn*, 104.

89. Ricœur, *Metapher*, 289. In the foreword to the German edition, Ricœur calls the primary objective of his book a "plea for metaphorical reference" (III).

90. Wittgenstein, *Tractatus*, 5.6 [trans. Ogden].

91. Ricœur, *Metapher*, III.

92. Ricœur, *Metapher*, 28.

93. Danz, *Begriff*, 209.

94. Tillich, *Überwindung*, 367.

of meaning:[95] "Because consciousness has no other forms than the conditional, then it must use these in order to express therein the unconditional, meaning that it must use scientific concepts symbolically, not authentically."[96]

In the metaphor—or, in Tillich's terminology the symbol—the structure of the consummation of meaning itself is expressed since meaningfulness cannot be attached to any empirical data. "Formulated in sign-theoretical terms, the symbol is a sign in which the use of a sign itself serves as a sign."[97] Tillich calls this sensory overload "transcendent signification."[98] The reflected interaction with this sensory overload distinguishes the religious consciousness which "uses [symbols] under constant remembrance of their symbolic character and the sense that they express vividly and graphically, albeit inadequately."[99] In short: "The symbol is the language of religion."[100]

Tillich's narrow determination is hardly productive for extracting a language-theoretic criterion for religious use of signs—but not because it cannot sufficiently separate the use of symbols in art, literature, and religion. Besides that, Tillich's approach involves the danger that with his differentiation of "authentic" and "symbolic" manner of speaking, the progress of Wittgenstein's language concept along with its overcoming of the picture theory is abandoned.

The language game perspective leads inevitably to an interaction theory of metaphor,[101] which does not define this as a three-figure relationship between subject, object, and *tertium comparationis* (Achilles–Lion–Strength), but as an encounter of two contexts whose connection is first created by the metaphor.[102] This expanded formulation of the term allows—in contrast to the substitution theory which concentrates on the single word—the inclusion of entire sentences and word families. Within the metaphors comprehended as interactionistic, one can differentiate

95. Tillich, *System*, 233.

96. Tillich, *System*, 254.

97. Danz, *Begriff*, 210.

98. Tillich, *Protestantismus*, 41.

99. Tillich, *Rechtfertigung und Zweifel* (unpublished manuscript from 1919)—cited in Danz, *Begriff*, 213.

100. Tillich, *Recht*, 237.

101. The main protagonists are Ivor A. Richards and Max Black (see van Noppen, *Einleitung*, 29).

102. On this see Buntfuß, *Metaphern*, 41–42.

conceptual from living.[103] For the former, the more common usage is typical with its stabilizing function of individual and collective convictions. By contrast, living metaphors are distinguished by their unusual nature and confined usability. "Thereby they have the effect of flipping the ignition switch for further unconventional possibilities of description [and] lead to unfamiliar perspectives of understanding."[104]

The proprium of religious imagery can then be described as the articulation of fundamental opposites which open themselves up to mankind reflecting on his existence: life and death, conditional and unconditional, eternal and temporal.[105] Markus Buntfuß suggests the term "fundamental distinctions" in "whose relationship halves in religious consummation are not fixed as separated, but are shifted into a relationship of interaction with one another."[106] He names as examples "God and man, heaven and earth, time and eternity, sin and grace, finite and infinite, sacred and profane, immanence and transcendence, contingency and sense."[107] That is expressed paradigmatically in Jesus' parables, in which "the transfer of God's sovereignty to human everyday reality" is consummated in innovative pictorial worlds.[108] Malte Dominik Krüger's analysis of human pictorial worlds arrives at four fundamental categories which can be made religiously fertile: integrity (all-encompassing unity), otherness (revelation), distance (unconditionality), and negation (freedom).[109] All suggestions are in the end alternatives which give an orientation to the human yearning toward the absolute.

6.3.3. Summary

The highlighting of different metaphor concepts may have been made clear in the fact that Ramsey's relatively simple approach possesses high explanation potential. His odd discernments can be understood in this sense as living metaphors which are created anew in a disclosure situation. They are religiously exact when they express a "total commitment

103. Buntfuß, *Metaphern*, 42–43.

104. Buntfuß, *Metaphern*, 43.

105. Korsch, *Theologie*, 230.

106. Buntfuß, *Metaphern*, 47.

107. Buntfuß, *Metaphern*, 47.

108. Buntfuß, *Metaphern*, 48.

109. See Krüger, *Das andere Bild*, 555–57.

to the entire universe"—or when they place in connection to one another the named "fundamental distinctions." The charm of the Ramsey model consists in the fact that it anchors the origin of religious communication, on the one hand, in subjective experience, thus experiential-theological, and on the other hand connects it to innovative language formation which one could interpret as revelatory-theological (on this see the following section).

With the connection of the features "linguistic innovation" and "interaction of fundamental distinctions," we have caught up with Luther's exact starting off point for *nova lingua* in this reconstruction. The relation of fundamental distinctions beyond which no greater is conceivable is *Christus vere deus et homo est*. In "*Christus*" this sentence brings into connection two contexts—God and man—which by definition lie as far apart as possible from one another. In the Christ-event "free selection of theological metaphors [has] its basis as well as its limit."[110] It enables us to speak "quite heavenly German."[111]

The introduction of these language game formative metaphors in the framework of a disclosure experience is arranged particularly vividly in Mark's gospel. After Jesus' death cry on the cross, the Roman centurion says: "Truly this man was God's Son! [Mark 15:39, NRSV]" The metaphor is previously introduced as a voice from heaven (Mark 1:11) or from the clouds (Mark 9:7) and as the cry of unclean spirits (Mark 3:11 and 5:7), but here it appears for the first time in human discourse. Thus the centurion becomes with his odd discernment the first "witness" in the sense of Barth. He creates a new language game in the narrative logic of Mark's gospel which can be productive in two ways:

a. Others can use the language game in order to formulate their experiences in the same fashion—an interpretation community emerges. Paul Ricœur gets to the heart of this in his article *Gott nennen*: "I can name God in my faith since the texts which were proclaimed to me already named him."[112] Subsequently texts can take on a normative, ecclesiological function for these interpretation communities.[113]

110. Jüngel, *Stellung*, 116.

111. Luther, *Predigten* 1532, WA 36, 644,25–26.

112. Ricœur, *Gott*, 155.

113. On this see Dalferth's suggestion to differentiate between "the word of God," "Scripture," and "Bible" (*Wirkendes Wort*, 76, 118–19, and 188–89).

b. Furthermore the language game can be the object of a disclosure situation if through it a hearer or reader gains a consciousness-altering insight. Odd discernment broadens the articulation scope of the recipients, their experience horizons, and finally their self- and world-understanding.

Section 6.2 concludes with the result that the word of God as a linguistic expression can be interpreted as an experience indicating God's address or God's presence which can initially individually and then collectively effect an attitude-change and rule-change. The word of God, then, can to a certain degree as a code switcher establish or alter a language game which can in turn have consequences for the form of life of a language community. In this section the interlacing of experience and linguistic expression can be refined:

a. the experience of a disclosure situation was defined as a "total commitment to the entire universe" in Ramsey's sense and as a result has a new self-understanding and
b. the spoken expression is to be comprehended as an interactively understood metaphor which sets the fundamental distinctions of the poles of our rudimentary existence in connection.

Thereby the preconditions have been sketched under which the word of God can come to pass. Metaphors understood in this way "create with the world, in the world, space for God."[114] They are necessary but inadequate conditions for the sacrosanct event of God's word. In a third step now, it must be clarified how God has his say—of what manner the language events are which mankind designates as "the word of God."

6.4. Barth's Theme: The Word as Language Event

6.4.1. Recapitulation

Already in Luther appear approaches of action-oriented language comprehension which somewhat emphasize the orality of the gospel[115] and interpret the biblical "read word" as "life word"[116]—an occurrence ac-

114. Jüngel, *Stellung*, 119.

115. Luther, *Weihnachtspostille*, WA 10.1.1., 17,7–12.

116. Luther, *Psalmenauslegungen* 1529/32, WA 31.1, 67,25.

tualized again and again which alters the recipients (see section 4.5.1). In Barth this aspect is fundamental. Here language never comes as an atemporal structure but generally only as an event, the result of actions in plain view.

This especially holds for the word of God whose semantic content can be reduced to this simple formula: "God becomes man."[117] This statement then first becomes the word of God when it is spoken "as *God's* word,"[118] thus of God himself by the mouth of mankind and effects a change among the addressees. Consequently Barth worked out the word of God as a language act, indeed as one in which different individual acts intertwine and whose success depends on mankind but is not guaranteed by mankind. That is less unusual than it may seem at first reading. In the end, all language acts in which it comes to the effect on the listeners depend on so many conditions for success that they cannot possibly be totally formalized.

The network of language acts constituting the word of God is most clearly seen when on the one hand its three-fold form—proclamation, canonical testimony, and revelation—and on the other hand the recognition with the aid of language act theory are reconstructed. These elements describe the sender and receiver sides of the communication situation in which, according to Barth, the word of God appears. Previous reflections on the semantics of religious language flow into the language act of bearing witness.

6.4.2. Reconstruction: From Event to Language Act

Barth's implicit understanding of language displays an astonishing proximity to the "philosophy of ordinary language" and the "philosophy of speaking" which were first formulated decades after the publication of the first volume of Barth's *KD* with two differing accentuations: one from Ludwig Wittgenstein (on this see section 6.2.2) and the other from John L. Austin.[119] The crucial publications for both authors appeared

117. Barth, *Wort Gottes*, 160.

118. Barth, *Wort Gottes*, 160. Emphasis in original.

119. Within analytical philosophy this impulse is understood as a reaction to the "philosophy of ideal language" and the "philosophy of language" with their two respective protagonists Bertrand Russell and Rudolf Carnap. See Dalferth, *Religiöse Rede*, 43 and Savigny, *John Langshaw Austin*, 208.

posthumously.[120] In his lecture from 1955 and published in 1962, *How to Do Things with Words*,[121] Austin uncovered a blind spot in the history of philosophy. The insight that speaking is a form of action is in no way as obvious as it seems at first hearing. Wolfgang Stegmüller speaks of a "shameful scandal for all those who in any way engaged themselves with languages over the past 2,500 years, that they did not make this discovery long before Austin which can be expressed in one simple sentence: with the help of linguistic utterances we can consummate the most different forms of actions."[122] According to Austin, it was just "an assumption as old as philosophy itself that *saying something* in all noteworthy cases . . . merely boils down to *stating something*."[123]

In his famous, paradigmatically maieutic arranged lecture, Austin first goes forward from the point that statements can be differentiated into "constative" (describing facts) and "performative," which first create the facts that they then describe. Examples of such language actions are sentences in the first person indicative present[124] with verbs like "baptize," "condemn," "bet, "congratulate," "wish," "promise," and "excuse"—finally with all verbs that can be strengthened in German by adding "hereby." For such performative statements the difference between "true" and "false" is mostly inapplicable. We speak more easily of "success" and "failure," of "succeeding" and "failing."[125] In the further course of his reflections Austin shows that the limit between "constative" and "performative" is not at all clearly drawn. Even seemingly simple statements are language actions which can succeed or fail.[126]

Let us consider the most often used example in analytical philosophy of language since Bertrand Russell for a supposedly simple declarative sentence:[127] "The cat sits on the mat." At first glance a simple constative which can still, according to the situation of the statement, uncover a colorful variety of language actions. The sentence can be intended as:

120. Wittgenstein's *Philosophische Untersuchungen* were finished in 1949 and appeared in 1955, four years after his death. Austin died in 1960.

121. Austin, *Theorie*.

122. Stegmüller, *Hauptströmungen*, 64–65.

123. Austin, *Theorie*, 35. Author's emphasis.

124. The number is not significant.

125. See Austin, *Theorie*, 28–29.

126. Austin, *Theorie*, 76 and 109–10.

127. See de Pater, *Sprechakt*, 34–35.

a. an *answer* to a question
b. an *accusation* if the speaker had just finished carefully cleaning the mat
c. an *invitation* to finally feed the animal
d. a *contradiction* to an opposing assertion
e. a *warning* to someone allergic to cat hair
f. a *threat* to an unexpected guest with a dog
g. a *password* to gain entry into a closed society
h. an *insult* if "cat" does not refer to an animal or the "mat," for example, refers to a very expensive prayer mat.

And if with the expression of the sentence a *statement* should actually be met, an intentional action which effects something becomes executed. "I hereby baptize this cat with the name 'Fee'" and "I hereby state: the cat sits on the mat" is only a gradual difference, one not satisfyingly nor distinctly articulated with formal criteria. There is no "null context," no "literal meaning" in which a statement can be determined independently of all background information on truth or falsehood, success or failure.[128] While we are saying something, we are doing something and we are causing something. For this observation Austin introduces the term "speech act" in which he differentiates three aspects: with a *locution* (a statement) we perform an *illocution* (an action), which has as a result a *perlocution* (an effect).[129]

Austin's point sounds like a generalization of Barth's description that the word of God "happens, holds true, and takes effect."[130] Is the word of God therefore a speech act, so to say the prototype of all language actions, as the priestly myth of creation suggests? In contrast to the anthropomorphism of the Genesis narrative, the word of God appears in Barth in the human language action of *proclamation*. This act lends itself to being illuminated according to speech act theory.

In the following, the rules will be formulated based on Barth, specifically the rules which are essential for the speech act of "proclamation." Corresponding to Barth's intention, these rules are intended as *constitutive* and not *regulative*. They define the speech act in the form

128. See Searle, *Ausdruck*, 139–47.

129. Austin, *Theorie*, 112–19.

130. Barth, *KD* 1/1:128.

of necessary and sufficient conditions, like chess rules for a chess game, and not to organize (like organizing street traffic) an event independent of them.[131] The speech act of "proclaiming" is not bound to a worship situation but leaps over "the walls of the church" with Barth.[132] His "proclamation" is—as Dietrich Korsch suggested—to be generally interpreted as "religious communication in Christianity."[133] Thereby one precludes the misapprehension that "proclaiming" is tantamount to "preaching." As a rule, a sermon is (hopefully) not a homogeneous speech act, but a combination of different language actions like explaining, comforting, narrating, edifying, and exhorting.[134] By contrast Barth's proclamation is presented, as has been shown, as an action with a very specific effect.

In a preliminary step, the speech act "proclaiming" is dissected into four individual acts. The illustration follows the further development of Austin's tripartite locution/illocution/perlocution as John Searle intended.[135] Within locution he differentiates the *statement act*, the phonetic (or gesture-based) speech process with comprehensible lexemic and syntax, from the statement, the so-called *propositional act*. As in Austin, next comes the *illocutionary act*, the type of statement, and the *perlocutive act*, the desired effect.

In order to explain "proclaiming," the first step is to match the relevant concepts to the individual acts from the *KD*:

a. illocutionary act: "proclaiming"
b. statement act: "human discourse"[136]
c. propositional act: "promise of future revelation on the basis of happened revelation"[137]
d. perlocutive act: the act of "acknowledgment" of the content of proclamation effects a new "human self-determination."[138]

131. On this differentiation see Searle, *Sprechakte*, 54–55.

132. Barth, *KD* 1/1:83. In a similar vein *KD* 4/3:593–94.

133. Korsch, *Religionsbegriff*, 203.

134. On this see Henning Luther, *Predigt*, 229–30.

135. Searle, *Sprechakte*, 40–42.

136. Barth, *KD* 1/1:94.

137. Barth, *KD* 1/1:93.

138. Barth, *KD* 1/1:213–14.

Here already it can be recognized that "proclaiming" is a fabric of several language actions. Hidden within are "promising," "acknowledging," as well as—implicit in recourse to the happened, recorded revelation—"remembering" and "bearing witness." This will be taken into account in discussing the constitutive rules.

In order for this speech act to succeed as a whole, meaning that the intended effect becomes the achieved effect, four types of rules (after Searle) are to be adhered to:[139]

1. The *rules of propositional content* specify which types of semantic contents are eligible. [Example: A promise necessarily has an action as content.]
2. The *rules of introduction* describe the facts which must be fulfilled in order for the consummation of the speech act to be sensible at all. [An apology presupposes that the speaker is responsible for that for which he is apologizing.]
3. The *rules of sincerity* are connected to mental preconditions, independent of language, which are necessary for success of the speech act. [Whoever issues an order assumes the hearers are capable of carrying out the order.]
4. The *essential rules* finally are the core conditions for success for the consummation of the speech act. They describe the actual intention and the specific results of any illocutionary act. [Whoever gives a promise is obligated to consummate the same.]

If the speech act "proclaiming" is formally grasped as [A,B;p(Z)]—Speaker A proclaims to Listener B (or Listener group $B_{1,}$ B_2 . . .) the content p with connection to Z, then the earlier Barth reconstruction can be updated in Searle's system with the following rules V1 to V4.

V1 Rule of propositional content

p(Z) = promise of the presence of God in B's experience

|→ α ←|→ β ←|

By remembrance of happened, witnessed experiences of God Z.

|→ γ ←|→ δ

On α: Firstly the language action "promising" is in need of explanation. Would it not be more sensible to speak of "pledging," especially if our most important neighbor languages in passing can make no difference

139. Searle, *Sprechakte*, 88–115. Examples following Krämer, *Sprache*, 62–66.

between the two verbs? Despite all this Barth's concept is adopted because he expresses, in comparison to "pledging," an important shift in meaning directly under a language-theoretical perspective. A commits itself to nothing—A finally prophesies something, which according to its view will come to pass with unconditional certainty. A delegates the guarantee for this occurrence of the promised to another instance to which he admits in this speech act. A is the speaker of the promise whose subject is God.

In this interpretation as *divine* commitment, "promise"/ἐπαγέλλω which has no direct equivalent in the Old Testament,[140] can be traced back to Judaic-Hellenistic writings[141] and in the Pauline letters gains a central significance as a counter term to the law.[142] In Luke's double work as well the conversation is only about—with one exception (Acts 23:21)—the ἐπαγγελὶα θεοῦ. In German, the difference between the profane "pledging" and the sacred "promising" was standardized only in the nineteenth century, as a comparison of the Luther Bible from 1545 and 1892 shows.[143] Of course, in Barth the significance is unambiguous in the explicit sense: "That is the promise of Christian proclamation: that we speak God's word."[144]

On β: The phrase "presence of God in B's experience" is a recommendation which tries to grasp the Barthian concept of revelation more realistically. In sections 5.7.2 and 5.7.3 it became clear that in the *KD* "revelation" is described as a "God with us experience"[145] and as "the presence of the word of God in our own presence."[146] Even the concept "religious experience" Barth finds appropriate in the *KD*—in contrast to the *Römerbrief*![147]—to the extent that no statement on the normative meaning of a "general religious capacity of experience of mankind"[148] is encountered. The religious nature of an experience is undoubtedly a specific feeling, but it is shown in linguistic formulation as the attested

140. See Schniewind/Friedrich, article ἐπαγέλλω, 575.

141. See for example 3 Macc 2:10, Ps. Sol. 12:8, Test. Jos. 20, sBar. 57:2.

142. Gal 3:15–29, Rom 4:13–14.

143. See the synopsis of the corresponding passages in Wonneberger/Hecht, *Verheißung*, 161–63.

144. Barth, *Not und Verheißung*, 249.

145. Barth, *KD* 1/1:110 and elsewhere.

146. Barth, *KD* 1/1:592.

147. See Barth, *Römerbrief*, 4.

148. Barth, *KD* 1/1:201.

word of God. This interplay of a religiously significant experience on the one hand, and an articulation as divine revelation on the other hand, attempts to make plain the suggested formulation. Insofar as such experiences remain inaccessible, the revelatory-theological aspect of the event is demonstrated,[149] and insofar as they require verbalization in order to qualify as a divine act, the experiential-theological aspect is demonstrated.

On γ: The act of remembering concerns more than a historical reference—it concerns a realization of the linguistically fixed experiences in Z. In Barth's words "the secondary extension" of a primary experience. Therefore the historical text must become "summoning" for present-day hearers.[150]

On δ: In Barth's model the manner of linguistic fixing describes the term "bearing witness" (see section 5.7.3). Here the variable Z stands for, in this sense, the witnessed experiences of God's presence as they are handed down to us by the canon with special authority (see section 5.7.2). The special nature of the successful speech act "bearing witness" lies in the sustainable claim to validity which corresponds to high credibility on the part of the hearers.

Nevertheless, the crucial point of this concept, with solely speech act theoretical means, is not expressed. Here is the interface to the semantic model of religious metaphor which stands at the center of section 6.3. In this reconstruction of the word of God, the linguistic transformation of experience—the multitude of certain sensory data—occurs in the act of "bearing witness" as linguistically articulated experience. That can happen in different ways, even if the propositional, illocutionary, and perlocutionary partial acts are respectively identical (Example: "I feel cold," "I am freezing," "I am shivering"). The concern here is fine nuances of significance which are not grounded in the language action itself but in the specific use of medium. This aspect is, however, central to the question of how religious language is formed, since it decides on the exact shape of articulation of transcendent experiences. With the results of section 6.3, "bearing witness" proves to be initialization or utilization of a community of interpretation.

149. See Dalferth, *Radikale Theologie*, 114–22.

150. Barth, *KD* 1/2:593.

V2 *Rule of introduction*: With "proclaiming," A has no need to communicate anything connected to facts, convictions, or moral value judgments.

This rule reflects Barth's postulate, according to which, that proclaimed word has no solely rationally explicable cause. The success of the speech act "proclaiming" is demonstrated in the reaching of a goal by the recipient, not in the fulfillment of a task. "Proclaiming" has a "final theme." That differentiates proclamation from explanation or proof which follow a "causal theme."[151] These can be successful even if none of the hearers understand them.

V3 *Rule of sincerity*: A believes in the sincerity of its prophecy and the authenticity of Z's experiences of God which are formulated in p(Z).

One could say it even more succinctly: A believes p(Z). The longer version still makes it clear that this accepting as true embraces two components: faith in the arrival of the promise which A prophesies, and the acceptance of the attested meaning Z which designates an experience as an encounter with God.

V4 *Essential rule*: If B acknowledges p(Z), "proclaiming" has a new (or renewed) determination of existence for B.

This rule condenses the reflections of section 3.3 on the effect of the word of God, and thereby the actual sense of the speech act "proclaiming." An explication of the conditional sentence phrase with "If B believes p(Z)" would be too weak. Here we adopt Barth's "acknowledgment" as the only appropriate description of the experience of the word of God,[152] in order to signalize that it is not only about the accepting as true of p(Z). It is also about the acknowledgment of interpretations expressed in the written testimonies. "Acknowledgment" here is intended as "faith that p(Z)" *and* as "declared belief in Z."

This acknowledgment can be expressed for its part in different speech acts. For these language actions Donald Evans coined the term "self-involving language."[153] It encompasses

a. Behabitives:[154] Statements which express an attitude toward a person. (Example: "I praise my God" expresses gratitude and awe.)

151. The concepts can be traced back to Albert Schweitzer (see Wintzer, *Homiletik*, 22–23).

152. Barth, *KD* 1/1:213–14.

153. Evans, *Logic*, 12 and 114.

154. Evans, *Logic*, 34–36.

b. Commissives:[155] Statements with which the speaker commits to a future action which is more than linguistic. (Example: pledging.)

c. Expressive language:[156] Statements that express feelings or attitudes. For religious language, the onlooks are of special significance, in which the speakers articulate an attitude in the fashion of "I look on x as y"[157] or "I look on God as my creator."[158]

In all of these cases, the speech act is based on an acknowledgment, a "self-involvement" that confirms the consummation of the interpretation and in which the subject who consummates the speech act determines himself. The acknowledgment of B appears in the reconstruction undertaken here as a mirror image of the acknowledgment of A, as it became clear in part α of the propositional content (V1). The conviction that the prophecy of God's presence is fulfilled with a transcendent claim to validity is essentially "promised" for the success of the speech act. The fulfillment of prophecy presupposes faith in that fulfillment.

The new determination of existence is then the necessary consequence of this acknowledgment. If I accept an interpretation which embraces my entire self-image, world-image, and God-image, my self-understanding is constructed anew. In Barth's words: In acknowledgment I discern my being acknowledged by God.[159] To this extent the promise begins to be fulfilled in the moment in which I believe in it. I become conscious of God's presence in my life. When it happens in this way, the speech act is successful. The proclaimed word has led to a disclosure experience and has become, according to Barth, a "revealed word of God."

This specific condition for success is not attached to Speaker A—that differentiates "proclaiming" for example from "pledging" or "proving." The consummation of the perlocutive act is not a necessary result of a rule-governed act of A, but depends on a rational, incompletely grounded, and thus inaccessible process of consciousness in B. The inaccessibility is a required quality of the communication process which is earthshaking for B and has a surprising impact.[160] *From B's perspective,*

155. Evans, *Logic*, 32.

156. Evans, *Logic*, 79–141.

157. Evans, *Logic*, 125.

158. "Onlook" is certainly stronger than "view" but less intellectual than "conception."

159. Barth, *KD* 1/1:217.

160. On this see Rosa, *Unverfügbarkeit*, 56–60.

successful proclamation—"God's word"—presents itself as an experience of a linguistically transmitted interpretation option which in the moment of acceptance changes the entire horizon of experience. In this sense, the "word of God" is a successful speech act.

6.4.3. Summary

The speech act theoretical analysis of the language action "proclaiming," as described by Barth in *KD*, clarified the network of individual acts which here are interwoven with one another. The proclaimed word shows itself as *prophecy* with an *acknowledgment* and a *remembrance* of a *testimony*. It becomes a "real proclamation,"[161] a proclaimed *and* revealed word of God, if the speech act succeeds, thus the prophecy arrives. This is exactly the case when the recipient *believes the prophecy* and *acknowledges the interpretation contained in the testimony*. This acknowledgment can be expressed in different speech acts—in profession of faith ("I believe . . ."), in gratitude, or in other forms of "self-involvement language."

In all these language actions it is not difficult to recognize the Christian virtues of *faith* (profession and bearing witness) and *hope* (prophecy). *Love* shines out in the communal parts of interpretation of self-understanding, world-understanding, and God-understanding. Under this rubric can be read the oldest canonical mention of the three virtues in 1 Thessalonians 1. Paul used the triad in order to describe the effect of his proclamation in Thessaloniki one year after founding the community[162] as a) work of faith (ἔργου τῆς πίστεως), b) steadfastness of hope (ὑπομονῆς τῆς ἐλπίδος), and c) labor of love (κόπου τῆς ἀγάπης), which are also demonstrated in "receiving the word" (1 Thess 1:3 and 6).

Is "proclaiming," then, the one "religious model of language action"[163] which in theological reception of speech act theory was being sought again and again?[164] It that were so, "proclaiming" would have to show an essential specific of religious communication independent of all other factors in consummation of the language action.

161. See Barth, *KD* 1/1:95.

162. See Schnelle, *Paulus*, 176.

163. Dalferth, *Religiöse Rede*, 176.

164. Literature survey in Dalferth, *Religiöse Sprechakte*, 116–18 and research report in Wagner, *Sprechakte*, 67–74. For criticism of the suggestions see Dalferth, *Religiöse Rede*, 326–35.

Oswald Bayer was one of the first, going out from Luther's *promissio* concept, to represent an analogous thesis. He understands the gospel as promise and thus as a "performative statement. It constitutes a set of facts; it declares them not as already existing, but lays them out."[165] In the same way the forgiveness of sins is "not a judgment that declares what already is" but "a language action which first constitutes a set of acts, a relationship (namely between him in whose name is being spoken and him who is being spoken to and believes the solace) laid down, created."[166] For Bayer, the central insight of Luther is that in going out from his word of God understanding as *verbum eficax* in the sense of Isaiah 55:11 and Hebrews 4:12, he replaces the constative understanding of biblical prophecy with a performative understanding. The language action itself, according to Bayer, is the "basis of faith."[167]

The first thing to criticize in this reasoning is an incorrect application of the term "performative statement," so harmonious for absolution, but not for prophecy. Prophecy is an illocutionary act, to be more exact, a special pledge—and a pledge is not already fulfilled the moment it has been spoken. Gottfried Hornig formulated this important objection. Religious performatives do not create faith, they demand it. "The consolation of the forgiveness of sins presupposes faith in the truth of the statement that there is a living and presently acting God who encounters us as demanding and judgmental, but for Christ's sake out of grace is ready to forgive mankind its sins."[168] The same argument holds for other typical performatives in the religious context, like baptizing or blessing.[169] So a context of interpretation is always presupposed in which the language actions make sense. Whoever does not share in these contexts remains untouched by the action.

Matthias Petzold tried to salvage Bayer's approach by connecting it to the proclamation of the historical Jesus. His authority, which some of his hearers sensed and which expresses itself later "understood reflexively"[170] in the majesty titles of the gospels, must have been an event "which first emerged between the one speaking and the one being

165. Bayer, *Was ist das?* 26.
166. Bayer, *Was ist das?* 28.
167. Bayer, *Was ist das?* 37.
168. Hornig, *Analyse*, 69.
169. See Searle, *Linguistik*, 117.
170. Petzold, *Offenbarung*, 139.

spoken to in consummation of the language action."[171] Jesus' interpretations were not decisive—his language aligned with the "everyday life of human language of connection"—but his discourse with "authority,"[172] as the gospels express it.[173] God reveals himself "in the linguistic reality of everyday life."[174] However, Petzold overlooks that this effect of Jesus' discourse, despite his everyday language, was not possible without the background of interpretation of Judaic expectation of the messiah[175] and that, at the very least, the synoptic gospels emphasize the affinity of Jesus with the Jewish canon and his religiously symbolic language.[176] Even Jesus' proclamation did not create *ex nihilo* a fellowship of believers by the word, but the proclamation was only comprehensible within the interpretative framework of Jewish theology.[177]

Back to Barth's proclamation. The analysis demonstrated that the acknowledgment of interpretation Z is an essential condition for success of the speech act (V4). To that extent proclamation can bring about faith. Still, it is the specifically religious element, which connects to the profession, and is contained in interpretation Z, not in the act, which communicates the interpretation. It is Z which first makes a "God with us" experience out of an experience in the stream of sensory data. And precisely this salient point, as the reflections on V1 (δ) reveal, does not come into view with speech act theory. While this describes a communication event, it is constitutive for Z, and a resource for language actions, namely the semantics of applied language. It is the language game founded on odd discernment and interactive metaphors which makes up religious language (see section 6.3).

With the help of speech act theory, on this basis the moments can be described in which, thanks to successful proclamation, recipients become fellow players. The word of God comes through mankind to mankind in a language event which comprehensively renews, with semantic means, his understanding of existence—and precisely at the moment when he reacts to the address with an act of acknowledgment. Then it holds true

171. Petzold, *Offenbarung*, 138.

172. Petzold, *Offenbarung*, 140.

173. Predominantly in Matt 7:29, 9:6, 21:23, and John 5:27.

174. Petzold, *Offenbarung*, 140.

175. See Theißen/Merz, *Jesus*, 139 and 467–69.

176. See Theißen, *Religion*, 256–57.

177. See Theißen/Merz, *Jesus*, 143–44.

for these language actions that they "are themselves forms of consummation in which personality emerges, namely in the opposition of an 'I am' which gives me to understand 'you are.'"[178]

6.5. Looking Back, Looking Forward

This concluding section attempts in the first part, in retrospect, to summarize in a compact characterization the gained insights into the "word of God" and then to describe these in two respects: one with a view to the three language theoretical aspects which concerned Augustine, Luther, and Barth, and then with a view to the five biblical lines of tradition of the term identified in chapter 2.

The second segment examines two possible objections against the suggested conception. Finally, the third points out some general implications extending beyond the theological debate and touching human understanding and thereby shows the unbroken, indeed actually increasing relevance of a conception of the word of God.

6.5.1. Categorized Summary

The path of thought forged in this work from the Christian canon through Augustine, Martin Luther, and Karl Barth to modern philosophy of language suggests the following ten-part explication of the concept "word of God."

1. A language event is intended with "word of God" which can occur in communication between people or in visual or auditory reception of a text.
2. This language event can be more closely characterized by the speech act of "proclaiming."
3. Proclamation consists in pledging to the perceptible presence of God which is connected with reference to other linguistically witnessed experiences of God. While the speaker himself (or the text) cannot himself vouch for the pledge but instead refers to a transcendent instance, the term "promise" is offered for this case.

178. Korsch, *Einführung*, 49.

4. A contingent event is intended by "the perceptible presence of God" in which the self- and world-understanding of the experiencing subject is oriented to a disclosure situation on an external instance, which itself is not a part of the world.
5. The reference to a linguistically witnessed experience of God serves as an articulation aid for this experience which becomes an experience of God in this linguistic interpretation.
6. The interpretation necessarily makes use of an absolutely metaphorical language form (odd discernment) which cannot be translated into an "actual" language form.
7. The metaphor initializes a new language game in which the fundamental opposites of our formation of consciousness—finite and infinite, conditional and absolute, individual and general—can be named and brought into relationship. The model for Christian language games sounds forth: "God became man."
8. In the moment at which the language game is separated from the subject, the reality described therein is disclosed to him—whether for the first time or anew.
9. Changing the language game results in a permanent change in the form of life.
10. If the speech act "proclaiming" succeeds, in this language game the comprehensive reorientation of self-, world-, and God-understanding is experienced as a personal address from God: as the word of God.

In these ten points, all three essential language-theoretical aspects of the "word of God" are raised which in thinking through the impulses of Augustine for semiotics, Luther for semantics, and Barth for pragmatics of the intended communication event, these results are:

1. Semiotics: The term "language game" makes clear that the formation of signs cannot be described by a classic triangle of object, interpretation, and sign, but that the ontologically neutral use of signs is the starting point. The "true reality,"[179] to take up Barth's concept, shows itself within the language game to the extent that it has achieved absolute relevance for the speakers.

179. Barth, *KD* 1/1:195.

2. Semantics: Initializing for the language game, within which the "word of God" is the topic, are disclosure or transcendent experiences whose adequate linguistic articulation makes the transgression of limits urgent.
3. Pragmatics: The "word of God" is fully grasped only with its situative components connected to the particular communication situation. For it describes the effect of a language event whose conditions for success alongside the speech act "proclaiming" can be refined.

When, as happens here, the "word of God" is interpreted as a language-theoretical concept, the experiential- and revelatory-theological approaches no longer stand diametrically in opposition. Every authentic use of language must be anchored in personal experience—particularly a religious one. The experience finds its expression in linguistic interpretation and thus becomes an experience, or a religious experience. On the other hand, because interpretations are not further deducible, they must be immediately evident in order to gain currency. This is consistently an individual and unplanned event. God does not speak for all in every discussion of God. The "word of God" and "piety"—these are not mutually exclusive alternatives[180]—but two "paths of reflection," which "in consideration of the philosophy of language" are placed in a context which "certainly permits the possibility of cross-pollination."[181]

In the suggested explication of points one to ten above, all five lines of tradition of the biblical word of God concept are recognizable. Like the presentation in section 2.7, the following survey is not oriented in the series to the canonical sequence, but to an inner context:

a. Creative word: By way of language a pathway is cleared to transcendence in which the disclosure experience can be articulated. In this new language sphere, previous and present experiences seem to have been placed in relation to the absolute (God). To apply a typical "odd discernment," reality appears "in a new light." Self-relation and world-relation become grounded in the God-relation.
b. Prophetic word: The achieved potential for interpretation especially permits the positioning of contingent experiences whose immanent causal explanation alone would be insufficiently meaningful.

180. See Korsch, *Dialektische Theologie*, 109–29.

181. Dietz, *Sprache als Dasein*, 88.

c. Personified word: The successful speech act "proclaiming" is experienced in its subjectivity-constituting effect as a "you are" and therefore experienced as a personal address. For Christians the testimonies of and about Jesus of Nazareth add up to the incomparable proclamation of the sentence "God became man."

d. Legal word: Language is a rule-governed attitude. A change in the language game means inevitably a change in attitude. As a member of a community of interpretation, I am only credible to the extent that I adhere to the rules.

e. Critical word: If in the word of God the promise is fulfilled, namely the steadfast presence of God in one's own life, one's own attitude towards this presence depends on this pledge. It becomes immediately true as soon as the range of interpretations has been acknowledged.

Even the later post-biblical differentiation of the word of God in the gospel and in the law is rediscovered in the submitted specification—and exactly in the constellation which Barth asserted against any possible misapprehension of Luther's (see section 5.2). The word of God is first and foremost a promise (point 3) which is fulfilled precisely when the recipient reacts to the promise in an act of profession (point 8). In other words: The new orientation to God proffered by the word—the gospel—presupposes the readiness to abandon the old self-image and world-image and to engage with a new rule-governed acknowledgment of reality (law).

6.5.2 Two Possible Objections

As a language phenomenon, the word of God stands paradigmatically for the possibilities of language with regard to a) its function for subjectification, b) communication between people, and c) disclosure of reality. It should not be surprising that both the word of God and language wish to mediate between the commonplace and the extraordinary. As the extraordinary can only be expressed if it is formulated in the commonality of language, in a special event of the divine word it opens the vista of the commonplace reconciled to the extraordinary.[182]

Understood in this way, the reconstruction of the word of God evades the important objection of Martin Laube that every attempt to

182. On this see Korsch, *Theologie*, 226–28.

grasp theoretically the connection of linguisticality and religiosity faces the aporetic alternative "of dissipating the religiosity either in a fog of non-linguistic irrationality, or acknowledging that even it is only mediated by commonplace linguisticality and therefore as the extraordinary, but cannot be defined as the other of this linguisticality."[183]

In the approach presented the word of God is not a special case of human communication, but conversely the model for the same. The recommended explication preserves the *otherness* of the word of God because it is, at any rate, our sole path to the totally other and nevertheless does not remove it from the context of common linguisticality (and rationality), but grounds it. This idea is found, as chapter 4 showed, in Luther's approach, and then programmatically in Gerhard Ebeling[184] and Eberhard Jüngel.[185] The idea can be refined in a linguistic-analytic fashion:

a. viewed epistemologically, the word of God marks the maximum of that which can be effectuated by language—identity founding, community building, ontologically and normatively, and
b. viewed genealogically, the word of God is always shifting the limits of linguistic capability of expression with its semantic innovation potential.

The word of God is the paradigm for all language use, a model for communication. That does not mean that the word of God would be a sort of exemplar for successful human accommodation which by this linguistic act and initiated process includes the radical convulsion of the previous self- and world-image, a radical No, in which is also included a Yes.[186] It can only be a model for communication insofar as in the word of God the possibilities of a language event in all dimensions have been exhausted. If one understands rationality as communicatively

183. Laube, *Im Bann*, 311.

184. Ebeling, *Wesen*, 184–85: "For with God's word nothing else is intended than simply word: pure, true word, in which that, what the word actually is and should impact, comes to fulfillment and happens."

185. Jüngel, *Gottes Sein*, 26: "The word of God brings language into its essence."

186. Barth, *Not und Verheißung*, 246.

constituted,[187] then the word of God is, as Barth wrote in *KD*, "a rational event,"[188] indeed the epitome of rationality.

A further fundamental objection could come from the philosophical direction, which for some time now has been practiced as "critical" or "new realism." It turns against the view represented in many places since Kant's transcendental philosophy that in epistemology one cannot deal with things or reality "in itself" but only with our access to them. As a matter of fact many empirical and linguistic-analytical thinkers would agree with this thesis, which plays a role in chapter 6, most prominently Ludwig Wittgenstein whose intellectual approach became the starting point of the radical constructivism of Ernst von Glasersfeld[189] as well as the neopragmatism of Donald Davidson and Richard Rorty.[190] The latter stands above all in the closing line of new realism, since Wittgenstein's language game concept leads here to a complete dissolution of the terms "meaning" and "language."[191] According to Davidson and Rorty, instead of a description of language, only "preliminary theories" on our observations of the attitude of our opposite number can be formulated for which there are no rules governing their assembly and correction. "Wittgenstein's line of thinking, which . . . Davidson elaborated for languages, naturalizes language, in that all questions on its relation to the rest of the universe are transformed into *causal* questions, no longer questions on the suitability of exposition or expression."[192]

Certainly, one could sensibly ask why we have come from the "relative incapacity of apes to think to the complete thinking apparatus of humans," but questions about the essence of our thought and language and its relation to facts are now meaningless.[193] That is obviously nothing more than a philosophical capitulation in the form of an assertion, which anyway is inconsistent. Obviously, "preliminary theories" have in the course of time been replaced by other theories, so that in the long run

187. On this see Habermas, *Theorie*, 25–71.

188. Barth, *KD* 1/1:139.

189. Initially in critical distance from the *Tractatus*, and then is agreement with the *Philosophische Untersuchungen* (see von Glasersfeld, *Radikaler Konstruktivismus*, 22–26 and 217–21).

190. See Davidson, *A Nice Derangement*, particularly 446, and Rorty, *Kontingenz*, 21–51.

191. See Rorty, *Kontingenz*, 37.

192. Rorty, *Kontingenz*, 40. Emphasis in original.

193. Rorty, *Kontingenz*, 40.

something like progress is demonstrated. Even if this has for us no recognizable telos, the question of the manner of progress must be allowed to remain. Now as before the old theories are disposable, but obviously there are reasons to no longer use them. These reasons, even if they are more complex than portrayed by scientific theory of the early twentieth century, can be researched and named.

Against the surrender of philosophical thought propagated by neopragmatism, Markus Gabriel, the main proponent of new realism in Germany,[194] asserts that there are different areas of facts, so-called "conceptual fields" whose existence and objectivity we can recognize and examine independently of our personal influences, convictions, and languages.[195] This position wants to distinguish itself from "naïve realism" by the fact that it does not assert *one* recognizable reality but the reality of our diverse recognition. Gabriel takes aim against the "postmodern flight from facts" which flows into the epistemological aporie of relativism—and he does that with theological pathos throughout. As his peak proposition, he cites John 8:32 (NRSV): "The truth will make you free."[196]

In the reasoning presented here, the word of God is the key to our understanding of reality. This is bound to a communication situation and to signs, whose meaning is revealed in their application. As Karl Barth emphasized, it would be wrong to want to push forward at "facts standing behind."[197] And still the truth of relativism is not left behind, but exactly the reverse—the moment and structure of human disclosure of reality is captured (see point 8). Therefore, in the *KD*, Barth speaks of "true reality,"[198] which becomes manifest in the moment of a successful speech act of the type "proclaiming." That this realization can be described and passed on does not mean that it has been delivered from the arbitrary nature of linguistic signs.

The question remains, if the diastasis between sensory *experience* of a disclosure of reality and the linguistic articulation of the same—the *explanation* of reality—is bridgeable tautologically. In other words: If in discourse one cannot transgress the limits of language, is there then at least something like a glance over this limit? The sociologist of religion

194. See Gabriel, *Warum es die Welt night gibt*, 87–95.

195. See Gabriel, *Existenz*, 195–97.

196. Gabriel, *Wider die postmoderne Flucht*.

197. See Barth, *KD* 1/2:545.

198. Barth, *KD* 1/1:195.

Hans Joas has made a convincing suggestion with his category, recovered in thinking beyond Émile Durkheim, of the "sacred"—exactly one hundred years after the appearance of Rudolf Otto's classic.[199] Connected to the conception advocated here, his reasoning can be integrated as follows. The new determination initiated by God of the self-, world-, and God-relation is the experience of self-transcendence in which the subject is torn from the limits of his ego. In this new orientation to an external source of power, a liberation of the self is experienced: "This passive dimension of being carried away in the experiences of self-transcendence is by necessity the experience of stirring forces. Something must be at work when individuals or collectives are torn from the previous limits of their ego. . . . Experiences of self-transcendence lead compellingly to the attribution of the quality of 'sacred'—naturally, not necessarily applying this designation."[200] This sacred is thus initially qualified by nothing further than through its externity and its effect which mankind experiences as something unconditional. That can be something unconditionally good or unconditionally evil. The valuation is initially achieved by connection to an articulated interpretation.[201]

The concept pair "sacred/profane" is therefore not synonymous with "transcendent/mundane" (or "immanent") and "religious/secular." Transcendence—in Joas not to be confused with the equivalent word component in "self-transcendence"—"indicates the ideas of a separation between the realms of the divine and the earthly, concurrently a localization of truth in the realm of the divine."[202] On the other hand, "religious" refers to traditional attempts "to understand, more closely systematize, and pass on" the experiences of mankind with the sacred.[203] While the sacred represents for Joas "a universal anthropological phenomenon"[204] and to that extent something objective, transcendence and religion are bound to specific places, times, and signs.

In this brief sketch it can be recognized that the argumentative outcome of a linguistic phenomenon—like the word of God here—must in no way lead to a constructivist or decisionist position. The experience of

199. Joas, *Die Macht des Heiligen*.

200. Joas, *Die Macht des Heiligen*, 434.

201. Joas, *Die Macht des Heiligen*, 435–38.

202. Joas, *Die Macht des Heiligen*, 253–54.

203. Joas, *Das Heilige*, 5.

204. Joas, *Die Macht des Heiligen*, 254.

the word of God is bound to a given, external power, independent of all human interpretation, which is stronger than that which mankind can bring about by the specific powers vested in itself.

6.5.3. Actual Relevance

What relevance does an actualization of the theologumenon of the word of God have in an era when so much is communicated as never before[205] and real understanding threatens concurrently to become even more difficult? In an era when the world has long coalesced ecologically, logistically, and economically but populist currents increasingly position national and individual interests against global solidarity and responsibility? What can this thousand year old concept evoke in us in contemporary religious and secular communication among persons? The seven following recommendations are to be read as arguments for a reconsideration of theology based on the word of God.

1. The Word of God as Resonance Event

First of all is the inherent reflection on the word of God as an authentic language event. It has to do with a situation of address and the personal being-spoken-to with permanent effect. This precisely is not a given in all modern communication processes. The hasty, often self-centered postings on social networks and messenger services could be compared to those existential conceptions of the absurd in which the world is summoned and a response is expected, which either never comes or at least indicates partial incomprehension.[206] As a result the world is perceived as "mute, cold, indifferent, and indeed repugnant."[207]

In the word of God the complementary idea is preserved which Hartmut Rosa defined as "resonance"[208] in his *Soziologie der Weltbezie-*

205. Currently more than fifty million texts per minute are sent just over mobile news services worldwide. See the summary and real time simulation at www.kaufda.de/info/apps-in-echtzeit/ (retrieved on 10 March 2018).

206. See Rosa, *Beschleunigung*, 147.

207. Rosa, *Beschleunigung*, 146. See Rosa, *Resonanz*, 25.

208. Rosa, *Resonanz*, 20.

hungen.[209] Resonance is "the positive connection to something outside of me, something I love and gives me something in return."[210]

Resonance is defined as a four-figure relation: a subject (1), that sends a message (2) to an opposite number (3), which gives a response (4) to this message.[211] The opposite number can be a person, a living or inanimate part of the world, or something extramundane, something transcendent. The opposite of a connection interpreted as resonance is reification or accessibility, an instrumentalization of the opposite number that expects no response. A resonance connection always contains the possibility that it or the other will respond differently than expected. Genuine resonances can only ensue where communication remains open-ended. The attempt to make the other accessible hushes it. Successful resonance, by contrast, alters the participating persons.

The special aspect of Rosa's suggestion is that it basically extends a communication model to all connections which can have a subject in its exterior experience. Not just all spoken language which reaches us in dealing with the world, but a diversity of forms of inner contact and addressability: the painted sunrise, the inviting look of a dog, becoming aware of a deep friendship, a fascinating work of art, a rousing symphony—or even a religious experience.[212] The idea that fulfilled life distinguishes itself by resonance connections which "touch us, move us, and grasp us . . . and concurrently cause the experience that in others—people, nature, art, religion—we can reach something and effectuate it"[213] connects Rosa's approach with the idea of the word of God. The talking God is the ideal of identity-founding and fulfilling resonance connection. Naturally, only so long as one does not fail to anticipate the response of the opposite number: "In the moment that I believe 'Now I know what God is saying,' I lose the resonance space. The danger of religions resides in that. If I proclaim 'God says . . . ' I am no longer in hearing and answering mode, but accessibility mode."[214]

209. See Rosa, *Beschleunigung*, 147 and Rosa, *Resonanz*, 24–25.

210. Rosa, *Ressourcensammler*, 4.

211. Rosa, *Resonanz*, 298.

212. See Rosa, *Resonanz*, 331–514.

213. Rosa, *Ressourcensammler*, 4.

214. Rosa, *Menschen*, 49.

The preserved ideal in the word of God of a designed connection based on inaccessible resonance[215] gains concurrently an ethical dimension in this sociological interpretation. It appears as a counter-model to an alienated world-connection construed as the gathering of resources in which it is predominantly concerned with accumulating reified object connections as (unlived) possibilities.[216] Where this expansion assumes a separate existence, things fall silent. No longer qualitative, but only quantitative goals become the measure of political and individual action.[217] By contrast the hope arises, in experience of the world of the strongest conceivable resonance axes ever, of encountering the word of God,[218] opening our eyes for what Christians have called since time immemorial "grace." "Resonance connections always have a moment of becoming a gift."[219]

2. *The Word of God as External Point of Reference*

Right alongside the resonance connection hangs a second corrective of the word of God. It posits the externity of an all-determining instance against the aporetic trend of perpetuated self-optimization which produces an absolutized society of expansion. This "fitter-richer-prettier" orientation revolving around one's self remains aporetic because an attempt at self-determination fixed on one's self enables no boundary between the I and the non-I. The range of interpretation of the word of God, by contrast, locates the I within the existential base relations and first enables the diversity of experiences which in turn form the basis for responsible discernment.

In actual societal and political debates, an ethical competence of judgment gained in this fashion becomes more and more important. The base relation "Life-Death" raises many ethical questions at both ends

215. On the relationship between resonance and inaccessibility see Rosa, *Unverfügbarkeit*, 48–68.

216. See Rosa, *Resonanz*, 316–28.

217. See Rosa, *Resonanz*, 725.

218. See Rosa, *Resonanz*, 441: "From the plea of Solomon to the cry of Jesus on the cross, [the Bible] appears as a peculiar document of human pleading, petitioning, and praying, waiting and awaiting, whispering and calling for an answer. And one could add that there is perhaps one single great counter-pledge to this pleading which sounds like this: *There is one who hears you, understands you, and can find the ways and means to reach you and answer you.*" Emphasis in original.

219. Rosa, *Menschen*, 47.

of the spectrum about the possibilities for reproductive medicine and prenatal diagnostics on the one hand, and on the other hand, palliative medicine and assisted suicide. Here only a moral standpoint liberated from individual interests (of an economic nature) can differentiate between welcome and unwelcome progress. The word of God is the offering of a point of reference from which the totality of the created world comes into view.

3. *The Word of God as Good News*

The third corrective emerges from the essence of the word of God as joyful good news. As numerous studies show, people are evolutionarily conditioned to react more strongly to bad news than good news.[220] This attitude contributes to the survival of the species. However this inclination threatens to turn in a counterproductive direction when bad news is multiplied by a fun house mirror in the media. For mercantile reasons the media aligns itself with this attitude, and the more channels are recorded, the bleaker becomes the impression which people have of the world situation.

And yet, we live in an era "in which we are profiting from the achievements of the Enlightenment as never before."[221] For leading psychologists like Steven Pinker, this discrepancy of perception has meanwhile reached the scale where it is a massive threat to further progress. Increasingly people are turning away from Enlightenment values and instead following irrational ideologies or so-called "authentic" leadership personalities.[222] The word of God reminds us that a self-and world-relation sustained by hope can be based solely on the comforting assurance of its presence. Perhaps Ernst Bloch's dictum is again as topical as it was in the years following the catastrophe of the Second World War. At the moment, "the so-called modern man [lives] on previous hopes and the foothold they once provided."[223]

220. See Baumeister et al., *Pragmatic Prospection*, 1–14.

221. Pinker, *Romantik*.

222. See Pinker, *Enlightenment*, especially 29–31.

223. Bloch, *Das Prinzip Hoffnung*, 1361.

4. *The Word of God as Standard*

In the word of God there are no "alternative facts"—the claim to absoluteness of truth is directly supported by the fact that for semantic fuzziness the delicate part of linguistic formulations is interpreted as a region of correctable interpretations. Without the ideal truth standing behind it, the "total commitment to the entire universe" which is constitutive for the disclosure experience would not be possible.

The problem of "fake news"[224] is more important today than at any other time in which people called them "rumors." The reason is related to the just mentioned phenomenon of faster dissemination of bad news. Obviously false news is disseminated faster than correct news. According to the result of a 2018 study published in *Science*, in which four and a half million Twitter tweets from approximately three million users from eleven years on roughly one hundred twenty six thousand different news items from different subject areas were analyzed.[225] False, mainly political information was shared on Twitter with substantially greater coverage and speed than true information. Certainly iterative computer programs (bots) play a role in this, but this comes predominantly from human users captivated by false reporting.

The systematic distortion to the disadvantage of truth threatens on the one hand all theories which are supported by rational accomplishment of consensus and coherence, and on the other hand theories of democratic form of government based on the responsibility of the individual—as associated attempts at manipulating votes show.

The "word of God," with its world-opening power, is virtually a counter-design to such rumor campaigns and conspiracy theories. The word of God posits the conviction of a—and indeed exactly one—all-determining reality against any postmodern "anything goes" attitude.

5. *The Word of God as Offer of Accommodation*

Since the language-theoretic setting of the word of God intrinsically includes the realm of human interpretations, it offers itself as a connecting bridge for inter-religion dialogue—especially where religions of

224. The *Rechtsschreib-Duden* incorporated the term in the twenty-seventh edition (2017). In American English its use can be traced back to 1890 (see www.merriam-webster.com/words-at-play/the-real-story-of-fake-news; retrieved on 15 April 2018).

225. Vosoughi, *The spread of true*, 1146–51.

revelation want to come into the discussion which derive from an address situation between God and mankind. The word of God contains the component "word" which can be argued over in different interpretations and languages, and it contains the component "God," whose independence from every human language formation must by necessity be presupposed (otherwise the conversation would be about something other than God).

Already in 1984, the American historian George A. Lindbeck, famous for his efforts in the ecumenical movement,[226] presented a recommendation with his *The Nature of Doctrine* as to how one can divide dogmas from different cultural horizons in a socio-cultural vocabulary on the one hand, and in a universally valid grammar on the other hand.[227] Even if Lindbeck's derivation is not always convincing,[228] his approach going forth from Wittgenstein proves to be practical. It lies at the basis of the *Malta Report*[229] from 1972 in which Lutherans and Catholics found for the first time a common understanding of the gospel.[230]

With this method, one will naturally not come to the same interpretations, but observe its structural similarities: the attempt to describe in symbolic and metaphoric signatures a power reaching out to mankind but superior to everything human. The specific Christian element does not come off badly because the God become man gets to the heart of the personal address of God to mankind most consequentially. What the "word of God" moreover gets to capture is comparable with the above mentioned sociologically achieved category of the "sacred" in Hans Joas. He also differentiates between a contingent experience space—religion—and the "anthropological universality of experiences of 'self-transcendence' and the attributions of 'sacredness' emerging from there."[231]

With this reflection on the essentials of revealed religion, namely the manner of the God-man connection, the "dramatic overdogmaticization

226. Lindbeck took part in all sessions of Vatican II as an official observer from the Lutheran World Federation and initiated, together with Catholic theologians, an ecumenical dialogue between the Federation and the Roman Catholic church on controversial questions of doctrine which led to astonishing agreements (see Tambour, *Ansatz*, 279–80).

227. See Lindbeck, *Nature*, 73–90.

228. Self-critically, Lindbeck admitted to understanding Wittgenstein differently than "those more knowledgable in Wittgenstein" (*Nature*, 24).

229. The Gospel and the Church (Malta Report) (christianunity.va)

230. On Lindbeck's contribution see Tambour, *Ansatz*, 279–80.

231. Joas, *Die Macht des Heiligen*, 440.

of Christianity" could also be countered, which Jörg Lauster has criticized as the legacy of confessional antagonism between Catholicism and Protestantism[232] and if nothing else is responsible for the "perceived de-Christianization" of society. Whoever measures religiosity by agreement on articles of faith or concurrence on traditional practices of piety may not wonder when he finds an additional declining trend: "While [polling agencies] and with them empirical sociologists of religion follow this line and explain an orthodox doctrine as the 'core collection of Christianity,' dismissing everything else about lived religion as 'vague spirituality,' it is hardly possible for them to perceive the complexity and ambivalence of the secularization or legitimization of individual religiosity. . . . Then, however, the decline of Christianity would, if nothing else, be owed its own definition."[233]

6. *The Word of God between Individuation and Society*

These reflections implicitly contain an answer to the question posed over and over again in an era of flight from the church—how much individuation can religion tolerate?[234] The word of God is not to be had without society, but also not without personal experience. When both first come together, the experience of self-transcendence in every person which feeds on other sensory data and the formative possibility of articulation in a community of interpretation, the word of God becomes the key to knowledge of reality.

7. *The Word of God as Gift*

For the thinkers dealt with here, Augustine, Luther, and Barth, language was the outstanding attribute of mankind, indeed for Luther the crucial evidence for the divine image of mankind.[235] Language opens the gate to the world and community with other people, language enables culture, interpretation, and religion—that ζωὴ περισσή of which John 10:10 speaks.

232. Lauster, *Verzauberung*, 329.

233. Claussen, *Kulturreligionen*, 5.

234. See for example Pohl-Patalong, *Glaube*.

235. See Luther, *Randbemerkungen*, WA 9, 67,15–18 and *Vorrede auf den Psalter*, WA DB 10.1, 100,12–13.

At the same time, language is always a gift—no one can create for themselves a language suitable for communication.[236] Whoever can stand before creation in nothing else but veneration, that person ought to feel that sacred awe in the use of language, which the poet Martin Walser once described: "The development of language leads totally of itself to creation in a manner akin to God. God is probably the purest word that there is. The pure literalness. The absolute essence of language. Simply the linguistic. In God, language comes into its own. . . . The supreme thing that we have is language. Think about this, please, when you pursue your essence with language."[237]

236. See Wittgenstein, *Philosophische Untersuchungen*, 258.

237. Walser, *Über Rechtfertigung*, 98.

Bibliography

Primary Sources

Augustine

De beata vita liber unus. Edited by Pius Knöll. CSEL 63. Vienna: Tempsky, 1922.

Bekenntnisse. Translated and edited by Kurt Flasch and Burkhard Mojsisch. Stuttgart: Reclam, 2009.

Die christliche Bildung. Translated by Karla Pollmann. Stuttgart: Reclam, 2013.

De civitate dei. Edited by Emanuel Hoffmann. CSEL 40/1 and 40/2. Vienna: Tempsky, 1899–1900.

Confessiones. Edited by Pius Knöll. CSEL[1] 33. Vienna: Tempsky, 1896.

Confessions. Translated by J.G. Pilkington. Nicene and Post-Nicene Fathers, First Series, Vol. 1. Edited by Philip Schaff. Buffalo, NY: Christian Literature, 1887.

Contra Academicos Libri Tres. Edited by Pius Knöll. CSEL 63. Vienna: Hölder-Pichler-Tempsky, 1922.

De dialectica. Edited by Jacques Paul Migne. PL[2] 32. Paris: Apud Garnier Fratres, 1861–62.

De dialectica. Translated and edited by B. Darrell Jackson and Jan Pinborg. Boston: Reidel, 1975.

De diversis quaestionibus octoginta tribus. Edited by Jacques Paul Migne. PL 40. Paris: Apud Garnier Fratres, 1861–62.

De doctrina christiana libri quattuor. Edited by William McAllen Green. CSEL 80. Vienna: Hölder-Pichler-Tempsky, 1963.

Dreiundachtzig verschiedene Fragen. Translated by Carl Johann Perl. Paderborn: Schöningh, 1972.

Epistula 102. Edited by Alois Goldbacher. CSEL 34/2. Vienna: Tempsky, 1895.

De fide et symbolo. Edited by Joseph Zycha. CSEL 41. Vienna: Tempsky, 1900.

De genesi ad litteram liber unus inperfectus. Edited by Joseph Zycha. CSEL 28. Vienna: Tempsky, 1894.

1. *Corpus Scriptorum Ecclesiaticorum Latinorum*. Vienna (to 2011), Berlin, (2012–).

2. *Patrologiae Cursus Completus, Series prima*. Edited by Jacques Paul Migne. Vol. 32–47. Paris, 1861/62. Text basis for the works of Augustine which had not yet been critically edited for inclusion in CSEL.

De genesi ad litteram libri duodecim. Edited by Joseph Zycha. CSEL 28. Vienna: Tempsky, 1894.

De genesi contra Manichaeos libri duo. Edited by Dorothea Weber. CSEL 91. Vienna: Austrian Academy of Sciences, 1998.

In evangelium Ioannis tractatus centrum viginti quatuor. Edited by Jacques Paul Migne. Paris: Migne, 1861–62.

Lectures on the Gospel of John. Translated by John Gibb. Revised and edited by Kevin Knight. Nicene and Post-Nicene Fathers, First Series, Vol. 7. Edited by Philip Schaff. Buffalo, NY: Christian Literature, 1888.

De libero arbitrio libri tres. Edited by William McAllen Green. CSEL 74. Vienna: Hölder-Pichler-Tempsky, 1956.

The Literal Interpretation of Genesis. Translated by Isabella Image. Edited by Roger Pearse. 2020. https:// www.roger-pearse.com/weblog/wp-content/uploads/2020/08/ Augustine-De_Genesi_Imperfectum_Image-v4.pdf.

The Literal Meaning of Genesis. Translated and annotated by John Hammond Taylor. Ancient Christian Writers 41, 23. New York: Newman, 1982.

De magistro liber unus. Edited by Günther Weigel. CSEL 77. Vienna: Hölder-Pichler-Tempsky, 1961.

On Faith and the Creed. Translated by S. D. F. Salmon. Nicene and Post-Nicene Fathers, First Series, Vol. 3. Edited by Philip Schaff. Buffalo, NY: Christian Literature, 1887.

The Philosophy of Teaching. A Study in the Symbolism of Language. A Translation of De magistro. Translated by Francis E. Tourscher, OSA. Lancaster: Villanova College, 1924.

Sechs Vorträge über das Evangelium des heiligen Johannes. Translated by Thomas Specht. Bibliothek der Kirchenväter 1,19. Munich: Kösel, 1913–14.

Sermo M 27/D 10 (*Super verbis apostolic ad Galatos*). In *Vingt-six sermons au peuple d'Afrique, retrouvés à Mayence*. Edited by François Dolbeau. Collection des ètudes Augustiniennes, Série Antiquité 147. Paris: Institute of Augustinian Studies, 1996.

Sermones. Edited by Jacques Paul Migne. PL 38. Paris: Migne, 1861–62.

Sermones selecti. Edited by Clemens Weidemann. CSEL 101. Berlin: de Gruyter, 2015.

Sermons. Translated by Edmund Hill, OP. Brooklyn: New City, 1991.

De trinitate. Edited by Jacques Paul Migne. PL 42. Paris: Migne, 1861–62.

De trinitate. Translated by Johann Kreuzer. Hamburg: Meiner, 2001.

De trinitate. Translated by Arthur West Haddan. Nicene and Post-Nicene Fathers, First Series, Vol. 3. Edited by Philip Schaff. Buffalo, NY: Christian Literature, 1887.

Two Books on Genesis Against the Manichees and On the Literal Interpretation of Genesis: An Unfinished Book. Translated by Roland J. Teske, SJ. Washington, DC: Catholic University of America, 1991.

Über den Lehrer. Translated by Burkhard Mojsisch. Stuttgart: Reclam, 1998.

De vera religione liber unus. Edited by Jacques Paul Migne. PL 34. Paris: Migne, 1861–62.

Vom Gottesstaat. Translated by Wilhelm Thimme. Edited by Carl Andresen. Munich: DTV, 2011.

Martin Luther

Adventspostille. WA[3] 10.1.2.
An die Ratsherren aller Städte deutschen Landes, daß sie christlichen Schulen aufrichten und erhalten sollen. WA 15.
Die Anfänge. Translated by Kurt Aland. Luther Deutsch—Studienausgabe in zehn Bänden und einem Registerband, Vol. 1. Göttingen: Vandenhoeck und Ruprecht, 1991.
Antwort auf Emser. WA 7.
Assertio omnium aerticulorum Martini Lutheri per bullam Leonis X novissimam damnatorum. WA 7.
Auslegung des dritten und vierten Kapitels Johannis, in *Predigten 1538–1540*. WA 48.
De captivitate babylonica ecclesiae. WA 6.
Christusglaube und Rechtfertigung. Translated by Tobias Goldhahn and Rudolf Mau. Martin Luther—lateinisch-deutsche Studienausgabe, Vol. 2. Edited by Johannes Schilling. Leipzig: Evangelische Verlagsanstalt, 2007.
Concerning Christian Liberty. Translation Philadelphia Edition. 1520-Concerning-Christian-Liberty.pdf (checkluther.com) No translator listed.
Crucigers Sommerpostille. WA 21.
Daß diese Worte Christi "Das ist mein Leib" noch fest stehen wider die Schwärmgeister. WA 23.
Deudsch Catechismus (Der große Katechismus). WA 30.1.
Dictata super Psalterium 1513/1515. WA 3 and WA 4.
Disputationen 1533/1538. WA 39.1.
De divinitate et humanitate Christi. WA 39.2.
Ennaratio Psalmi XC. WA 40.3.
Festpostille. WA 17.2.
First Lectures on the Psalms. Psalms 1–75. Translated by Herbert J.A. Bouman. Edited by Hilton C. Oswald. *Luther's Works.* Edited by Jaroslav Pelikan, Vol. 10. Saint Louis: Concordia, 1958-.
First Lectures on the Psalms. Psalms 76–126. Translated by Herbert J.A. Bouman. Edited by Hilton C. Oswald. *Luther's Works.* Edited by Jaroslav Pelikan, Vol. 11. Saint Louis: Concordia, 1958-.
Galatervorlesung 1531. WA 40.1.
Genesisvorlesung 1535–1545. WA 42–44.
Glaube und Leben. Translated by Notger Slenczka. Martin Luther—deutsch-deutsche Studienausgabe, Vol. 1. Edited by Dietrich Korsch. Leipzig: Evangelische Verlagsanstalt, 2007.
Der große und der kleine Katechismus. Translated by Kurt Aland. Luther Deutsch—Studienausgabe in zehn Bänden und einem Registerband. Vol. 3. Göttingen: Vandenhoeck and Ruprecht, 1991.
Hauspostille. WA 52.
Heidelberger Disputation. WA 1.
Die Kirche und ihre Ämter. Translated by Renate und Reiner Preul. Martin Luther—lateinisch-deutsche Studienausgabe, Vol. 3. Edited by Günther Wartenberg. Leipzig: Evangelische Verlagsanstalt, 2007.

3. *Weimarer Ausgabe. Martin Luthers Werke—kritische Gesamtausgabe.* 220 volumes. Weimar: Böhlau, 1883–2009.

Ein klein Unterricht was man in den Evangeliis suchen und gewarten soll. Translated by Dietrich Korsch. Martin Luther—deutsch-deutsche Studienausgabe, Vol. 1. Edited by Dietrich Korsch. Leipzig: Evangelische Verlagsanstalt, 2007.

Lectures on Genesis. Chapters 1–5. Translated by George V. Schick. Edited by Jaroslav Pelikan. Luther's Works. Edited by Jaroslav Pelikan, Vol. 1. Saint Louis: Concordia, 1958–.

De libertate christiana. WA 7.

Das Magnificat Vorteutschet und ausgelegt. WA 7.

Der Mensch vor Gott. Translated by Sibylle Rolf and Athina Lexutt. Martin Luther—lateinisch-deutsche Studienausgabe, Vol. 1. Edited by Wilfred Härle. Leipzig: Evangelische Verlagsanstalt, 2007.

Operationes in Psalmos. WA 5.

Predigten 1519–1521 (Sammlung Poliander). WA 9.

Predigten 1522. WA 10.3.

Predigten 1523. WA 12.

Predigten 1525. WA 17.1.

Predigten 1529. WA 29.

Predigten 1532. WA 36.

Predigten 1533/1534. WA 37.

Predigten 1538. WA 46.

Predigten 1540/1545. WA 49.

Predigten und Schriften 1523. WA 11.

Der Prophet Jona ausgelegt. WA 19.

Psalmenauslegungen 1529/1532. WA 31.1.

Rationis Latomianae pro incendiariis Lovanieensis scholae sophistis redditae Lutheriana confutatio. WA 8.

Reihenpredigten Johannes 3–4. WA 47.

Reihenpredigten Johannes 6–8. WA 33.

Reihenpredigten 1. Mose 1523/1524. WA 14.

Reihenpredigten 1. Mose 1523/1524—Druckfassung 1627. WA 24.

Reihenpredigten 5. Mose 1529. WA 28.

Reihenpredigten 1. Petrus 1522. WA 12.

Römervorlesung 1515/1516. WA 56.

Roths Sommerpostille. WA 10.1.2.

Die Schmalkaldischen Artikel. WA 50.

Sendbrief vom Dolmetschen. WA 30.2.

Sermon vom neuen Testament, das heißt: von der heiligen Messe. WA 6.

Sermon von dem Sakrament des Leibes Christi. WA 2.

De servo arbitrio. WA 18.

Tischreden. WA TR 1–6.

Tischreden aus dem cod. Besoldi. WA 48.

Eine Unterrichtung, wie sich die Christen nach Mose richten sollen. WA 16.

Verbum caro factum est. Disputation von 1539. WA 39.2.

Vom Abendmahl Christi. WA 26.

Von der Freiheit eines Christenmenschen. WA 7.

Von der Freiheit eines Christenmenschen. Translated by Reinhold Rieger. Kommentare zu Schriften Luthers, Vol. 1. Tübingen: Mohr Siebeck, 2007.

Von der Freyheit eynisz Christen Menschen. Translated and edited by Henrike Lähnemann, Howard Jones, Anna Linton, and Sharon Baker. Oxford: Taylor, 2020.
Vorlesung über *Jesaja 1527/1529*. WA 25.
Vorlesung über *die Kleinen Propheten 1524/1526*. WA 13.
Vorrede auff das Newe Testament. WA DB 6.
Vorrede auff den Psalter 1528. WA DB 10.1.
Vorrede auff die Epistel S. Jacobi und Jude. WA DB 7.
Weihnachtspostille WA 10.1.1.
Wider die himmlischen Propheten. WA 18.
Wort und Sakrament. Translated by Björn Slenczka. Martin Luther—deutsch-deutsche Studienausgabe, Vol. 2. Edited by Dietrich Korsch and Johannes Schilling. Leipzig: Evangelische Verlagsanstalt, 2007.

Karl Barth

Ansatz und Absicht in Luthers Abendmahlslehre. GA[4] 19.
Barmer Theologische Erklärung. GA 52.
Biblische Fragen, Einsichten und Ausblicke. GA 48.
Christliche Dogmatik im Entwurf. 1. Band: *Die Lehre vom Worte Gottes—Prolegomena zur christlichen Dogmatik*. GA 14.
Church Dogmatics. 1/1. *The Doctrine of the Word of God*. Translated by G. W. Bromiley, G. T. Thomason, and Harold Knight. London: T. & T. Clark, 2009.
Church Dogmatics. 4/3. *The Doctrine of Reconciliation*. Translated by G. W. Bromiley, G. T. Thomason, and Harold Knight. London: T. & T. Clark, 2009.
Dogmatik im Grundriss. Zürich: Theologischer Verlag Zürich, 2011.
Das erste Gebot als theologisches Axiom. GA 49.
Evangelium und Gesetz. Munich: Kaiser, 1935.
Fides quaerens intellectum—Anselms Beweis der Existenz Gottes im Zusammenhang seines theologischen Programms. Edited by Eberhard Jüngel and Ingolf U. Dalferth. GA 13.
Die Gerechtigkeit Gottes. GA 48.
How My Mind Has Changed. In *Der Götze wackelt: zeitkritische Aufsätze, Reden und Briefe von 1930 bis 1960*. Edited by Karl Kupisch. Berlin: Vogt, 1961.
Kirchliche Dogmatik. 1/1: *Die Lehre vom Worte Gottes: Prolegomena zur kirchlichen Dogmatik*. Zollikon-Zürich: Evangelischer Verlag, 1955.
Kirchliche Dogmatik. 2/2: *Die Lehre vom Gott*. Zollikon-Zürich: Evangelischer Verlag, 1948.
Kirchliche Dogmatik. 4/1 and 4/3: *Die Lehre von der Versöhnung*. Zollikon-Zürich: Evangelischer Verlag, 1959.
Menschenwort und Gotteswort in der christlichen Predigt. GA 19.
Die Menschlichkeit Gottes. Theologische Studien 48. Zollikon-Zürich: Evangelischer Verlag, 1956.
Not und Verheißung der christlichen Verkündigung. GA 19.
Der Römerbrief—erste Fassung. GA 16.
Der Römerbrief—zweite Fassung. GA 47.

4. *Karl Barth Gesamtausgabe*. Edited by Hinrich Stoevesandt and Hans-Anton Drewes. Zürich: Theologischer Verlag Zürich, 1951–.

Unterricht in der christlichen Religion. 1. Prolegomena. GA 17.
Unterricht in der christlichen Religion. 2. Die Lehre von Gott / Die Lehre vom Menschen. GA 20.
Das Wort Gottes als Aufgabe der Theologie. GA 19.

Secondary Literature

Aland, Kurt and Barbara Aland. *Der Text des Neuen Testaments: Einführung in die wissenschaftlichen Ausgaben sowie in Theorie und Praxis der modernen Textkritik.* 2nd ed. Stuttgart: Deutsche Bibelgesellschaft, 2006.

Anderas, Philip. *Martin Luther, Augustinianism, and Augustine.* Oxford Research Encyclopedia of Religion (religion.oxfordre.com), 2017.

Anderegg, Johannes. "Sprache des Alltags—Sprache des Glaubens." *Sprachwissenschaft* 8.4 (1983) 413–28.

Anzinger, Herbert. *Glaube und kommunikative Praxis: eine Studie zur "vordialektischen" Theologie Karl Barths.* Beiträge zur evangelischen Theologie 110. Munich: Kaiser, 1991.

Apel, Karl-Otto. *Die Idee der Sprache in der Tradition des Humanismus von Dante bis Vico.* Archiv für Begriffsgeschichte 8. Bonn: Bouvier, 1963.

Aristoteles. *Poetik.* Translated and edited by Manfred Fuhrmann. Stuttgart: Reclam, 1994.

———. *Rhetorik.* Translated and edited by Franz G. Sieveke. Munich: Fink, 1993.

Assmann, Jan. *Das kulturelle Gedächtnis: Schrift, Erinnerung, und politische Identität in frühen Hochkulturen.* 2nd ed. Munich: Beck, 1997.

Austin, John L. *Zur Theorie von Sprechakte (How to Do Things with Words).* Translated by Eike von Savigny. Stuttgart: Reclam, 1972.

Ayer, Alfred. *Language, Truth and Logic.* London: Gollancz, 1936.

Bächli, Otto. *Das Alte Testament in der Kirchlichen Dogmatik von Karl Barth.* Neukirchen: Neukirchener Verlag, 1987.

Badiou, Alain. *Paulus: die Begründung des Universalismus.* Zürich: Diphanes, 2009.

Barth, Ulrich. *Aufgeklärter Protestantismus.* Tübingen: Mohr Siebeck, 2004.

———. "Theoriedimensionen des Religionsbegriffs—die Binnenrelevanz der sogenannten Außenperspektiven." In *Religion in der Moderne,* edited by Ulrich Barth, 29–87. Tübingen: Mohr Siebeck, 2003.

Baumeister, Roy, et al. "Pragmatic Prospection: How and Why People Think About the Future." In *Review of General Psychology.* Special issue: The Science of Prospection. www.psych.nyu.edu/oettingen/baumeister-vohs-oettingen-2016-pdf.

Bayer, Oswald. *Promissio: Geschichte der reformatorischen Wende in Luthers Theologie.* Forschungen zur Kirchen- und Dogmengeschichte 24. Göttingen: Vandenhoeck und Ruprecht, 1971.

———. *Schöpfung als Anrede: zu einer Hermeneutik der Schöpfung.* Tübingen: Mohr, 1986.

———. *Theologie.* Handbuch systematischer Theologie 1. Gütersloh: Gütersloher Verlagshaus, 1994.

———. *Was ist das: Theologie? Eine Skizze.* Stuttgart: Calwer, 1973.

Beintker, Michael, ed. *Barth-Handbuch.* Tübingen: Mohr Siebeck, 2016.

Beintker, Michael, Christian Link, and Michael Trowitzsch, eds. *Karl Barth in Deutschland (1921–1935): Aufbruch—Klärung—Widerstand.* Beiträge zum Internationalen Symposion vom 1. bis 4. Mai 2003 in Emden. Zürich: Theologischer Verlag Zürich, 2005.

Die Bekenntnisschriften der evangelisch-lutherischen Kirche: Quellen und Materialen. Edited by Irene Dingel. Volume 2: Die Konkordienformel. Göttingen: Vandenhoeck und Ruprecht, 2014.

Bergjan, Silke-Petra. "Die Liebe zu Gott als erste Regel der Schriftauslegung—Tyconius und die Struktur von Augustin, *De doctrina christiana.*" In *Patristica et Oecumenica.* Festschrift für Wolfgang A. Bienert zum 65. Geburtstag, edited by Peter Gemeinhardt and Uwe Kühneweg, 65–75. Marburger Theologische Studien 85. Marburg: Elwert, 2004.

Bergner, Gerhard. *Um der Sache willen: Karl Barths Schriftauslegung in der Kirchlichen Dogmatik.* Forschungen zur systematischen und ökumenischen Theologie 148. Göttingen: Vandenhoeck und Ruprecht, 2015.

Beutel, Albrecht. *In dem Anfang war das Wort: Studien zu Luthers Sprachverständnis.* Hermeneutische Untersuchungen zur Theologie 27. Tübingen: Mohr Siebeck, 1991.

———, ed. *Luther-Handbuch.* Tübingen: Mohr Siebeck, 2005.

———. "Sprache." In *Luther-Handbuch*, 249–56. Tübingen: Mohr Siebeck, 2005.

Bloch, Ernst. *Das Prinzip Hoffnung*, Vol. 3. 7th ed. Frankfurt am Main: Suhrkamp, 1980.

Blumenberg, Hans. "Paradigmen zu einer Metaphorologie." *Archiv für Begriffsgeschichte* 8 (1960) 5–142.

Bornkamm, Heinrich. "Das Wort Gottes bei Luther." In *Luther: Gestalt und Wirkungen; gesammelte Aufsätze*, 147–86. Gütersloh: Mohn, 1975.

Borsche, Tilman. "Macht und Ohnmacht der Wörter—Bemerkungen zu Augustins *De magistro.*" In *Sprachphilosophie in Antike und Mittelalter*, edited by Burkhard Mojsisch, 121–61. Bochumer Studien zur Philosophie 3. Amsterdam: Grüner, 1986.

Brachtendorf, Johannes. "Der menschliche Geist als Bild des trinitarischen Gottes—Ähnlichkeiten und Unähnlichkeiten." In *Gott und sein Bild: Augustins De trinitate im Spiegel gegenwärtiger Forschung*, 155–70. Paderborn: Schöningh, 2000.

———, ed. *Gott und sein Bild: Augustins De trinitate im Spiegel gegenwärtiger Forschung.* Paderborn: Schöningh, 2000.

———. *Die Struktur des menschlichen Geistes nach Augustinus: Selbstreflexion und Erkenntnis Gottes in De trintate.* Paradeigmata 19. Hamburg: Meiner, 2000.

Briggs, Richard. *Words in Action: Speech Act Theory and Biblical Interpretation; Towards a Hermeneutic of Self-Involvement.* Edinburgh: T. & T. Clark, 2004.

Brinkschmidt, Egon. *Martin Buber und Karl Barth: Theologie zwischen Dialogik und Dialektik.* Neukirchen-Vluyn: Neukirchener, 2000.

Bromand, Joachim, and Guido Kreis, eds. *Gottesbeweise von Anselm bis Gödel.* Berlin: Suhrkamp, 2011.

Brown, Peter. *Augustinus von Hippo: eine Biografie.* Translated by Johannes Bernard. 3rd ed. Frankfurt am Main: Societäts-Verlag, 1982.

Bultmann, Rudolf. "Der Begriff des Wortes Gottes im Neuen Testament." In *Glauben und Verstehen: gesammelte Aufsätze.* 4th ed., Vol. 1, 268–93. Tübingen: Mohr Siebeck, 1961.

———. *Glauben und Verstehen: gesammelte Aufsätze*. 4th ed. Tübingen: Mohr Siebeck, 1961.

———. "Welchen Sinn hat es, von Gott zu reden?" In *Glauben und Verstehen: gesammelte Aufsätze*, Vol. 1, 26–37. 4th ed. Tübingen: Mohr Siebeck, 1961.

Buntfuß, Markus. "Metaphern—Schlüssel zur religiösen Kommunikation." In *Religion und symbolische Kommunikation*, edited by Klaus Tanner, 38–57. Leipzig: Evangelische Verlags Anstalt, 2004.

Buren, Paul M. van. *Reden von Gott: in der Sprache der Welt; zur säkularen Bedeutung des Evangeliums*. Zürich: Zwingli Verlag, 1965.

Busch, Eberhard. *Die große Leidenschaft: Einführung in die Theologie Karl Barths*. Gütersloh: Kaiser, 1998.

———. *Karl Barths Lebenslauf: nach seinen Briefen und autobiografischen Texten*. 4th ed. Munich: Kaiser, 1986.

Carl, Wolfgang. "Bertrand Russell—die *Theory of Descriptions*; ihre logische und erkenntnistheoretische Bedeutung." In *Grundproblemen der großen Philosophen: Philosophie der Gegenwart 1*, edited by Josef Speck. 3rd ed., 220–68. Göttingen: Vandenhoeck und Ruprecht, 1985.

Cassirer, Ernst. *Philosophie der symbolischen Formen. 1. Teil. Die Sprache*. 4th ed. Darmstadt: Wissenschaftliche Buchgesellschaft, 1964.

Cassirer, Ernst. *Philosophie der symbolischen Formen. 3. Teil. Phänomenologie der Erkenntnis*. 4th ed. Darmstadt: Wissenschaftliche Buchgesellschaft, 1964.

Cicero, Marcus Tullius. *Orator*. Translated by Harald Merklin. Stuttgart: Reclam, 2004.

Claussen, Johann Hinrich. "Lob der Kulturreligion." *Süddeutsche Zeitung*, 3 April 2018, 5.

Coseriu, Eugenio. *Geschichte der Sprachphilosophie: von den Anfängen bis Rousseau*. Newly revised by Jörn Albrecht. Tübingen: Francke, 2003.

Dalferth, Ingolf U. "Einführung in die analytische Religionsphilosophie und Theologie." In *Sprachlogik des Glaubens: Texte analytischer Religionsphilosophie und Theologie zur religiösen Sprache*, 9–60. Munich: Kaiser, 1974.

———. "Ereignis und Transcendenz." *Zeitschrift für Theologie und Kirche* 110 (2013) 475–500.

———. *Jenseits von Mythos und Logos: die christliche Transformation der Theologie*. Quaestiones Disputatae 142. Freiburg im Breisgau: Herder, 1993.

———. *Radical Theology*. Translated by William D. Howden. Minneapolis: Fortress, 2016.

———. *Radikale Theologie*. Leipzig: Evangelische Verlagsanstalt, 2010.

———. *Religiöse Rede von Gott*. Munich: Kaiser, 1981.

———. "Religiöse Sprechakte als Kriterien der Religiosität? Kritik einer Konfusion." *Linguistica Biblica* 44 (1979) 101–16.

———, ed. *Sprachlogik des Glaubens: Texte analytischer Religionsphilosophie und Theologie zur religiösen Sprache*. Munich: Kaiser, 1974.

———. "Theologischer Realismus und realistische Theologie bei Karl Barth." *Evangelische Theologie* 46 / New Series 41 (1986) 402–22.

———. *Wirkendes Wort: Bibel, Schrift und Evangelium im Leben der Kirche und im Denken der Theologie*. Leipzig: Evangelische Verlagsanstalt, 2018.

Danz, Christian. "Der Begriff des Symbols bei Paul Tillich und Ernst Cassirer." In *Die Prägnanz der Religion in der Kultur: Ernst Cassirer und die Theologie*, edited by Dietrich Korsch and Enno Rudolph, 201–28. Tübingen: Mohr Siebeck, 2000.

Davidson, Donald. "A Nice Derangement of Epitaphs." In *Truth and Interpretation: Perspectives on the Philosophy of Donald Davidson*, edited by Ernest LePore, 433–46. Oxford: Blackwell, 1986.

Deiser, Oliver. *Einführung in die Mengenlehre: die Mengenlehre Georg Cantors und ihre Axiomatisierung durch Ernst Zermelo*. 2nd ed. Berlin: Springer, 2004.

Demut, André. *Evangelium und Gesetz: eine systematisch-theologische Reflexion zu Karl Barths Predigtwerk*. Theologische Bibliothek Töpelmann 145. Berlin: De Gruyter, 2008.

Denkmal memphitischer Theologie. In *Schöpfung: biblische Theologie im Kontext altorientalischer Religionen* by Othmar Keel and Silvia Schroer, 255–57. Göttingen: Vandenhoeck und Ruprecht, 2002.

Derrida, Jacques. "Die differánce." Translated by Eva Pfaffenberger-Brückner. In *Die differánce: ausgewählte Texte*, edited by Peter Engelmann, 110–49. Stuttgart: Reclam, 2004.

Dettwiler, Andreas, and Jean Zumstein, eds. *Kreuzestheologie im Neuen Testament*. Wissenschaftliche Untersuchungen zum Neuen Testament 151. Tübingen: Mohr Siebeck, 2002.

Dierken, Jörg. "Wort Gottes 3." In *Evangelisches Kirchenlexikon*, Vol. 4, 1329–33. Göttingen: Vandenhoeck und Ruprecht, 1986–97.

Dietz, Thorsten. "Die Sprache als Dasein des Glaubens—erkenntnistheoretische und sprachphilosophische Voraussetzungen der Dogmatik." In *Dogmatik im Diskurs: mit Dietrich Korsch im Gespräch*, edited by Cornelia Richter et al., 73–88. Leipzig: Evangelische Verlagsanstalt, 2014.

Doeker, Andrea. *Die Funktion der Gottesrede in den Psalmen: eine poetologische Untersuchung*. Bonner biblische Beiträge 135. Berlin: Philo, 2002.

Drecoll, Volker Henning, ed. *Augustin-Handbuch*. Tübingen: Mohr Siebeck, 2014.

———. "Zur Chronologie der Werke." In *Augustin-Handbuch*, 250–60. Tübingen: Mohr Siebeck, 2014.

Duchrow, Ulrich. *Sprachverständnis und biblisches Hören bei Augustin*. Hermeneutische Untersuchungen zur Theologie 5. Tübingen: Mohr, 1965.

———. "Zum Prolog von Augustins *De doctrina christiana*." *Viviliae Christianae* 17 (1953) 165–72.

Dürr, Lorenz. *Die Wertung des göttlichen Wortes im Alten Testament im antiken Orient: zugleich ein Beitrag zur Vorgeschichte des neutestamentlichen Logosbegriffes*. Mitteilungen der Vorderasiatisch-Aegyptischen Gesellschaft 42/1. Leipzig: Hinrichs, 1938.

Ebeling, Gerhard. "Die Anfänge von Luthers Hermeneutik." In *Lutherstudien*, Vol. 1, 1–68. Tübingen: Mohr, 1971.

———. *Dogmatik des christlichen Glaubens*, Vol. 2, *Der Glaube an Gott den Versöhner der Welt*. 4th ed. Tübingen: Mohr Siebeck, 2012.

———. *Evangelische Evangelienauslegung: eine Untersuchung zu Luthers Hermeneutik*. 3rd ed. Darmstadt: Wissenschaftliche Buchgesellschaft, 1991.

———. "Karl Barths Ringen mit Luther." In *Lutherstudien*, Vol. 3, Begriffsuntersuchungen—Textinterpretationen—Wirkungsgeschichtliches, 428–537. Tübingen: Mohr, 1985.

———. *Luther. Einführung in sein Denken*. 4th ed. Tübingen: Mohr, 1981.

———. "Luther und die Bibel." In *Lutherstudien*, Vol. 1, 286–301. Tübingen: Mohr, 1971.

———. *Lutherstudien*, Vol. 1. Tübingen: Mohr, 1971.

———. *Lutherstudien*, Vol. 2, Disputation de homine. Part 3. Die theologische Definition des Menschen—Kommentar zu These 20–40. Tübingen: Mohr Siebeck, 1989.

———. "Das *sola scriptura* und das Problem der Tradition." In *Wort Gottes und Tradition: Studien zu einer Hermeneutik der Konfessionen*, 91–143. Kirche und Konfession 7. Göttingen: Vandenhoeck und Ruprecht, 1964.

———. *Das Wesen des christlichen Glaubens*. 2nd ed. Munich: Siebenstern, 1965.

———. "Wort Gottes und Hermeneutik." In *Wort und Glaube*, Vol. 1, 319–48. Tübingen: Mohr, 1960.

Eco, Umberto. "Two Models of Interpretation." In *The Limits of Interpretation*, 8–22. Bloomington, IN: Indiana University, 1990.

———. *Zeichen: Einführung in einen Begriff und seine Geschichte*. Translated by Günter Memmert. Frankfurt am Main: Suhrkamp, 1977.

Enderman, Heinz. "Anmerkungen zu Luthers Sprachphilosophie." In *Luthers Sprachschaffen: gesellschaftliche Grundlagen, geschichtliche Wirkungen*, edited by Joachim Schildt, 281–94. Linguistische Studien, Reihe A: Arbeitsberichte 119/1. Berlin: Akademie der Wissenschaften der DDR, 1984.

Enuma Eliš. Das babylonische Weltschöpfungsepos *Enuma eliš*. Edited by Thomas Kämmerer and Kai Metzler. Alter Orient und Altes Testament 375. Münster: Ugarit, 2012.

Erasmus Roterodamus, Desiderius and Martin Luther. *Discourse on Free Will*. Translated and edited by Ernst F. Winter. New York: Continuum, 1961.

Erasmus Roterodamus, Desiderius. *De libero arbitrio diatribe sive collatio*. Edited by Johannes von Walter. Leipzig: Deichert, 1935.

———. *Vom freien Willen*. Translated by Otto Schumacher. Göttingen: Vandenhoeck und Ruprecht, 1956.

Evans, Donald. *The Logic of Self-Involvement: a Philosophical Study of Everyday Language with Special Reference to the Christian Use of Language about God as Creator*. London: SCM, 1963.

Fee, Gordon D. *The First Epistle to the Corinthians*. The New International Commentary on the New Testament. Grand Rapids: Eerdmans, 1987.

Fischer, Helmut. *Glaubensaussage und Sprachstruktur*. Hamburg: Furche, 1972.

Fischer, Johannes. "Behaupten oder Bezeugen? Zum Modus des Wahrheitsanspruchs christlicher Rede von Gott." *Zeitschrift für Theologie und Kirche* 87 (1990) 224–44.

Fischer, Norbert, and Cornelius Mayer, eds. *Die Confessiones des Augustinus von Hippo: Einführung und Interpretation zu den 13 Büchern*. Freiburg: Herder, 2004.

Flasch, Kurt. *Augustin: Einführung in sein Denken*. 4th ed. Stuttgart: Reclam, 2013.

Frederiksen, Paula. "Die *Confessiones*." Translated by Michael Zank. In *Augustin-Handbuch*, edited by Volker Henning Drecoll, 294–309. Tübingen: Mohr Siebeck, 2014.

Führer, Werner. *Das Wort Gottes in Luthers Theologie*. Göttinger theologische Arbeiten 30. Göttingen: Vandenhoeck und Ruprecht, 1984.

Fuhrer, Therese. "Die Schöpfung als Modus göttlicher Rede—Augustin über Religion und Hermeneutik." In *Von Rom nach Bagdad: Bildung und Religion von der römischen Kaiserzeit bis zum klassischen Islam*, edited by Peter Gemeinhardt and Sebastian Günther, 219–41. Tübingen: Mohr Siebeck, 2013.

Gabriel, Markus. "Existenz realistisch gedacht." In *Der neue Realismus*, 171–99. Berlin: Suhrkamp, 2014.

———. *Warum es die Welt night gibt*. 8th ed. Berlin: Ullstein, 2013.

———. "Wider die postmoderne Flucht vor den Tatsachen." In *Neue Zürcher Zeitung*, 19 June 2016 (https://goo.gl/ZQpsG6).

Gadamer, Hans-Georg. *Truth and Method*. Translated and edited by Garrett Bowden and John Cumming. New York: Seabury, 1975.

———. *Wahrheit und Methode: Grundzüge einer philosophischen Hermeneutik*. 5th ed. Tübingen: Mohr, 1986.

Gaß, Erasmus. *Menschliches Handeln und Sprechen im Horizont Gottes: Aufsätze zur biblischen Theologie*. Tübingen: Mohr Siebeck, 2015.

Gerber, Uwe, and Rudolf Hoberg, eds. *Sprache und Religion*. Darmstadt: Wissenschaftliche Buchgesellschaft, 2009.

Gerber, Uwe, and Erhardt Güttgemanns, eds. *"Linguistische" Theologie: biblische Texte, christliche Verkündigung und theologische Sprache*. Forum Theologiae Linguisticae 3. Bonn: Linguistica Biblica, 1972.

Gertz, Jan Christian, ed. *Grundinformation Altes Testament: eine Einführung in Literatur, Religion und Geschichte des Alten Testaments*. 5th ed. Göttingen: Ullstein, 2016.

Gese, Hartmut. "Der Johannesprolog." In *Zur biblischen Theologie: alttestamentliche Vorträge*, 152–201. Beiträge zur evangelischen Theologie 78. Munich: Kaiser, 1977.

Glasersfeld, Ernst von. *Radikaler Konstruktivismus: Ideen, Ergebnisse, Probleme*. Translated by Wolfram Karl Köck. Frankfurt am Main: Suhrkamp, 1997.

Goebel, Hans Theodor. *Wort Gottes als Auftrag: zur Theologie von Rudolf Bultmann, Gerhard Ebeling und Wolfhart Pannenberg*. Neukirchen-Vluyn: Neukirchener Verlag, 1972.

Goethe, Johann Wolfgang. *Italienische Reise*. In *Werke*, Hamburger Ausgabe in vierzehn Bänden, edited by Erich Trunz, Vol. 11: Autobiographische Schriften 3. Munich: Beck, 1981.

Gogarten, Friedrich. *Jesus Christus Wende der Welt: Grundfragen zur Christologie*. 2nd ed. Tübingen: Mohr, 1967.

Grabner-Haider, Anton. *Glaubenssprache: ihre Struktur und Anwendbarkeit in Verkündigung und Theologie*. Freiburg: Herder, 1975.

Grether, Oskar. *Name und Wort Gottes im Alten Testament*. Zeitschrift für die alttestamentliche Wissenschaft; Beiheft 64. Gießen: Töpelmann, 1934.

Grözinger, Albrecht. *Die Sprache des Menschen: ein Handbuch; Grundwissen für Theologinnen und Theologen*. Munich: Kaiser, 1991.

Grosshans, Hans-Peter. "Wahrheit—VI. Religionsphilosophisch." In *Religion in Geschichte und Gegenwart*, Vol. 8, edited by Eberhard Jüngel et al., 1254–56. 4th ed. Tübingen: Mohr Siebeck, 2008.

Haacker, Klaus. "Wort Gottes II." In *Theologisches Realenzyklopädie*, Vol. 36, edited by Gerhard Müller, Horst Balz, and Gerhard Krause, 298–311. Berlin: de Gruyter, 1976–2004.

Habermas, Jürgen. *Theorie des kommunikativen Handelns*, Vol. 1, *Handlungsrationalität und gesellschaftliche Rationalisierung*. Frankfurt am Main: Suhrkamp, 1981.

Hafstad, Kjetil. *Wort und Geschichte: das Geschichtsverständnis Karl Barths*. Beiträge zur evangelischen Theologie 98. Translated by Dietrich Harbsmeier. Munich: Kaiser, 1985.

Halbfas, Hubertus. *Religiöse Sprachlehre: Theorie und Praxis*. Ostfildern: Patmos, 2012.

Harnack, Adolf von. *Augustin's Confessionen: ein Vortrag*. 2nd ed. Gießen: Ricker'sche Buchhandlung, 1895.

Hart, Herbert L. A. *Der Begriff des Rechts: mit dem Postscriptum von 1994 und einem Nachwort von Christoph Möllers*. Translated by Alexander von Baeyer. Frankfurt: Suhrkamp, 2009.

Hartenstein, Friedhelm. *Das Angesicht JHWHs: Studien zu seinem höfischen und kultischen Bedeutungshintergrund in den Psalmen und in Exodus 32–34*. Forschungen zum Alten Testament 55. Tübingen: Mohr Siebeck, 2008.

Hegel, Georg Wilhelm Friedrich. *Phänomenologie des Geistes*. In *Werkausgabe*, Vol. 3, edited by Eva Moldenhauer and Karl Markus Michel. Frankfurt am Main: Suhrkamp, 1983.

Hennigfeld, Jochem. *Geschichte der Sprachphilosophie: Antike und Mittelalter*. Berlin: de Gruyter, 1993.

Hermisson, Hans-Jürgen. *Studien zu Prophetie und Weisheit: gesammelte Aufsätze*. Forschungen zum Alten Testament 23. Edited by Jörg Barthel. Tübingen: Mohr Siebeck, 1998.

Herms, Eilert. *Offenbarung und Glaube: zur Bildung des christlichen Lebens*. Tübingen: Mohr, 1992.

Herzog, Reinhart. "*Non in sua voce*—Augustins Gespräch mit Gott in den *Confessiones*." In *Das Gespräch*, edited by Karlheinz Stierle and Reiner Warning, 213–50. Poetik und Hermeneutik XI. Munich: Fink, 1984.

Hilgenfeld, Hartmut. *Mittelalterlich-traditionelle Elemente in Luthers Abendmahlsschriften*. Zürich: Theologischer Verlag, 1971.

Hintikka, Merill B., and Jaako Hintikka. *Untersuchungen zu Wittgenstein*. Translated by Joachim Schulte. Frankfurt am Main: Suhrkamp, 1996.

Hirsch, Emanuel. *Leitfaden zur christlichen Lehre*. Tübingen: Mohr, 1938.

Hofmann, Frank. *Radikal-empiristische Wahrheitstheorie: Eine Studie* über *Otto Neurath, den Wiener Kreis und das Wahrheitsproblem*. Vienna: Hölder-Pichler-Tempsky, 1988.

———. *Sören Kierkegaard: wie der dänische Dichter das Christentum vor der Kirche retten wollte*. Wichern Porträts. Berlin: Wichern, 2012.

Holl, Adolf. *Die Welt der Zeichen bei Augustin: religionsphänomenologische Analyse des 13. Buches der Confessiones*. Wiener Beiträge zur Theologie 2. Vienna: Herder, 1963.

Hornig, Gottfried. "Analyse und Problematik der religiösen Performative." *Neue Zeitschrift für systematische Theologie und Religionsphilosophie* 24 (1982) 53–70.

Hunsinger, George. *Karl Barth lesen: eine Einführung in sein theologisches Denken*. Translated by Marianne Mühlenberg. Neukirchen-Vluyn: Neukirchener Verlag, 2009.

Hunziker, Andreas. "Der Andere als Ende der Metaphysik." In *Gott denken—ohne Metaphysik? Zu einer aktuellen Kontroverse in Theologie und Philosophie*, edited by Ingolf U. Dalferth and Andreas Hunziker, 183–202. Tübingen: Mohr Siebeck, 2014.

———. "Ludwig Wittgensteins Hermeneutik menschlicher Lebensformen." In *Das Leben: historisch-systematische Studien zur Geschichte eines Begriffs*, Vol. 2, edited by Stephan Schaede et al., 441–61. Tübingen: Mohr Siebeck, 2012.

———. *Das Wagnis des Gewöhnlichen: ein Versuch über den Glauben im Gespräch mit Ludwig Wittgenstein und Stanley Cavell*. Religion in Philosophy and Theology 32. Tübingen: Mohr Siebeck, 2008.

Iser, Wolfgang. *Der Akt des Lesens: Theorie ästhetischer Wirkung*. 4th ed. Munich: Fink, 1994.

———. "Die Appellstruktur der Texte." In *Rezeptionsästhetik: Theorie und Praxis*, edited by Rainer Warning, 228–52. 4th ed. Munich: Fink, 1994.

———. "Der Lesevorgang." In *Rezeptionsästhetik: Theorie und Praxis*, edited by Rainer Warning, 253–76. 4th ed. Munich: Fink, 1994.

Iwand, Hans Joachim. "Die 1. Barmer These und die Theologie Martin Luthers." *Evangelische Theologie* 46 (1986) 214–31.

———. *Luthers Theologie*. Edited by Johann Haar. Munich: Kaiser, 1974.

Jackson, B. Darrell. "The Theory of Signs in St. Augustine's *De doctrina christiana*." *Revue des Ètudes Augustiniennes* 15 (1969) 9–49.

James, William. *Die Vielfalt religiöser Erfahrung: eine Studie über die menschliche Natur*. Translated by Eilert Herms and Christian Stahlhut. Frankfurt am Main: Insel, 1997.

Jeremias, Jörg. "Das Gottesbild des Alten Testaments." In *Studien zur Theologie des Alten Testaments*, edited by Friedhelm Hartenstein and Jutta Krispenz, 52–61. Forschungen zum Alten Testament 99. Tübingen: Mohr Siebeck, 2015.

———. *Theologie des Alten Testaments*. Grundrisse zum Alten Testament 6. Göttingen: Vandenhoeck und Ruprecht, 2015.

Joas, Hans. "Braucht der Mensch Religion?" In *Braucht der Mensch Religion? Über Erfahrungen der Selbsttranszendenz*, 12–31. Freiburg: Herder, 2004.

———. "'Das Heilige ist jedem zugänglich.' Im Gespräch mit Frank Hofmann." *Andere Zeiten—Magazine zum Kirchenjahr* 19 (2018) Heft 2, 4–5.

———. *Die Macht des Heiligen: eine Alternative zu der Geschichte von der Entzauberung*. Frankfurt am Main: Suhrkamp, 2017.

Johnson, Douglas W. "*Verbum* in the Early Augustine (386–97)." *Recherches Augustiniennes* 8 (1972) 25–53.

Jüngel, Eberhard. *Barth-Studien*. Zürich: Mohn, 1982.

———. *God as the Mystery of the World*. Translated by Darrell L. Guder. Grand Rapids: Eerdmans, 1983.

———. *Gott als Geheimnis der Welt: zur Begründung der Theologie des gekreuzigten im Streit zwischen Theismus und Atheismus*. 8th ed. Tübingen: Mohr Siebeck, 2010.

———. "Gott—als Wort unserer Sprache." In *Unterwegs zur Sache: theologische Bemerkungen*, 80–104. Beiträge zur evangelischen Theologie 61. Munich: Kaiser, 1972.

———. *Gottes Sein ist im Werden: verantwortliche Rede vom Sein Gottes bei Karl Barth; eine Paraphrase*. 4th ed. Tübingen: Mohr Siebeck, 1986.

———. "Metaphorische Wahrheit—Erwägungen zur theologischen Relevanz der Metapher als Beitrag zur Hermeneutik einer narrativen Theologie." In Jüngel and Paul Ricœur, *Metapher: zur Hermeneutik religiöser Sprache*, 71–122. Munich: Kaiser, 1974.

———. "*Quae supra nos, nihil ad nos*—eine Kurzformel der Lehre vom verborgenen Gott; im Anschluß an Luther interpretiert." In *Entsprechungen: Gott—Wahrheit—Mensch; theologische Erörterungen*, 202–51. Beiträge zur evangelischen Theologie 88. Munich: Kaiser, 1980.

———. "Zur Bedeutung Luthers für die gegenwärtige Theologie." In *Luther und die Theologie der Gegenwart: Referate und Berichte des Fünften Internationalen Kongresses für Lutherforschung*, edited by Leif Grane and Bernhard Lohse, 17–80. Göttingen: Vandenhoeck und Ruprecht, 1980.

———. *Zur Freiheit eines Christenmenschen: eine Erinnerung an Luthers Schrift*. 3rd ed. Munich: Kaiser, 1991.

Jung, Matthias. *Erfahrung und Religion: Grundzüge einer hermeneutisch-pragmatischen Religionsphilosophie*. Alber Thesen Philosophie 2. Freiburg: Alber, 1999.

Junghans, Helmar. "Das Wort Gottes bei Luther während seiner ersten Psalmenvorlesung." *Theologische Literaturzeitung* 100 (1975) 161–74.

———. "Die Worte Christi geben das Leben." In *Wartburg-Jahrbuch*. Sonderband 1996: Wissenschaftliches Kolloquium "Der Mensch Luther und sein Umfeld," edited by Wartburg-Stiftung Eisenach, 154–75. Eisenach: Wartburg-Stiftung, 1996.

Just, Wolf-Dieter. *Religiöse Sprache und analytische Philosophie: Sinn und Unsinn religiöser Aussagen*. Stuttgart: Kohlhammer, 1975.

Kaempfert, Manfred, ed. *Probleme der religiösen Sprache*. Darmstadt: Wissenschaftliche Buchgesellschaft, 1983.

Käsemann, Ernst. *Paulinische Perspektiven*. Tübingen: Mohr, 1969.

Kahnert, Klaus. *Entmachtung der Zeichen? Augustin über Sprache*. Bochumer Studien zur Philosophie 29. Amsterdam: Grüner, 2000.

Kaiser, Otto. *Der Gott des Alten Testaments: Theologie des Alten Testaments*. Part 2: *Jahwe, der Gott Israels, Schöpfer der Welt und des Menschen*. Göttingen: Vandenhoeck und Ruprecht, 1988.

———. "Die Schöpfungsmacht des Wortes Gottes." *Communio* 30 (2001) 6–17.

Kamlah, Wilhelm. *Christentum und Geschichtlichkeit: Untersuchungen zur Entstehung des Christentums und zu Augustins "Bürgerschaft Gottes."* 2nd ed. Stuttgart: Kohlhammer, 1951.

Kant, Immanuel. *Critique of Pure Reason*. Translated and edited by Paul Guyer and Allen W. Wood. Cambridge: Cambridge University Press, 1999.

———. *Grundlegung zur Metaphysik der Sitten*. In *Werkausgabe*, Vol. 7. Edited by Wilhelm Weischedel. Frankfurt am Main: Suhrkamp, 1981.

———. *Kritik der reinen Vernunft*. In *Werkausgabe*. Edited by Wilhelm Weischedel. Vol. 3. Frankfurt am Main: Suhrkamp, 1981.

Kany, Roland. "Typen und Tendenzen der *De trinitate*-Forschung seit Ferdinand Christian Bauer." In *Gott und sein Bild: Augustins De trinitate im Spiegel gegenwärtiger Forschung*, edited by Johannes Brachtendorf, 13–28. Paderborn: Schöningh, 2000.

Kierkegaard, Søren. *Einübung ins Christentum: Zwei kurze ethisch-religiöse Abhandlungen—Das Buch Adler*. Edited by Walter Rest. Munich: Deutscher Taschenbuch Verlag, 2005.

———. *Philosophische Brosamen und Unwissenschaftliche Nachschrift*. Edited by Hermann Diem and Walter Rest. Munich: Deutscher Taschenbuch Verlag, 2005.

Kinder, Ernst. "Was bedeutet 'Wort Gottes' nach dem Verständnis der Reformation?" *Kerygma und Dogma* 12 (1966) 14–26.

Klappert, Berthold. "λόγος III [NT]." In *Theologisches Wörterbuch zum Neuen Testament*, edited by Gerhard Kittel, Otto Bauernfeind, and Gerhard Friedrich, 1938–48. Stuttgart: Kohlhammer, 1933–79.

Körtner, Ulrich H. J. "Schriftwerdung des Wortes und Wortwerdung der Schrift—die Schriftlehre Karl Barths im Kontext der Krise des protestantischen Schriftprinzips." *Zeitschrift für dialektische Theologie* 15.2 (1999) 107–30.

———. *Theologie des Wortes Gottes: Positionen, Probleme, Perspektiven*. Göttingen: Vandenhoeck und Ruprecht, 2001.

———, ed. *Wort Gottes—Kerygma—Religion; zur Frage nach dem Ort der Theologie*. Neukirchen-Vluyn: Neukirchener, 2003.

Korsch, Dietrich. "Apriori, religiöses." In *Religion in Geschichte und Gegenwart*, Vol. 1, edited by Eberhard Jüngel et al., 660–62. 4th ed. Tübingen: Mohr Siebeck, 2008.

———. *Einführung in die Evangelische Dogmatik im Anschluß an Martin Luthers Kleinen Katechismus*. Leipzig: Evangelische Verlagsanstalt, 2016.

———. *Dialektische Theologie nach Karl Barth*. Tübingen: Mohr, 1996.

———, ed. *Karl Barth: Dialektische Theologie (= Schriften 1). Kirchliche Dogmatik (= Schriften 2)*. Edited and commentated by Dietrich Korsch. Leipzig: Evangelische Verlagsanstalt, 2009.

———. "Kommunikation des Wortes Gottes—eine Theologie des 20. Jahrhunderts." In *Karl Barth*, 1039–49. Leipzig: Evangelische Verlagsanstalt, 2009.

———. *Martin Luther: eine Einführung*. 2nd ed. Tübingen: Mohr Siebeck, 2007.

———, ed. *Martin Luther: Von der Freiheit eines Christenmenschen*. Große Texte der Christenheit 1. Deutsch-deutsche Ausgabe. Leipzig: Evangelische Verlagsanstalt, 2016.

———. *Paul Ricœur und die evangelische Theologie*. Religion in Philosophy and Theology 76. Tübingen: Mohr Siebeck, 2016.

———. "Die religiöse Leitidee." In *Luther-Handbuch*, edited by Albrecht Beutel, 91–97. Tübingen: Mohr Siebeck, 2005.

———. *Religionsbegriff und Gottesglaube: Dialektische Theologie als Hermeneutik der Religion*. Tübingen: Mohr Siebeck, 2005.

———. "Theologie als Theologie des Wortes Gottes—eine programmatische Skizze." In *Transformationsprozesse des Protestantismus: zur Selbstreflexion einer christlichen Konfession an der Jahrtausendwende; Falk Wagner (1939–1998) zu Ehren*, edited by Martin Berger and Michael Murmann-Kahl, 226–37. Gütersloh: Kaiser, 1999.

———. "Theologische Prinzipienfrage." In *Luther-Handbuch*, edited by Albrecht Beutel, 353–62. Tübingen: Mohr Siebeck, 2005.

Korsch, Dietrich, and Enno Rudolph, eds. *Die Prägnanz der Religion in der Kultur: Ernst Cassirer und die Theologie*. Religion und Aufklärung 7. Tübingen: Mohr Siebeck, 2000.

Krämer, Sibylle. *Sprache, Sprechakt, Kommunikation: sprachtheoretische Positionen des 20. Jahrhunderts*. Frankfurt am Main: Suhrkamp, 2001.

Kraus, Hans-Joachim. "Vorwort." In *Karl Barth: Exegese von 1. Könige 13*, 5–11. Neukirchen: Neukirchener Verlag, 1955.

Krause, Gerhard. *Studien zu Luthers Auslegung der kleinen Propheten*. Beiträge zur historischen Theologie 33. Tübingen: Mohr, 1962.

Kreuzer, Johann. "Einleitung." In Augustin, *De trinitate* (translated by Kreuzer), VII-LXVII. Hamburg: Meiner, 2003.

———. "*Et ecce est ante nos*—zur Kritik der Sprache bei Augustinus." In *Zeit und Zeichen*, edited by Tilman Borsche et al., 31–46. Schriften der Académie du Midi 1. Munich: Fink, 1993.

———. *Pulchritudo: vom Erkennen Gottes bei Augustin; Bemerkungen zu den Büchern IX, X, und XI der Confessiones*. Munich: Fink, 1985.

———. "Die Sprachlichkeit der Erinnerung—Überlegungen zum *verbum intimum* in Buch XV von *De Trinitate*." In *Gott und sein Bild: Augustins De trinitate im Spiegel gegenwärtiger Forschung*, edited by Johannes Brachtendorf, 183–203. Paderborn: Schöningh, 2000.

Kreuzer, Siegfried. "λόγος II (AT)." In *Theologisches Wörterbuch zum Neuen Testament*, edited by Gerhard Kittel, Otto Bauernfeind, and Gerhard Friedrich, 1930–38. Stuttgart: Kohlhammer, 1933–79.

Kripke, Saul. "Identity and Necessity." In *Identity and Individuation*, edited by Milton Munitz, 135–64. New York: New York University Press, 1971.

Krispenz, Jutta. "Wortereignisformel/Wortempfangsformel." In *Wissenschaftliche Bibellexikon*, 2014. www.bibelwissenschaft.de/stichwort/35010/.

Krötke, Wolf. "Wort Gottes V/VI." In *Religion in Geschichte und Gegenwart,* Vol. 8, edited by Eberhard Jüngel et al., 1700–1706. 4th ed. Darmstadt: Wissenschaftliche Buchgesellschaft, 2008.

Krüger, Malte Dominik. *Das andere Bild Christi: spätmoderner Protestantismus als kritische Bildreligion*. Dogmatik in der Moderne 18. Tübingen: Mohr Siebeck, 2017.

Kuypers, Karel. *Der Zeichen- und Wortbegriff im Denken Augustins*. Amsterdam: Swets & Zeitlinger, 1934.

Lachenmann, Hans. *Das Wort in der Welt: Perspektiven einer neuen Theologie des Wortes Gottes*. Stuttgart: Steinkopf, 1987.

Lange, Armin. *Vom prophetischen Wort zur prophetischen Tradition: Studien zur Traditions- und Redaktionsgeschichte innerprophetischer Konflikte in der Hebräischen Bibel*. Forschungen zum Alten Testament 34. Tübingen: Mohr Siebeck, 2002.

Latomus, Jacobus. *Articulorum doctrinae fratris Martini Lutheri per theologis Lova neinses damnatorum Ratio ex sacris literis et veteribus tractatoribus*. Iacobi Latomi sacrae theologiae apud Lavanienses professoris calaberrimi opera. Leuven: Birckmans, 1550.

Laube, Martin. *Im Bann der Sprache: die analytische Religionsphilosophie im 20. Jahrhundert*. Berlin: de Gruyter, 1999.

Lauster, Jörg. *Prinzip und Methode: die Transformation des protestantischen Schriftprinzips durch die historische Kritik von Schleiermacher bis zur Gegenwart*. Hermeneutische Untersuchungen zur Theologie. Tübingen: Mohr Siebeck, 2004.

———. *Religion als Lebensdetung: theologische Hermeneutik heute*. Darmstadt: Wissenschaftliche Buchgesellschaft, 2005.

———. *Die Verzauberung der Welt: ein Kulturgeschichte des Christentums*. 5th ed. Munich: Beck, 2017.

———. *Zwischen Entzauberung und Remythisierung: zum Verhältnis von Bibel und Dogma*. Theologische Literaturzeitung Forum 21. Leipzig: Evangelische Verlagsanstalt, 2008.

Lettieri, Gaetano. "*De doctrina christiana* (Über die christliche Wissensaneignung und Lehre)." Translated by Margitta Berghaus. In *Augustin-Handbuch*, edited by Volker Henning Drecoll, 377–93. Tübingen: Mohr Siebeck, 2012.

Lienhard, Marc. *Martin Luthers christologisches Zeugnis: Entwicklung und Grundzüge seiner Christologie*. Göttingen: Vandenhoeck und Ruprecht, 1980.

Lindbeck, George A. *The Nature of Doctrine: Religion and Theology in a Postliberal Age*. Philadelphia: Westminster, 1984.

Link, Christian. "Karl Barths Verständnis der 'wahren Worte.'" In *Karl Barth als Lehrer der Versöhnung (1950–1968): Vertiefung–Öffnung–Hoffnung*. Beiträge zum Internationalen Symposion im Mai 2014 in Emden, edited by Michael Beintker et al., 363–79. Zürich: Theologischer Verlag Zürich, 2016.

Löfgren, David. *Die Theologie der Schöpfung bei Luther*. Translated by Christiane Boehncke-Sjöberg. Forschungen zur Kirchen- und Dogmengeschichte 3. Göttingen: Vandenhoeck und Ruprecht, 1960.

Lohmann, Johann Friedrich. *Karl Barth und der Neukantianismus: die Rezeption des Neukantianismus im "Römerbrief" und ihre Bedeutung für die weitere Ausarbeitung der Theologie Karl Barths*. Theologische Bibliothek Töpelmann 72. Berlin: de Gruyter, 1995.

Lorenz, Rudolf. "Die Wissenschaftslehre Augustins. II. Teil." *Zeitschrift für Kirchengeschichte* 67 (1955/56) 213–51.

Luther, Henning. "Predigt als Handlung—Überlegungen zur Pragmatik des Predigens." *Zeitschrift für Theologie und Kirche* 80 (1983) 233–43.

Luz, Ulrich. "Theologia crucis als Mitte der Theologie im Neuen Testament." *Evangelische Theologie* 34 (1974) 116–41.

Maier, Christl. "Jeremia am Ende—Prophetie als Schriftgelehrsamkeit." *Evangelische Theologie* 77 (2017) 44–56.

Markus, Robert Austin. "Communication and Transcendence in Augustine's *De Trinitate*." In *Gott und sein Bild*, edited by Johannes Brachtendorf, 173–81. Paderborn: Schöningh, 2000.

———. "St. Augustine on signs." *Phronesis* 2 (1957) 60–83.

Maurer, Ernstpeter. "Biblisches Reden von Gott—ein Sprachspiel? Anmerkungen zu einem Vergleich von Karl Barth und Ludwig Wittgenstein." *Evangelische Theologie* 50 (1990) 71–82.

———. *Der Mensch im Geist: Untersuchungen zur Anthropologie bei Hegel und Luther*. Beiträge zur evangelischen Theologie 116. Gütersloh: Kaiser, 1996.

———. "Sprache bei Barth." In *Barth-Handbuch*, edited by Michael Beintker, 165–71. Tübingen: Mohr Siebeck, 2016.

Mayer, Cornelius Petrus. "*Confessiones* 12—*caelum caeli*; Ziel und Bestimmung des Menschen nach der Auslegung von Genesis 1:1–2" In *Die Confessiones des Augustinus von Hippo: Einführung und Interpretation zu den 13 Büchern*, edited by Mayer and Norbert Fischer, 553–601. Freiburg: Herder, 2004.

———. *Die Zeichen in der geistigen Entwicklung und in der Theologie des jungen Augustinus*, Vol. 1. Cassiciacum 24.1. Würzburg: Augustinus-Verlag, 1969.

———. *Die Zeichen in der geistigen Entwicklung und in der Theologie des jungen Augustinus*, Vol. 2. Die antimanichäische Epoche. Cassiciacum 24.2. Würzburg: Augustinus-Verlag, 1974.

McCormack, Bruce Lindley. "Der theologiegeschichtliche Ort Karl Barths." In *Barth-Handbuch*, edited by Michael Beintker, 15–40. Tübingen: Mohr Siebeck, 2016.

———. *Theologische Dialektik und kritischer Realismus: Entstehung und Entwicklung von Karl Barths Theologie 1909–1936*. Translated by Matthias Gockel. Zürich: Theologischer Verlag Zürich, 2006.

Meckenstock, Günter. "Karl Barths Prolegomena zur Dogmatik—Entwicklungslinien vom 'Unterricht in der christlichen Religion' bis zur 'Kirchlichen Dogmatik.'"

Neue Zeitschrift für Systematische Theologie und Religionsphilosophie 28 (1986) 296–310.

Meier, Samuel A. *Speaking of Speaking: Marking Direct Discourse in the Hebrew Bible.* New York: Brill, 1992.

Meinhold, Peter. *Die Genesisvorlesung Luthers und ihre Herausgeber.* Forschungen zur Kirchen- und Geistesgeschichte 8. Stuttgart: Kohlhammer, 1936.

———. *Luthers Sprachphilosophie.* Berlin: Lutherisches Verlagshaus, 1958.

Meyer, Harding, et al., eds. *Dokumente wachsender Übereinstimmung: Sämtliche Berichte und Konsenstexte interkonfessioneller Gespräche auf Weltebene,* Vol. 1, *1931–1982.* Frankfurt: Lembeck, 1991.

Meyer-Blanck, Michael. "Ernst Cassirers Symbolbegriff—zeichentheoretisch gegengelesen." In *Die Prägnanz der Religion in der Kultur: Ernst Cassirer und die Theologie,* edited by Dietrich Korsch and Enno Rudolph, 91–99. Tübingen: Mohr Siebeck, 2000.

Metzke, Erwin. "Sakrament und Metaphysik—eine Lutherstudie über das Verhältnis des christlichen Denkens zum Leiblich-Materiellen." In *Coincidentia oppositorum: gesammelte Studien zur Philosophiegeschichte,* edited by Karlfried Gründer Witten, 158–204. Stuttgart: Klett-Cotta, 1961.

Meyer zu Hörste-Bührer, Raphaela J. *Gott und Menschen in Beziehungen: Impulse Karl Barths für relationale Ansätze zum Verständnis christlichen Glaubens.* Forschungen zur reformierten Theologie 6. Neukirchen-Vluyn: Neukirchener Theologie, 2016.

Miles, Jack. *God: A Biography.* New York: Knopf, 1995.

———. *Gott: eine Biografie.* Translated by Martin Pfeiffer. Munich: Deutscher Taschenbuch Verlag, 1996.

Mojsisch, Burkhard. "Nachwort." In Augustin, *Über den Lehrer,* translated by Burkhard Mojsisch, 143–54. Stuttgart: Reclam, 1998.

Moxter, Michael. *Kultur als Lebenswelt: Studien zum Problem einer Kulturtheologie.* Tübingen: Mohr Siebeck, 2000.

Neumann, Karl E. "Ernst Cassirer—das Symbol." In *Grundprobleme der großen Philosophen: Philosophie der Gegenwart* 2, edited by Josef Speck, 102–45. Göttingen: Vandenhoeck und Ruprecht, 1973.

Noort, Ed. "Wort Gottes I (AT)." In *Theologisches Realenzyklopädie,* Vol. 36, edited by Gerhard Müller, Horst Balz, and Gerhard Krause, 291–98. Berlin: de Gruyter, 1976–2004.

Van Noppen, Jean-Pierre. "Einleitung: Metapher und Religion." Translated by Irmhild Rehkämper and Martina Wiese. In *Erinnern, um Neues zu sagen: die Bedeutung der Metapher für die religiöse Sprache,* 7–51. Frankfurt am Main: Athenäum, 1988.

Novum testamentum Graece. Edited by Barbara and Kurt Aland, et al. Stuttgart: Deutsche Bibelgesellschaft, 2012.

Ott, Wendelin. *Über die Schrift des heiligen Augustinus: De magistro.* Beilage zum Jahresbericht der Königlichen Realschule in Hechingen. Hechingen: Kleinmeier, 1898.

Otto, Rudolf. *Das Heilige: über das Irrationale in der Idee des Göttlichen und sein Verhältnis zum Rationalen.* Munich: Beck, 1963.

Pannenberg, Wolfhart. "Nachwort zur zweiten Auflage." In *Offenbarung als Geschichte,* 132–48. 5th ed. Göttingen: Vandenhoeck und Ruprecht, 1982.

———. *Problemgeschichte der neueren evangelischen Theologie in Deutschland: von Schleiermacher bis zu Barth and Tillich*. Göttingen: Vandenhoeck und Ruprecht, 1979.

Parker, David C. *The Living Text of the Gospels*. Cambridge: Cambridge University Press, 1997.

De Pater, Wim. "Erschließungssituationen und religiöse Sprache." In *Probleme der religiösen Sprache*, edited by Manfred Kaempfert, 184–210. Darmstadt: Wissenschaftliche Buchgesellschaft, 1983.

———. "Der Sprechakt, seinen Glauben zu bekennen—Gottes Gegenwart in der Erschließungssprache christlicher Religion." In *Möglichkeiten des Redens über Gott*, edited by Heinrich Fries et al., 31–56. Düsseldorf: Patmos, 1978.

Pesch, Otto Hermann. *Hinführung zu Luther*. Mit einer Einleitung von Volker Leppin. 4th ed. Ostfildern: Matthias Grünewald Verlag, 2017.

Petzold, Matthias. "Offenbarung—in sprechakttheoretischen Perspektive." In *Gottes Offenbarung in der Welt*. Festschrift für Horst Georg Pöhlmann, edited by Friedhelm Krüger, 129–48. Gütersloh: Kaiser, 1998.

Phillips, Dewi. "Religiöser Glaube und philosophische Untersuchung." Translated by Ingolf U. Dalferth. In *Sprachlogik des Glaubens*, edited by Ingolf U. Dalferth, 247–57. Munich: Kaiser, 1974.

Pinborg, Jan. "Das Sprachdenken der Stoa und Augustins Dialektik." *Classica et Mediaevalia* 23 (1962) 148–77.

Pinker, Steven. *Enlightenment Now: The Case for Reason, Science, Humanism, and Progress*. New York: Viking, 2018.

———. "Verfluchte Romantik. Im Gespräch mit Andrian Kreye." *Süddeutsche Zeitung* 15 February 2018 http://sz.de/1.3867113.

Pintarič, Drago. *Sprache und Trinität: semantische Probleme in der Trinitätslehre des heiligen Augustinus*. Salzburger Studien zur Philosophie 15. Salzburg: Pustet, 1983.

Pohl-Patalong, Uta. *Glaube im 21. Jahrhundert: attraktiv und zeitgemäß?* Vortrag in der ESG Kiel am 21. Januar 2015. Published online at https://www.theol.uni-kiel.de/de/professuren/pt-pohl-patalong/team.patalong/dateien=vortraege/glaube-im-21-jh.

Pollmann, Karla. *Doctrina christiana: Untersuchungen zu den Anfängen der christlichen Hermeneutik unter besonderer Berücksichtigung von Augustinus, De doctrina christiana*. Freiburg/Schweiz: Universitätsverlag, 1996.

———. "Nachwort." In Augustin, *De doctrina christiana*, translated by Karla Pollmann, 260–88. Stuttgart: Reclam, 2013.

Polman, Andries R. *The Word of God According to St. Augustine*. Translated by Arnold J. Pomerans. Grand Rapids: Hodder & Stoughton, 1962.

Quine, Willard Van Orman. *Wort und Gegenstand*. Translated by Joachim Schulte. Stuttgart: Reclam, 1980.

Rad, Gerhard von. *Theologie des Alten Testaments*, Vol. 1, *Die Theologie des geschichtlichen Überlieferungen Israels*. 4th ed. Munich: Kaiser, 1962. Vol. 2, *Die Theologie der prophetischen Überlieferungen Israels*. 4th ed. Munich: Kaiser, 1965.

Ramsey, Ian T. *Models and Mystery: The Whidden Lectures for 1963*. London: Oxford University Press, 1964.

———. *Religious Language: An Empirical Placing of Theological Phrases*. New York: MacMillan, 1963

Reichel, Hanna. *Theologie als Bekenntnis: Karl Barths kontextuelle Lektüre des Heidelberger Katechismus*. Forschungen zur systematischen und ökumenischen Theologie 149. Göttingen: Vandenhoeck und Ruprecht, 2015.

Reiffen, Hannelotte. "Vorwort." In Karl Barth, *Unterricht in der christlichen Religion*, GA 17, VII–IX. Zürich: Theologischer Verlag Zürich, 1951–.

Rendtorff, Trutz. "Radikale Autonomie Gottes—zum Verständnis der Theologie Karl Barths und ihrer Folgen." In *Theorie des Christentums: historisch-theologische Studien zu seiner neuzeitlichen Verfassung*, 161–81. Gütersloh: Mohn, 1972.

Reventlow, Henning Graf von. *Epochen der Bibelauslegung*. 4 vols. Munich: Beck, 1990–2001.

Richter, Cornelia. "Symbol, Mythos, Religion—zum Status der Religion in der Philosophie Ernst Cassirers." In *Die Prägnanz*, edited by Dietrich Korsch and Enno Rudolph, 5–32. Tübingen: Mohr Siebeck, 2000.

Ricœur, Paul. "Gott nennen." Translated by Peter Welsen. In *Vom Text zur Person: hermeneutische Aufsätze (1970–1999)*, 153–82. Hamburg: Meiner, 2005.

———. *Die lebendige Metapher*. Translated by Rainer Rochlitz. Übergänge 12. 3rd ed. Munich: Fink, 2004.

———. *Das Selbst als ein Anderer*. Translated by Jean Greisch. Übergänge 26. 2nd ed. Munich: Fink, 2005.

———. "Stellung und Funktion der Metapher in der biblischen Sprache." In Ricœur and Eberhard Jüngel, *Metapher: zur Hermeneutik religiöser Sprache*, 45–70. Munich: Kaiser, 1974.

Ricœur, Paul, and Eberhard Jüngel. *Metapher: zur Hermeneutik religiöser Sprache*. Evangelische Theologie Sonderheft. Munich: Kaiser, 1974.

Rieger, Reinhold. *Von der Freiheit eines Christenmenschen: De libertate christiana*. Kommentare zu Schriften Luthers 1. Tübingen: Mohr Siebeck, 2007.

Ringleben, Joachim. *Gott im Wort: Luthers Theologie von der Sprache her*. Hermeneutische Untersuchungen zur Theologie 57. Tübingen: Mohr Siebeck, 2010.

———. *Sprachloses Wort? Zur Kritik an Barths und Tillichs Worttheologie—von der Sprache her*. Forschungen zur systematischen und ökumenischen Theologie 150. Göttingen: Vandenhoeck und Ruprecht, 2015.

———. "Wort II." In *Historisches Wörterbuch der Philosophie*, edited by Joachim Ritter, Karlfried Gründer, and Gottfried Gabriel, Vol. 12, 1030–36. Darmstadt: Wissenschaftliche Buchgesellschaft, 2005.

———. "Wort Gottes IV." In *Theologisches Realenzyklopädie*, edited by Gerhard Müller, Horst Balz, and Gerhard Krause, Vol. 36, 315–29. Berlin: de Gruyter, 1976–2004.

Rorty, Richard. *Kontingenz, Ironie, und Solidarität*. Translated by Christa Krüger. 11th ed. Frankfurt am Main: Suhrkamp, 2016.

Rosa, Hartmut. *Beschleunigung und Entfremdung: Entwurf einer kritischen Theorie spätmoderner Zeitlichkeit*. Translated by Robin Celikates. Frankfurt am Main: Suhrkamp, 2013.

———. *Resonanz: eine Soziologie der Weltbeziehung*. Frankfurt am Main: Suhrkamp, 2016.

———. *Unverfügbarkeit*. Unruhe bewahren 2. Salzburg: Residenz, 2018.

———. "Was Menschen wirklich brauchen—im Gespräch mit Eva-Maria Lerch und Michael Schrom." *Publik-Forum* 47 (2017) Heft 24 44–49.

———. "'Wir sind Ressourcensammler'—im Gespräch mit Frank Hofmann." *Andere Zeiten—Magazin zum Kirchenjahr* 16 (2015) Heft 3 4–5.

Rückert, Hanns. "Luthers Anschauung von der Verborgenheit Gottes." In *Vorträge und Aufsätze zur historischen Theologie*, 96–107. Tübingen: Mohr, 1972.

Ruef, Hans. *Augustin über Semiotik und Sprache: sprachtheoretische Analysen zu Augustins Schrift De dialectica; mit einer deutschen Übersetzung*. Bern: Wyss, 1981.

Saarinen, Risto. "Metapher und biblische Redefiguren als Elemente der Sprachphilosophie Luthers." *Neue Zeitschrift für systematische Theologie* 30 (1988) 18–39.

Savigny, Eike von. "John Langshaw Austin: Hat die Wahrnehmung eine Basis?" In *Grundprobleme der großen Philosophen: Philosophie der Gegenwart III*, edited by Josef Speck, 208–49. Göttingen: Vandenhoeck und Ruprecht, 1991.

———. *Zum Begriff der Sprache: Konvention, Bedeutung, Zeichen*. Stuttgart: Reclam, 1983.

Schart, Aaron. "Prophetie (AT)." In *Wissenschaftliches Bibellexikon*. 2014. www.bibelwissenschaft.de/stichwort/31372/.

Scheel, Otto. *Die Anschauung Augustins über Christi Person und Werk: unter Berücksichtigung ihrer verschiedenen Entwicklungsstufen und ihrer dogmengeschichtlichen Stellung*. Tübingen: Mohr, 1901.

Schildt, Joachim, ed. *Luthers Sprachschaffen: gesellschaftliche Grundlagen, geschichtliche Wirkungen*. Linguistische Studien, Reihe A: Arbeitsberichte 119/1. Berlin: Akademie der Wissenschaften der DDR, 1984.

Schindler, Alfred. *Wort und Analogie in Augustins Trinitätslehre*. Hermeneutische Untersuchungen zur Theologie 4. Tübingen: Mohr Siebeck, 1965.

Schleiermacher, Friedrich D. E. *Über die Religion: Reden an die Gebildeten unter ihren Verächtern*. In *Kritische Gesamtausgabe*, Vol. 1/2, *Schriften aus der Berliner Zeit 1769–1799*, edited by Günter Meckenstock. Berlin: de Gruyter, 1984.

Schmaus, Michael. *Die psychologische Trinitätslehre des Heiligen Augustinus*. Münsterische Beiträge zur Theologie 11. Münster: Aschendorff, 1967.

Schnelle, Udo. *Einleitung in das Neue Testament*. 7th ed. Stuttgart: UTB, 2011.

———. *Die ersten 100 Jahre des Christentums 30–130 nach Christus: die Entstehungsgeschichte einer Weltreligion*. Göttingen: Vandenhoeck und Ruprecht, 2015.

———. *Paulus: Leben und Denken*. 2nd ed. Berlin: de Gruyter, 2014.

Schniewind, Julius. *Das Evangelium nach Matthäus*. Texte zum Neuen Testament 2. 12th ed. Göttingen: Vandenhoeck und Ruprecht, 1968.

Schniewind, Julius, and Gerhard Friedrich. "ἐπαγγέλλω." In *Theologisches Wörterbuch zum Neuen Testament*, edited by Gerhard Kittel, Otto Bauernfeind, and Gerhard Friedrich, Vol. 2, 573–83. Stuttgart: Kohlhammer, 1933–79.

Schottroff, Luise. *Der erste Brief an die Gemeinde Korinth*. Theologischer Kommentar zum Neuen Testament 7. Stuttgart: Kohlhammer, 2013.

Schrage, Wolfgang. *Der erste Brief an die Korinther*. 1. Teilband: I Cor 1:1—6:11. Evangelisch-Katholischer Kommentar zum Neuen Testament 7/1. Neukirchen-Vluyn: Neukirchener Theologie, 2001.

Schröter, Jens. *Von Jesus zum Neuen Testament: Studien zur urchristlichen Theologiegeschichte und zur Entstehung des neutestamentlichen Kanons*. Wissenschaftliche Untersuchungen zum Neuen Testament 204. Tübingen: Mohr Siebeck, 2007.

Schulte, Andrea. *Religiöse Rede als Sprachhandlung: eine Untersuchung zur performativen Funktion der christlichen Glaubens- und Verkündigungssprache*. Europäische Hochschulschriften 464. Frankfurt am Main: Lang, 1992.

Schulthess, Peter. "Die Bedeutung von *De magistro* für die moderne Philosophie." In Augustin: *De magistro—Der Lehrer. Zweisprachige Ausgabe* (= *Opera—Werke* 11), edited by Therese Fuhrer, 91–97. Paderborn: Schöningh, 2002.

Schwanke, Johannes. *Creatio ex nihilo: Luthers Lehre von der Schöpfung aus dem Nichts in der Großen Genesisvorlesung (1535–1545)*. Theologische Bibliothek Töpelmann 126. Berlin: de Gruyter, 2004.

Schwarz, Reinhard. *Martin Luther: Lehrer der christlichen Religion*. Tübingen: Mohr Siebeck, 2015.

Searle, John R. *Ausdruck und Bedeutung: Untersuchungen zur Sprechakttheorie*. Translated by Andreas Kemmerling. 2nd ed. Frankfurt am Main: Suhrkamp, 1990.

———. "A Classification of Illocutionary Acts." *Language in Society* 5 (1976) 1–23.

———. "Linguistik und Sprachphilosophie." In *Linguistik und Nachbarwissenschaften*, edited by Renate Bartsch and Theo Vennemann, 113–25. Kronberg: Hellhof, 1973.

———. *Sprechakte: ein sprachphilosophischer Essay*. Translated by Renate und Rolf Wiggershaus. 3rd ed. Frankfurt am Main: Suhrkamp, 1988.

Sellin, Gerhard. *Allegorie-Metapher-Mythos-Schrift: Beiträge zur religiösen Sprache im Neuen Testament und in seiner Umwelt*. Edited by Dieter Sänger. Novum testamentum et orbis antiquus/Studien zur Umwelt des Neuen Testaments 90. Göttingen: Vandenhoeck und Ruprecht, 2011.

———. *Der Streit um die Auferstehung der Toten: eine religionsgeschichtliche und exegetische Untersuchung von 1 Korinther 15*. Göttingen: Vandenhoeck und Ruprecht, 1986.

Simone, Raffaele. "Sémiologie augustinienne." *Semiotica* 6 (1972) 1–31.

Smend, Rudolf. "Karl Barth als Ausleger der Heiligen Schrift." In *Epochen der Bibelkritik. Gesammelte Studien*, Vol. 3. Beiträge zur evangelischen Theologie 109. Munich: Kaiser, 1991.

Steck, Odil Hannes. *Die Prophetenbücher und ihr theologisches Zeugnis: Wege der Nachfrage und Fährten zur Antwort*. Tübingen: Mohr, 1996.

———. *Der Schöpfungsbericht der Priesterschrift: Studien zur literarkritischen und überlieferungsgeschichtlichen Problematik von Genesis 1:1—2:4a*. Forschungen zur Religion und Literatur des Alten und Neuen Testamentes 115. 2nd ed. Göttingen: Vandenhoeck und Ruprecht, 1981.

Stegmüller, Wolfgang. *Hauptströmungen der Gegenwartsphilosophie: eine kritische Einführung*, Vol. 2. 6th ed. Stuttgart: Kröner, 1979.

Stoellger, Philipp. "Vom vierfachen Sinn der Metapher—eine Orientierung über ihre Formen und Funktionen." In *Interpretation of Texts: Sacred and Secular*, edited by Pierre Bühler and Tibor Fabiny, 87–116. Zürich: Pano Verlag, 1999.

Stoevesandt, Hinrich. "Die Göttinger Dogmatikvorlesung—Grundriß der Theologie Karl Barths." In *Karl Barth in Deutschland*, edited by Michael Beintker, Christian Link, and Michael Trowitzsch, 77–98. Zürich: Theologischer Verlag Zürich, 2005.

Stolt, Birgit. *Martin Luthers Rhetorik des Herzens*. Tübingen: Mohr Siebeck, 2000.

———. "Luther, die Bibel und das menschliche Herz." In *Luthers Sprachschaffen*, edited by Joachim Schildt, 154–77. Berlin: Akademie der Wissenschaften der DDR, 1984.

Strauss, Gerhard. *Schriftgebrauch, Schriftauslegung und Schriftbeweis bei Augustin*. Beiträge zur Geschichte der biblischen Hermeneutik 1. Tübingen: Mohr, 1959.

Streiff, Stefan. *Novis linguis loqui: Martin Luthers Disputation über Johannes 1:14 verbum caro factum est aus dem Jahr 1539*. Forschungen zur systematischen und ökumenischen Theologie 70. Göttingen: Vandenhoeck und Ruprecht, 1993.

Tambour, Hans-Joachim. "Der kulturell-sprachliche Ansatz—religionsphilosophische Perspektiven." In *Leben im Geist: Perspektiven der Spiritualität*, edited by Paul Imhof et al., 276–90. Scheidegg: Via verbis-Verlag, 2005.

Tanner, Klaus, ed. *Religion und symbolische Kommunikation*. Leipzig: Evangelische Verlagsanstalt, 2004.

Theissen, Gerd. *Die Religion der ersten Christen: eine Theorie des Urchristentums*. 2nd ed. Gütersloh: Gütersloher Verlagshaus, 2001.

Theissen, Gerd, and Annette Merz. *Der historische Jesus: ein Lehrbuch*. 4th ed. Göttingen: Vandenhoeck und Ruprecht, 2011.

Tillich, Paul. *Der Protestantismus als kritisches und gestaltendes Prinzip*. In *Gesammelte Werke VII: Der Protestantismus als Kritik und Gestaltung* (= Schriften zur Theologie 1). Edited by Renate Albrecht. Stuttgart: Evangelisches Verlags-Werk, 1962.

———. *Recht und Bedeutung religiöser Symbole*. In *Gesammelte Werke V: Die Frage nach dem Unbedingten* (= Schriften zur Religionsphilosophie). Edited by Renate Albrecht. 2nd ed. Stuttgart: Evangelisches Verlags-Werk, 1978.

———. *Das System der Wissenschaften nach Gegenständen und Methoden*. In *Gesammelte Werke I: Frühe Hauptwerke*. Edited by Renate Albrecht. 2nd ed. Stuttgart: Evangelisches Verlags-Werk, 1959.

———. *Die Überwindung des Religionsbegriffs in der Religionsphilosophie*. In *Gesammelte Werke I: Frühe Hauptwerke*. Edited by Renate Albrecht. 2nd ed. Stuttgart: Evangelisches Verlags-Werk, 1959.

Tobler, Stefan. "Vielgestaltiges Wort—theologiegeschichtliche Stationen von Justin bis Meister Eckhart." In *Wort Gottes*, edited by Ulrich H.J. Körtner, 41–75. Neukirchen-Vluyn: Neukirchener, 2003.

Track, Joachim. *Sprachkritische Untersuchungen zum christlichen Reden von Gott*. Forschungen zur systematischen und ökumenischen Theologie 37. Göttingen: Vandenhoeck und Ruprecht, 1977.

Trowitzsch, Michael. "Hermeneutik." In *Barth-Handbuch*, edited by Michael Beintker, 158–65. Tübingen: Mohr Siebeck, 2016.

Van Hooff, Anton. "*Confessiones* 8—die Dialektik der Umkehr." In *Confessiones des Augustinus von Hippo*, edited by Norbert Fischer and Cornelia Mayer, 343–88. Freiburg: Herder, 2004.

Vollenweider, Samuel. "Weisheit am Kreuzweg—zum theologischen Programm von 1 Kor 1 und 2." In *Kreuzestheologie im Neuen Testament*, edited by Andreas Dettwiler and Jean Zumstein, 43–58. Tübingen: Mohr Siebeck, 2002.

Vosoughi, Sourush et al. "The Spread of True and False News Online." *Science* 359 (2018) 1146–51.

Vouga, François. "Ist die Kreuzestheologie das hermeneutische Zentrum des NT?" In *Kreuzestheologie im Neuen Testament*, edited by Andreas Dettwiler and Jean Zumstein, 283–326. Tübingen: Mohr Siebeck, 2002.

Wabel, Thomas. *Sprache als Grenze in Luthers theologischer Hermeneutik und Wittgensteins Sprachphilosophie*. Theologische Bibliothek Töpelmann 92. Berlin: de Gruyter, 1998.

Wagner, Andreas. *Prophetie als Theologie: die "so spricht Jhwh"-Formel und das Grundverständnis alttestamentlicher Prophetie*. Forschungen zur Religion und

Literatur des Alten und Neuen Testaments 207. Göttingen: Vandenhoeck und Ruprecht, 2004.

———. *Sprechakte und Sprechaktanalyse im Alten Testament: Untersuchungen an der Nahtstelle zwischen Handlungsebene und Grammatik*. Berlin: de Gruyter, 1997.

Wagner, Falk. "Geht die Umformungskrise des deutschsprachig-modernen Protestantismus weiter?" *Zeitschrift für Neuere Theologiegeschichte* 2 (1995) 225–54.

Walser, Martin. *Über Rechtfertigung: eine Versuchung*. Reinbek: Rowohlt, 2012.

Walter, Christoph. *Der Ertrag der Auseinandersetzung mit den Manichäern für das hermeneutische Problem bei Augustin*. Munich: Schön, 1972.

Ward, Graham. *Barth, Derrida and the Language of Theology*. Cambridge: Cambridge University Press, 1995.

Warnach, Viktor. "Erleuchtung und Einsprechung bei Augustinus." In *Augustinus Magister: Congrès International Augustinien; Communications (= Ètudes Augustiniennes)*, edited by Fulbert Cayré, 429–50. Paris: Ètudes Augustiniennes, 1954.

Warning, Rainer, ed. *Rezeptionsästhetik: Theorie und Praxis*. 4th ed. Munich: UTB, 1994.

Watson, Philip S. *Um Gottes Gottheit: eine Einführung in Luthers Theologie*. Translated by Gerhard Gloege. 2nd ed. Berlin: Lutherisches Verlagshaus, 1967.

Weber, Max. *Briefe 1909–1910. Gesammelte Aufsätze* II/6. Edited by M. Rainer Lepsius and Wolfgang J. Mommsen. Tübingen: Mohr, 1994.

Webster, John. "Theologische Theologie." Translated by Jan Günter Jackisch. *Zeitschrift für Theologie und Kirche* 97 (2000) 238–58.

Westermann, Claus. *Basic Forms of Prophetic Speech*. Translated by Hugh Clayton White. Philadelphia: Westminster, 1967.

———. *Grundformen prophetischer Rede*. Beiträge zur evangelischen Theologie 31. Munich: Kaiser, 1978.

Wieland, Wolfgang. *Offenbarung bei Augustin*. Tübinger Theologische Studien 12. Mainz: Matthias Grünewald Verlag, 1978.

Williams III, H. H. Drake. *The Wisdom of the Wise: The Presence and Function of Scripture within 1 Cor 1:18–23*. Boston: Brill, 2001.

Williams, Rowan. "Language, Reality, and Desire in Augustine's *De doctrina christiana*." *Journal of Literaure and Theology* 3 (1989) 138–50.

Wintzer, Friedrich. *Die Homiletik seit Schleiermacher bis in die Anfänge der dialektischen Theologie in Grundzügen*. Göttingen: Vandenhoeck und Ruprecht, 1969.

Wischmeyer, Oda. "Das 'Wort Gottes' im Neuen Testament—eine theologische Problemanzeige." In *Wort Gottes*, edited by Ulrich H.J. Körtner, 27–40. Neukirchen-Vluyn: Neukirchener, 2003.

Wittgenstein, Ludwig. *Philosophical Investigations*. Translated by Gertrude Elizabeth Margaret Anscombe, Peter Michael Stephan Hacker, and Joachim Schulte. Oxford: Wiley-Blackwell, 2009.

———. *Philosophische Untersuchungen*. Edited by Gertrude Elizabeth Margaret Anscombe et al. In *Werkausgabe*, Vol. 1. Frankfurt am Main: Suhrkamp, 1989.

———. *Tractatus logico-philosophicus: logisch-philosophische Abhandlung*. Edited by Gertrude Elizabeth Margaret Anscombe, et al. In *Werkausgabe*, Vol. 1. Frankfurt am Main: Suhrkamp, 1989.

———. *Tractatus logico-philosophicus*. Translated by Charles Kay Ogden. New York: Harcourt, Brace & Company, 1922.

———. *Vermischte Bemerkungen: eine Auswahl aus dem Nachlass*. Edited by Georg Henrik von Wright. In *Werkausgabe*, Vol. 8. Frankfurt am Main: Suhrkamp, 1984.

———. *Vorlesungen über den religiösen Glauben*. In *Vorlesungen und Gespräche über Ästhetik, Psychoanalyse und religiösen Glauben*. Edited by Yorick Smythies, et al. 3rd ed. Frankfurt am Main: Suhrkamp, 2005.

———. *Vortrag über Ethik*. In *Vortrag über Ethik and andere kleine Schriften*. Edited by Joachim Schulte. Frankfurt am Main: Suhrkamp, 1989.

———. *Zettel*. Edited by Gertrude Elizabeth Margaret Anscombe and Georg Henrik von Wright. In *Werkausgabe*, Vol. 8. Frankfurt am Main: Suhrkamp, 1984.

Wonneberger, Reinhard, and Hans Peter Hecht. *Verheißung und Versprechen: eine theologische und sprachanalytische Klärung*. Göttingen: Vandenhoeck und Ruprecht, 1986.

Zaborowski, Holger. "'Aber sprich nur ein Wort, so wird meine Seele gesund.' Zur Theologie der Sprache und zur Sprache der Dichtung." *Communio* 30 (2001) 58–76.

Zimmerli, Walther. *Ezechiel*. Biblischer Kommentar Altes Testament XIII/1. 2nd ed. Neukirchen-Vluyn: Neukirchener, 1979.

Zur Mühlen, Karl-Heinz. *Nos extra nos: Luthers Theologie zwischen Mystik und Scholastik*. Tübingen: Mohr Siebeck, 1972.

Zwingli, Huldrych. *Über D. Martin Luthers Buch, Bekenntnis genannt, zwei Antworten von Johannes Oekolampad und Huldrych Zwingli*. In *Huldreich Zwinglis sämtliche Werke*, Vol. 6.2. *Corpus Reformatorum* 93.2. Edited by Emil Egli et al. Zürich: Theologischer Verlag, 1968.